W9-BWI-620

ORATIONS

WILLIAM M. EVARTS

Orations—Volume seventeen

ORATIONS

FROM HOMER TO
WILLIAM McKINLEY

EDITED BY

MAYO W. HAZELTINE, A.M

ILLUSTRATED

IN TWENTY-FIVE VOLUMES

VOL. XVII

NEW YORK
P. F. COLLIER AND SON
MCMII

CONTENTS

VOLUME SEVENTEEN

ORATIONS

SUMNER

CHARLES SUMNER was born at Boston, Massachusetts, in January, 1811. He graduated at Harvard College in 1830, and four years later was admitted to the bar. For the next three years he was a lecturer in the Harvard Law School, after which he spent three years in Europe. On his return he began the practice of law, but gradually drifted into politics during the anti-slavery struggle. In 1851 he was sent from Massachusetts to the Federal Senate, to which he was regularly re-elected for the rest of his life. A long series of speeches bristling with invective brought about an attack upon him in May, 1856, by Preston S. Brooks, a Representative from South Carolina, in retaliation for Sumner's criticism of Brooks' uncle, a Senator from his State. Sumner never fully recovered from the effects of the assault, yet, when his party assumed control of the Senate in 1861, he became one of its foremost members. His special field of service in the Senate was the Committee on Foreign Relations, of which he was chairman for ten years. He opposed the re-election of Grant to the Presidency in 1872, and his later years were passed out of accord with the party which he had helped to organize. He died at Washington on March 11, 1874.

ON THE CRIME AGAINST KANSAS

UNITED STATES SENATE, MAY 19-20, 1856

Mr. President:

YOU are now called to redress a great transgression. Seldom in the history of nations has such a question been presented. Tariffs, army bills, navy bills, land bills, are important, and justly occupy your care; but these all belong to the course of ordinary legislation. As means and instruments only, they are necessarily subordinate to the conservation of government itself. Grant them or deny them, in greater or less degree, and you will inflict no shock. The machinery of government will continue to

move. The State will not cease to exist. Far otherwise
is it with the eminent question now before you, involving,
as it does, liberty in a broad territory, and also involving
the peace of the whole country, with our good name in history forever more.

Take down your map, sir, and you will find that the
Territory of Kansas, more than any other region, occupies
the middle spot of North America, equally distant from the
Atlantic on the east, and the Pacific on the west; from
the frozen waters of Hudson's Bay on the north, and the
tepid Gulf Stream on the south, constituting the precise
territorial centre of the whole vast continent. To such advantages of situation, on the very highway between two
oceans, are added a soil of unsurpassed richness, and a
fascinating, undulating beauty of surface, with a health-
giving climate, calculated to nurture a powerful and generous people, worthy to be a central pivot of American institutions. A few short months only have passed since this
spacious and mediterranean country was open only to the
savage who ran wild in its woods and prairies; and now it
has already drawn to its bosom a population of freemen
larger than Athens crowded within her historic gates, when
her sons, under Miltiades, won liberty for mankind on the
field of Marathon; more than Sparta contained when she
ruled Greece, and sent forth her devoted children, quickened by a mother's benediction, to return with their shields,
or on them; more than Rome gathered on her seven hills,
when, under her kings, she commenced that sovereign sway,
which afterward embraced the whole earth; more than London held, when, on the fields of Crecy and Agincourt, the
English banner was carried victoriously over the chivalrous
hosts of France.

Against this Territory, thus fortunate in position and population, a crime has been committed, which is without example in the records of the past. Not in plundered provinces or in the cruelties of selfish governors will you find its parallel; and yet there is an ancient instance, which may show at least the path of justice. In the terrible impeachment by which the great Roman orator has blasted through all time the name of Verres, amid charges of robbery and sacrilege, the enormity which most aroused the indignant voice of his accuser, and which still stands forth with strongest distinctness, arresting the sympathetic indignation of all who read the story, is, that away in Sicily he had scourged a citizen of Rome—that the cry, "I am a Roman citizen," had been interposed in vain against the lash of the tyrant governor. Other charges were that he had carried away productions of art, and that he had violated the sacred shrines. It was in the presence of the Roman Senate that this arraignment proceeded; in a temple of the Forum; amid crowds—such as no orator had ever before drawn together—thronging the porticos and colonnades, even clinging to the housetops and neighboring slopes—and under the anxious gaze of witnesses summoned from the scene of crime. But an audience grander far—of higher dignity— of more various people, and of wider intelligence—the countless multitude of succeeding generations, in every land, where eloquence has been studied, or where the Roman name has been recognized—has listened to the accusation, and throbbed with condemnation of the criminal. Sir, speaking in an age of light, and a land of constitutional liberty, where the safeguards of elections are justly placed among the highest triumphs of civilization, I fearlessly assert that the wrongs of much-abused Sicily, thus memorable in history, were small by the side of the wrongs of Kansas, where the very shrines of popular institutions, more sacred than any heathen altar, have been desecrated; where the ballot-box, more precious than any work, in ivory or marble, from the cunning hand of art, has been plundered; and where the cry, "I am an American citizen," has been interposed in vain against outrage of every kind, even upon life itself. Are you against sacrilege? I present it for your execration. Are you against robbery? I hold it up to your scorn. Are you for the protection of American citizens? I show you how their dearest rights have been cloven down, while a tyrannical usurpation has sought to instal itself on their very necks!

But the wickedness which I now begin to expose is immeasurably aggravated by the motive which prompted it. Not in any common lust for power did this uncommon tragedy have its origin. It is the rape of a virgin Territory, compelling it to the hateful embrace of slavery; and it may be clearly traced to a depraved longing for a new slave State, the hideous offspring of such a crime, in the hope of adding to the power of slavery in the National Government. Yes, sir, when the whole world, alike Christian and Turk, is rising up to condemn this wrong, and to make it a hissing to the nations, here in our Republic, *force*—ay, sir, FORCE—has been openly employed in compelling Kansas to this pollution, and all for the sake of political power. There is the simple fact, which you will in vain attempt to deny, but which in itself presents an essential wickedness that makes other public crimes seem like public virtues.

But this enormity, vast beyond comparison, swells to dimensions of wickedness which the imagination toils in

vain to grasp, when it is understood that for this purpose
are hazarded the horrors of intestine feud not only in this
distant Territory, but everywhere throughout the country.
Already the muster has begun. The strife is no longer
local, but national. Even now, while I speak, portents
hang on all the arches of the horizon threatening to darken
the broad land, which already yawns with the mutterings
of civil war. The fury of the propagandists of slavery, and
the calm determination of their opponents, are now diffused
from the distant Territory over widespread communities;
and the whole country, in all its extent—marshalling hostile divisions, and foreshadowing a strife which, unless
happily averted by the triumph of Freedom, will become
war—fratricidal, parricidal war—with an accumulated wickedness beyond the wickedness of any war in human annals;
justly provoking the avenging judgment of Providence and
the avenging pen of history, and constituting a strife, in the
language of the ancient writer, more than *foreign*, more
than *social*, more than *civil;* but something compounded
of all these strifes, and in itself more than war; sed potius
commune quoddam ex omnibus, et plus quam bellum.

Such is the crime which you are to judge. But the
criminal also must be dragged into day, that you may see
and measure the power by which all this wrong is sustained.
From no common source could it proceed. In its perpetra-
tion was needed a spirit of vaulting ambition which would
hesitate at nothing; a hardihood of purpose which was insensible to the judgment of mankind; a madness for slavery
which would disregard the Constitution, the laws, and all
the great examples of our history; also a consciousness of
power such as comes from the habit of power; a combination of energies found only in a hundred arms directed by

a hundred eyes; a control of public opinion through venal
pens and a prostituted press; an ability to subsidize crowds
in every vocation of life—the politician with his local importance, the lawyer with his subtle tongue, and even the
authority of the judge on the bench; and a familiar use of
men in places high and low, so that none, from the President to the lowest border postmaster, should decline to be
its tool; all these things and more were needed, and they
were found in the slave power of our Republic. There, sir,
stands the criminal, all unmasked before you—heartless,
grasping, and tyrannical—with an audacity beyond that of
Verres, a subtlety beyond that of Machiavel, a meanness
beyond that of Bacon, and an ability beyond that of Hast-
ings. Justice to Kansas can be secured only by the pros-
tration of this influence; for this the power behind—greater
than any President—which succors and sustains the crime.
Nay, the proceedings I now arraign derive their fearful
consequences only from this connection.

In now opening this great matter, I am not insensible
to the austere demands of the occasion; but the dependence
of the crime against Kansas upon the slave power is so
peculiar and important, that I trust to be pardoned while
I impress it with an illustration, which to some may seem
trivial. It is related in Northern mythology that the god
of Force, visiting an enchanted region, was challenged by
his royal entertainer to what seemed a humble feat of
strength—merely, sir, to lift a cat from the ground. The
god smiled at the challenge, and, calmly placing his hand
under the belly of the animal with superhuman strength
strove, while the back of the feline monster arched far upward, even beyond reach, and one paw actually forsook the
earth, until at last the discomfited divinity desisted; but

he was little surprised at his defeat when he learned that this creature, which seemed to be a cat, and nothing more, was not merely a cat, but that it belonged to and was a part of the great Terrestrial Serpent, which, in its innumerable folds, encircled the whole globe. Even so the creature, whose paws are now fastened upon Kansas, whatever it may seem to be, constitutes in reality a part of the slave power, which, in its loathsome folds, is now coiled about the whole land. Thus do I expose the extent of the present contest, where we encounter not merely local resistance, but also the unconquered sustaining arm behind. But out of the vastness of the crime attempted, with all its woe and shame, I derive a well-founded assurance of a commensurate vastness of effort against it by the aroused masses of the country, determined not only to vindicate right against wrong, but to redeem the Republic from the thraldom of that oligarchy which prompts, directs, and concentrates the distant wrong.

Such is the crime, and such is the criminal, which it is my duty in this debate to expose, and, by the blessing of God, this duty shall be done completely to the end. . . .

But, before entering upon the argument, I must say something of a general character, particularly in response to what has fallen from Senators who have raised themselves to eminence on this floor in championship of human wrongs. I mean the Senator from South Carolina (Mr. Butler), and the Senator from Illinois (Mr. Douglas), who, though unlike as Don Quixote and Sancho Panza, yet, like this couple, sally forth together in the same adventure. I regret much to miss the elder Senator from his seat; but the cause, against which he has run a tilt, with such activity of animosity, demands that the opportunity of exposing him should not be lost; and it is for the cause that I speak. The Senator from South Carolina has read many books of chivalry, and believes himself a chivalrous knight, with sentiments of honor and courage. Of course he has chosen a mistress to whom he has made his vows, and who, though ugly to others, is always lovely to him; though polluted in the sight of the world, is chaste in his sight—I mean the harlot, Slavery. For her, his tongue is always profuse in words. Let her be impeached in character, or any proposition made to shut her out from the extension of her wantonness, and no extravagance of manner or hardihood of assertion is then too great for this Senator. The frenzy of Don Quixote, in behalf of his wench, Dulcinea del Toboso, is all surpassed. The asserted rights of Slavery, which shock equality of all kinds, are cloaked by a fantastic claim of equality. If the slave States cannot enjoy what, in mockery of the great fathers of the Republic, he misnames equality under the Constitution—in other words, the full power in the National Territories to compel fellow men to unpaid toil, to separate husband and wife, and to sell little children at the auction block—then, sir, the chivalric Senator will conduct the State of South Carolina out of the Union! Heroic knight! Exalted Senator! A second Moses come for a second exodus!

But not content with this poor menace, which we have been twice told was "measured," the Senator, in the unrestrained chivalry of his nature, has undertaken to apply opprobrious words to those who differ from him on this floor. He calls them "sectional and fanatical"; and opposition to the usurpation in Kansas he denounces as "an uncalculating fanaticism." To be sure these charges lack all grace of originality, and all sentiment of truth; but the adventurous Senator does not hesitate.   He is the uncompromising, unblushing representative on this floor of a flagrant *sectionalism*, which now domineers over the Republic, and yet with a ludicrous ignorance of his own position—unable to see himself as others see him—or with an effrontery which even his white head ought not to protect from rebuke, he applies to those here who resist his *sectionalism* the very epithet which designates himself.   The men who strive to bring back the government to its original policy, when Freedom and not Slavery was sectional, he arraigns as *sectional*.   This will not do.   It involves too great a perversion of terms.   I tell that Senator that it is to himself, and to the "organization" of which he is the "committed advocate," that this epithet belongs.   I now fasten it upon them.   For myself, I care little for names; but since the question has been raised here, I affirm that the Republican party of the Union is in no just sense *sectional*, but, more than any other party, *national;* and that it now goes forth to dislodge from the high places of the government the tyrannical sectionalism of which the Senator from South Carolina is one of the maddest zealots. . . .

As the Senator from South Carolina is the Don Quixote, the Senator from Illinois (Mr. Douglas) is the Squire of Slavery, its very Sancho Panza, ready to do all its humiliating offices.   This Senator, in his labored address, vindicating his labored report—piling one mass of elaborate error upon another mass—constrained himself, as you will remember, to unfamiliar decencies of speech.   Of that address I have nothing to say at this moment, though before I sit down I shall show something of its fallacies.   But I go back now to an earlier occasion, when, true to his native impulses, he threw into this discussion, "for a charm of powerful trouble," personalities most discreditable to this body. I will not stop to repel the imputations which he cast upon myself; but I mention them to remind you of the "sweltered venom sleeping got," which, with other poisoned ingredients, he cast into the caldron of this debate. Of other things I speak. Standing on this floor, the Senator issued his rescript, requiring submission to the Usurped Power of Kansas; and this was accompanied by a manner—all his own—such as befits the tyrannical threat. Very well. Let the Senator try. I tell him now that he cannot enforce any such submission. The Senator, with the slave power at his back, is strong; but he is not strong enough for this purpose. He is bold. He shrinks from nothing. Like Danton, he may cry, "*l'audace! l'audace! toujours l'audace!*" but even his audacity cannot compass this work. The Senator copies the British officer who, with boastful swagger, said that with the hilt of his sword he would cram the "stamps" down the throats of the American people, and he will meet a similar failure. He may convulse this country with a civil feud. Like the ancient madman, he may set fire to this Temple of Constitutional Liberty, grander than the Ephesian dome; but he cannot enforce obedience to that Tyrannical Usurpation.

The Senator dreams that he can subdue the North. He disclaims the open threat, but his conduct still implies it. How little that Senator knows himself or the strength of the cause which he persecutes! He is but a mortal man; against him is an immortal principle. With finite power he wrestles with the infinite, and he must fall. Against him are stronger battalions than any marshalled by mortal arm —the inborn, ineradicable, invincible sentiments of the human heart; against him is nature in all her subtle forces; against him is God. Let him try to subdue these. . . .

With regret, I come again upon the Senator from South Carolina (Mr. Butler), who, omnipresent in this debate, overflowed with rage at the simple suggestion that Kansas had applied for admission as a State; and, with incoherent phrases, discharged the loose expectoration of his speech, now upon her Representative, and then upon her people. There was no extravagance of the ancient parliamentary debate which he did not repeat; nor was there any possible deviation from truth which he did not make, with so much of passion, I am glad to add, as to save him from the suspicion of intentional aberration. But the Senator touches nothing which he does not disfigure—with error, sometimes of principle, sometimes of fact. He shows an incapacity of accuracy, whether in stating the Constitution or in stating the law whether in the details of statistics or the diversions of scholarship. He cannot ope his mouth, but out there flies a blunder. Surely he ought to be familiar with the life of Franklin; and yet he referred to this household character, while acting as agent of our fathers in England, as above suspicion; and this was done that he might give point to a false contrast with the agent of Kansas—not knowing that, however they may differ in genius and fame, in this experience they are alike; that Franklin, when intrusted with the petition of Massachusetts Bay, was assaulted by a foul-mouthed speaker, where he could not be heard in defence, and denounced as a "thief," even as the agent of Kansas has been assaulted on this floor, and denounced as a "forger." And let not the vanity of the Senator be inspired by the parallel with the British statesman of that day; for it is only in hostility to Freedom that any parallel can be recognized.

But it is against the people of Kansas that the sensibilities of the Senator are particularly aroused. Coming, as he announces, "from a State"—ay, sir, from South Carolina—he turns with lordly disgust from this newly-formed community, which he will not recognize even as a "body politic." Pray, sir, by what title does he indulge in this egotism? Has he read the history of "the State" which he represents? He cannot surely have forgotten its shameful imbecility from Slavery, confessed throughout the Revolution, followed by its more shameful assumptions for Slavery since. He cannot have forgotten its wretched persistence in the slave trade as the very apple of its eye, and the condition of its participation in the Union. He cannot have forgotten its Constitution, which is Republican only in name, confirming power in the hands of the few, and founding the qualifications of its legislators on "a settled freehold estate and ten negroes." And yet the Senator, to whom that "State" has in part committed the guardianship of its good name, instead of moving, with backward treading steps, to cover its nakedness, rushes forward in the very ecstasy of madness, to expose it by provoking a comparison with Kansas. South Carolina is old; Kansas is young. South Carolina counts by centuries, where Kansas counts by years. But a beneficent example may be born in a day; and I venture to say, that against the two centuries of the older "State," may be already set the two years of trial, evolving corresponding virtue, in the younger community. In the one, is the long wail of Slavery; in the other, the hymns of Freedom. And if we glance at special achievements, it will be difficult to find anything in the history of

South Carolina which presents so much of heroic spirit in
a heroic cause as appears in that repulse of the Missouri
invaders by the beleaguered town of Lawrence, where even
the women gave their effective efforts to Freedom. The
matrons of Rome, who poured their jewels into the treas-
ury for the public defence—the wives of Prussia, who, with
delicate fingers, clothed their defenders against French invasion—the mothers of our own Revolution, who sent forth
their sons, covered with prayers and blessings, to combat
for human rights, did nothing of self-sacrifice truer than
did these women on this occasion. Were the whole history of South Carolina blotted out of existence, from its
very beginning down to the day of the last election of the
Senator to his present seat on this floor, civilization might
lose—I do not say how little; but surely less than it has
already gained by the example of Kansas, in its valiant
struggle against oppression, and in the development of a
new science of emigration. Already, in Lawrence alone,
there are newspapers and schools, including a High School,
and throughout this infant Territory there is more mature
scholarship far, in proportion to its inhabitants, than in all
South Carolina. Ah, sir, I tell the Senator that Kansas,
welcomed as a free State, will be a "ministering angel" to
the Republic, when South Carolina, in the cloak of darkness which she hugs, "lies howling."

The Senator from Illinois (Mr. Douglas) naturally joins
the Senator from South Carolina in this warfare, and gives
to it the superior intensity of his nature. He thinks that
the national government has not completely proved its
power, as it has never hanged a traitor; but, if the occasion requires, he hopes there will be no hesitation; and
this threat is directed at Kansas, and even at the friends

of Kansas throughout the country. Again occurs the parallel with the struggle of our fathers, and I borrow the language of Patrick Henry, when, to the cry from the Senator, of "treason," "treason," I reply, "if this be treason, make the most of it." Sir, it is easy to call names; but I beg to tell the Senator that if the word "traitor" is in any way applicable to those who refuse submission to a Tyrannical Usurpation, whether in Kansas or elsewhere, then must some new word, of deeper color, be invented, to designate those mad spirits who could endanger and degrade the Republic, while they betray all the cherished sentiments of the fathers and the spirit of the Constitution, in order to give new spread to slavery. Let the Senator proceed. It will not be the first time in history that a scaffold erected for punishment has become a pedestal of honor. Out of death comes life, and the "traitor" whom he blindly executes will live immortal in the cause.

"For Humanity sweeps onward; where to-day the martyr stands,
On the morrow crouches Judas, with the silver in his hands;
While the hooting mob of yesterday in silent awe return,
To glean up the scattered ashes into History's golden urn."

Among these hostile Senators, there is yet another, with all the prejudices of the Senator from South Carolina, but without his generous impulses, who, on account of his character before the country, and the rancor of his opposition, deserves to be named. I mean the Senator from Virginia (Mr. Mason), who, as the author of the Fugitive Slave Bill, has associated himself with a special act of inhumanity and tyranny. Of him I shall say little, for he has said little in this debate, though within that little was compressed the bitterness of a life absorbed in the support of slavery. He holds the commission of Virginia; but he does not represent

that early Virginia, so dear to our hearts, which gave to us
the pen of Jefferson, by which the equality of men was declared, and the sword of Washington, by which Independence was secured; but he represents that other Virginia,
from which Washington and Jefferson now avert their
faces, where human beings are bred as cattle for the
shambles, and where a dungeon rewards the pious ma-
tron who teaches little children to relieve their bondage
by reading the Book of Life. It is proper that such a
Senator, representing such a State, should rail against
free Kansas.

Senators such as these are the natural enemies of Kansas, and I introduce them with reluctance, simply that the
country may understand the character of the hostility
which must be overcome. Arrayed with them, of course,
are all who unite, under any pretext or apology, in the
propagandism of human slavery. To such, indeed, the
time-honored safeguards of popular rights can be a name
only, and nothing more. What are trial by jury, *habeas
corpus*, the ballot-box, the right of petition, the liberty of
Kansas, your liberty, sir, or mine, to one who lends himself, not merely to the support at home, but to the propagandism abroad, of that preposterous wrong, which denies
even the right of a man to himself! Such a cause can be
maintained only by a practical subversion of all rights. It
is, therefore, merely according to reason that its partisans
should uphold the Usurpation in Kansas.

To overthrow this Usurpation is now the special, impor-
tunate duty of Congress, admitting of no hesitation or post-
ponement. To this end it must lift itself from the cabals
of candidates, the machinations of party, and the low level
of vulgar strife. It must turn from that Slave Oligarchy

which now controls the Republic, and refuse to be its tool.
Let its power be stretched forth toward this distant Territory, not to bind, but to unbind; not for the oppression of
the weak, but for the subversion of the tyrannical; not for
the prop and maintenance of a revolting Usurpation, but
for the confirmation of Liberty.

"These are imperial arts and worthy thee!"

Let it now take its stand between the living and dead,
and cause this plague to be stayed. All this it can do;
and if the interests of slavery did not oppose, all this it
would do at once, in reverent regard for justice, law, and
order, driving away all the alarms of war; nor would it
dare to brave the shame and punishment of this great refusal. But the slave power dares anything; and it can be
conquered only by the united masses of the people. From
Congress to the People I appeal. . . .

The contest, which, beginning in Kansas, has reached
us, will soon be transferred from Congress to a broader
stage, where every citizen will be not only spectator, but
actor; and to their judgment I confidently appeal. To
the People, now on the eve of exercising the electoral
franchise, in choosing a Chief Magistrate of the Republic,
I appeal, to vindicate the electoral franchise in Kansas.
Let the ballot-box of the Union, with multitudinous might,
protect the ballot-box in that Territory. Let the voters
everywhere, while rejoicing in their own rights, help to
guard the equal rights of distant fellow citizens; that the
shrines of popular institutions, now desecrated, may be
sanctified anew; that the ballot-box, now plundered, may
be restored; and that the cry, "I am an American citizen," may not be sent forth in vain against outrage of
every kind. In just regard for free labor in that Terri-

tory, which it is sought to blast by unwelcome association with slave labor; in Christian sympathy with the slave, whom it is proposed to task and sell there; in stern condemnation of the crime which has been consummated on that beautiful soil; in rescue of fellow citizens now subjugated to a Tyrannical Usurpation; in dutiful respect for the early fathers, whose aspirations are now ignobly thwarted; in the name of the Constitution, which has been outraged —of the laws trampled down—of Justice banished—of Humanity degraded—of Peace destroyed—of Freedom crushed to earth; and, in the name of the Heavenly Father, whose service is perfect Freedom, I make this last appeal."

MAY 20, 1856

Mr. Douglas—I shall not detain the Senate by a detailed reply to the speech of the Senator from Massachusetts. Indeed, I should not deem it necessary to say one word, but for the personalities in which he has indulged, evincing a depth of malignity that issued from every sentence, making it a matter of self-respect with me to repel the assaults which have been made.

As to the argument, we have heard it all before. Not a position, not a fact, not an argument has he used, which has not been employed on the same side of the Chamber, and replied to by me twice. I shall not follow him, therefore, because it would only be repeating the same answer which I have twice before given to each of his positions. He seems to get up a speech as in Yankee land they get up a bed-quilt. They take all the old calico dresses of various colors, that have been in the house from the days of their grandmothers, and invite the young ladies of the neighborhood in the afternoon, and the young men to meet them at a dance in the evening. They cut up these pieces of old dresses and make pretty figures, and boast of what beautiful ornamental work they have made, although there was not a new piece of material in the whole quilt. Thus it is with the speech which we have had rehashed here to-day, in regard to matters of fact, matters of law, and matters of argument—everything but the personal assaults and the malignity. . . .

His endeavor seems to be an attempt to whistle to keep up his courage by defiant assaults upon us all. I am in doubt as to what can be his object. He has not hesitated to charge three-fourths of the Senate with fraud, with swindling, with crime, with infamy, at least one hundred times over in his speech. Is it his object to provoke some of us to kick him as we would a dog in the street, that he may get sympathy upon the just chastisement? What is the object of this denunciation against the body of which we are members? A hundred times he has called the Nebraska Bill a "swindle," an act of crime, an act of infamy, and each time went on to illustrate the complicity of each man who voted for it in perpetrating the crime. He has brought it home as a personal charge to those who passed the Nebraska Bill, that they were guilty of a crime which deserved the just indignation of heaven, and should make them infamous among men.

Who are the Senators thus arraigned? He does me the honor to make me the chief. It was my good luck to have such a position in this body as to enable me to be the author of a great, wise measure, which the Senate has approved, and the country will indorse. That measure was sustained by about three-fourths of all the members of the

Senate. It was sustained by a majority of the Democrats and a majority of the Whigs in this body. It was sustained by a majority of Senators from the slaveholding States, and a majority of Senators from the free States. The Senator, by his charge of crime, then, stultifies three-fourths of the whole body, a majority of the North, nearly the whole South, a majority of Whigs, and a majority of Democrats here. He says they are infamous. If he so believed, who could suppose that he would ever show his face among such a body of men? How dare he approach one of those gentlemen to give him his hand after that act? If he felt the courtesies between men he would not do it. He would deserve to have himself spit in the face for doing so. . . .

The attack of the Senator from Massachusetts now is not on me alone. Even the courteous and the accomplished Senator from South Carolina (Mr. Butler) could not be passed by in his absence.

Mr. Mason—Advantage was taken of it.

Mr. Douglas—It is suggested that advantage is taken of his absence. I think that this is a mistake. I think the speech was written and practiced, and the gestures fixed; and, if that part had been stricken out the Senator would not have known how to repeat the speech. All that tirade of abuse must be brought down on the head of the venerable, the courteous, and the distinguished Senator from South Carolina. I shall not defend that gentleman here. Every Senator who knows him loves him. The Senator from Massachusetts may take every charge made against him in his speech, and may verify by his oath, and by the oath of every one of his confederates, and there is not an honest man in this Chamber who will not repel it as a slander. Your oaths cannot make a Senator feel that it was not an outrage to assail the honorable gentleman in the terms in which he has been attacked. He, however, will be here in due time to speak for himself, and to act for himself, too. I know what will happen. The Senator from Massachusetts will go to him, whisper a secret apology in his ear, and ask him to accept that as satisfaction for a public outrage on his character! I know the Senator from Massachusetts is in the habit of doing those things. I have had some experience of his skill in that respect. . . .

Why these attacks on individuals by name, and two-thirds of the Senate collectively? Is it the object to drive men here to dissolve social relations with political opponents? Is it to turn the Senate into a bear garden, where Senators cannot associate on terms which ought to prevail between gentlemen? These attacks are heaped upon me by man after man. When I repel them, it is intimated that I show some feeling on the subject. Sir, God grant that when I denounce an act of infamy I shall do it with feeling, and do it under the sudden impulses of feeling, instead of sitting up at night writing out my denunciation of a man whom I hate, copying it, having it printed, punctuating the proof-sheets, and repeating it before the glass, in order to give refinement to insult, which is only pardonable when it is the outburst of a just indignation.

Mr. President, I shall not occupy the time of the Senate. I dislike to be forced to repel these attacks upon myself, which seem to be repeated on every occasion. It appears that gentlemen on the other side of the Chamber think they would not be doing justice to their cause if they did not make myself a personal object of bitter denunciation and malignity. I hope that the debate on this bill may be brought to a close at as early a day as possible. I shall do no more in these side discussions than vindicate myself and repel unjust attacks, but I shall ask the Senate to permit me to close the debate, when it shall close, in a calm, kind summary of the whole question, avoiding personalities.

Mr. Sumner—Mr. President, To the Senator from Illinois, I should willingly leave the privilege of the common scold—the last word; but I will not leave to him, in any discussion with me, the last argument, or the last semblance of it. He has crowned the audacity of this debate by venturing to rise here and calumniate me. He said that I came here, took an oath to support the Constitution, and yet determined not to support a particular clause in that Constitution. To that statement I give, to his face, the flattest denial. When it was made on a former occasion on this floor by the absent Senator from South Carolina (Mr. Butler), I then repelled it. I will read from the debate of the 28th of June, 1854, as published in the "Globe," to show what I said in response to that calumny when pressed at that hour. Here is what I said to the Senator from South Carolina:

"This Senator was disturbed, when to his inquiry, personally, pointedly, and vehemently addressed to me, whether I would join in returning a fellow-man to slavery? I exclaimed, 'Is thy servant a dog, that he should do this thing?'"

You will observe that the inquiry of tne Senator from South Carolina, was whether I would join in returning a fellow-man to slavery. It was not whether I would support any clause of the Constitution of the United States—far from that. . . .

Sir, this is the Senate of the United States, an important body, under the Constitution, with great powers. Its members are justly supposed, from age, to be above the intemperance of youth, and from character to be above the gusts of vulgarity. They are supposed to have something of wisdom, and something of that candor which is the handmaid of wisdom. Let the Senator bear these things in mind, and let him remember hereafter that the bowie-knife and bludgeon are not the proper emblems of Senatorial debate. Let him remember that the swagger of Bob Acres and the ferocity of the Malay cannot add dignity to this body. The Senator has gone on to infuse into his speech the venom which has been sweltering for months—ay, for years; and he has alleged facts that are entirely without foundation, in order to heap upon me some personal obloquy. I will not go into the details which have flowed out so naturally from his tongue. I only brand them to his face as false. I say, also, to that Senator, and I wish him to bear it in mind, that no person with the upright form of man can be allowed—(Hesitation).

Mr. Douglas—Say it.

Mr. Sumner—I will say it—no person with the upright form of man can be allowed, without violation to all decency, to switch out from his tongue the perpetual stench of offensive personality. Sir, that is not a proper weapon of debate, at least, on this floor. The noisome, squat, and nameless animal, to which I now refer, is not a proper model for an American Senator. Will the Senator from Illinois take notice?

Mr. Douglas—I will; and therefore will not imitate you, sir.

Mr. Sumner—I did not hear the Senator.

Mr. Douglas—I said if that be the case I would certainly never imitate you in that capacity, recognizing the force of the illustration.

Mr. Sumner—Mr. President, again the Senator has switched his tongue, and again he fills the Senate with its offensive odor. . . .

Mr. Douglas—I am not going to pursue this subject further. I will only say that a man who has been branded by me in the Senate, and convicted by the Senate of falsehood, cannot use language requiring a reply, and therefore I have nothing more to say.

ORATION ON THE TRUE GRANDEUR OF NATIONS

DELIVERED IN BOSTON, JULY 4, 1845

IN OBEDIENCE to an uninterrupted usage of our community, we have all, on this Sabbath of the Nation, put aside the common cares of life, and seized a respite from the never-ending toils of labor, to meet in gladness and congratulation, mindful of the blessings transmitted from the past, mindful, also, I trust, of the duties to the present and the future. May he who now addresses you be enabled so to direct your minds, that you shall not seem to have lost a day!

All hearts first turn to the Fathers of the Republic. Their venerable forms rise before us, in the procession of successive generations. They come from the frozen rock of Plymouth, from the wasted bands of Raleigh, from the heavenly companionship of William Penn, from the anxious councils of the Revolution, and from all those fields of sacrifice, on which, in obedience to the spirit of their age, they sealed their devotion to duty with their blood. They seem to speak to us, their children: " Cease to vaunt yourselves of what you

do, and of what has been done for you.   Learn to walk humbly, and to think meekly of yourselves.   Cultivate habits of
self-sacrifice and of devotion to duty.   May our words be
always in your minds, never aim at aught which is not right,
persuaded that without this, every possession and all knowledge will become an evil and a shame.   Strive to increase
the inheritance which we have bequeathed; know, that, if we
excel you in virtue, such a victory will be to us a mortification, while defeat will bring happiness.   It is in this way,
that you may conquer us.   Nothing is more shameful for a
man than to found his title to esteem, not on his own merits,
but on the fame of his ancestors.   The glory of the fathers is
doubtless to their children a most precious treasure; but to
enjoy it without transmitting it to the next generation, and
without adding to it yourselves, this is the height of imbecility.   Following these counsels, when your days shall be
finished on earth, you will come to join us, and we shall
receive you as friends receive friends; but if you neglect our
words, expect no happy greeting then from us."

Honor to the memory of our fathers!   May the turf lie
gently on their sacred graves!   But not in words only, but
in deeds also, let us testify our reverence for their name.
Let us imitate what in them was lofty, pure, and good; let
us from them learn to bear hardship and privation.   Let us,
who now reap in strength what they sowed in weakness, study
to enhance the inheritance we have received.   To do this, we
must not fold our hands in slumber, nor abide content with
the past.   To each generation is committed its peculiar task;
nor does the heart, which responds to the call of duty, find
rest except in the world to come.

Be ours, then, the task which, in the order of Providence,
has been cast upon us!   And what is this task?   How shall

we best perform our appointed part? What can we do to make our coming welcome to our fathers in the skies, and to draw to our memory hereafter the homage of a grateful posterity? How may we add to the inheritance we have received? The answer to these questions cannot fail to interest all minds, particularly on this festival of the nativity of the republic. In truth, it well becomes the patriot citizen, on this anniversary, to meditate on the national character, and the way in which it may be advanced — as the good man dedicates his birthday to meditation on his life, and to aspirations for its improvement. Avoiding, then, all customary exultation in the abounding prosperity of the land, and in that freedom whose influence is widening to the uttermost circles of the earth, let us turn our thoughts on the character of our country, and humbly endeavor to learn what it belongs to us to do, to the end that the Republic may best secure the rights and happiness of the people committed to its care — that it may perform its great part in the world's history — that it may fulfil the aspirations of generous hearts — and, practising that righteousness which exalteth a nation, thus attain to the Christian heights of true grandeur.

With this aim, and believing that I can in no other way so fitly fulfill the trust reposed in me, when I was selected as the voice of the City of Boston, on this welcome Anniversary, I propose to consider what, in our age, are the true objects of ational ambition — what is truly national honor — national glory — what is the true grandeur of nations. I hope to contribute something to rescue these terms, so powerful over the minds of men, from the mistaken objects to which they are applied, from deeds of war, and the extension of empire, that henceforward they may be attached only to works of justice and beneficence.

The subject may be novel, particularly on an occasion like the present; but it is comprehensive and transcendent in importance. It raises us to the contemplation of things that are not temporary or local in their character; but which belong to all ages and all countries; which are as lofty as truth, as universal as humanity. Nay more; it practically concerns the general welfare, not only of our own cherished Republic, but of the whole federation of nations. Besides, at this moment, it derives a peculiar and urgent interest from transactions in which we are unhappily involved. On the one side, by an act of unjust legislation, extending our power over Texas, we have endangered peace with Mexico; while on the other, by a presumptuous assertion of a disputed claim to a worthless territory beyond the Rocky Mountains, we have kindled anew on the hearth of our mother country, the smothered fires of hostile strife. Mexico and England both aver the determination to vindicate what is called the national honor; and our government now calmly contemplates the dread arbitrament of war, provided it cannot obtain what is called an honorable peace.

Far be it from our country and our age the sin and shame of contests hateful in the sight of God and all good men, having their origin in no righteous though mistaken sentiment, in no true love of country, in no generous thirst for fame, that last infirmity of noble minds, but springing in both cases from an ignorant and ignoble passion for new territories; strengthened, in one case, by an unnatural desire, in this land of boasted freedom, to fasten by new links the chains which promise soon to fall from the limbs of the unhappy slave! In such contests, God has no attribute which can join with us. Who believes that the national honor will be promoted by a war with Mexico or with England? What just man would sacrifice a single human life, to bring under our rule both Texas and Oregon? An ancient Roman, a stranger to Christian truth, touched only by the relations of fellow countrymen, and not of fellow man, said, as he turned aside from a career of Asiatic conquest, that he would rather save the life of a single citizen than become master of all the dominions of Mithridates.

A war with Mexico would be mean and cowardly; with England it would be bold at least, though parricidal. The heart sickens at the murderous attack upon an enemy, distracted by civil feuds, weak at home, impotent abroad; but it recoils in horror from the deadly shock between children of a common ancestry, speaking the same language, soothed in infancy by the same words of love and tenderness, and hardened into vigorous manhood under the bracing influence of institutions drawn from the same ancient founts of freedom. "Curam acuebat, quod adversus Latinos bellandum erat, lingua, moribus, armorum genere, institutis ante omnia militaribus, congruentes; milites militibus, centurionibus centuriones, tribuni tribunis compares, collegæque, iisdem præsidiis, sæpe iisdem manipulis permixti fuerant."

In our age there can be no peace that is not honorable; there can be no war that is not dishonorable. The true honor of a nation is to be found only in deeds of justice and beneficence, securing the happiness of its people, all of which are inconsistent with war. In the clear eye of Christian judgment vain are its victories; infamous are its spoils. He is the true benefactor and alone worthy of honor, who brings comfort where before was wretchedness; who dries the tear of sorrow; who pours oil into the wounds of the unfortunate; who feeds the hungry and clothes the naked; who unlooses the fetter of the slave; who does justice; who enlightens the

ignorant; who, by his virtuous genius, in art, in literature, in
science, enlivens and exalts the hours of life; who, by words
or actions, inspires a love for God and for man.   This is the
Christian hero, this is the man of honor in a Christian land.
He is no benefactor, nor deserving of honor, whatever his
worldly renown, whose life is passed in acts of brute force;
who renounces the great law of Christian brotherhood; whose
vocation is blood.   Well may old Sir Thomas Browne
exclaim, " The world does not know its greatest men; " for
thus far it has chiefly discerned the violent brood of battle,
the armed men springing up from the dragon's teeth sown
by hate, and cared little for the truly good men, children of
love, guiltless of their country's blood, whose steps on earth
have been noiseless as an angel's wing.

It cannot be disguised that these views differ from the
opinions most popular with the world down to this day.   The
voice of man is yet given to the praise of military chieftains,
and the honors of victory are chanted even by the lips of
woman.   The mother, while rocking her infant on her knees,
stamps upon his tender mind, at that age more impressible
than wax, the images of war; she nurses his slumbers with its
melodies; she pleases his waking hours with its stories; and
selects for his playthings the plume and the sword.   From
the child is formed the man; and who can weigh the influence
of a mother's spirit on the opinions of later life?   The mind
which trains the child is like the hand that commands the
end of a long lever; a gentle effort at that time suffices to
heave the enormous weight of succeeding years.   As the boy
advances to youth, he is fed like Achilles, not on honey and
milk only, but on bear's flesh and lion's marrow.   He draws
the nutriment of his soul from a literature whose beautiful
fields have been moistened by human blood.   Fain would I

2 offer my tribute to the father of poetry, standing with harp of immortal melody, on the misty mountain top of distant antiquity; to those stories of courage and sacrifice which emblazon the annals of Greece and Rome; to the fulminations of Demosthenes and the splendors of Tully; to the sweet verse of Virgil and the poetic prose of Livy. Fain would I offer my tribute to the new literature, which shot up in modern times as a vigorous forest from the burnt site of ancient woods; to the passionate song of the troubadour of France, and the minnesinger of Germany; to the thrilling ballads of Spain, and the delicate music of the Italian lyre. But from all these has breathed the breath of war, that has swept the heart strings of the thronging generations of men!

And when the youth becomes a man, his country invites his services in war, and holds before his bewildered imagination the prizes of worldly honor. For him is the pen of the historian and the verse of the poet. His soul is taught to swell at the thought that he also is a soldier; that his name shall be entered on the list of those who have borne arms in the cause of their country; and perhaps he dreams that he too may sleep, like the great captain of Spain, with a hundred trophies over his grave. The law of the land throws its sanction over this madness. But the contagion spreads beyond those bands on whom is imposed any positive obligation. Respectable citizens volunteer to look like soldiers, and to affect in dress, in arms, and deportment, what is called "the pride, pomp, and circumstance of glorious war." The ear-piercing fife has to-day filled our streets, and we have come together to this church on this national Sabbath, by the thump of drum and with the parade of bristling bayonets.

It is not strange, then, that the spirit of war still finds a home among us; nor that its honors continue to be regarded.

All this may seem to give point to the bitter philosophy of Hobbes, who held, that the natural state of mankind was war, and to sustain the exulting language of the soldier in our own day, who has said, "War is the condition of this world. From man to the smallest insect, all are at strife, and the glory of arms, which cannot be obtained without the exercise of honor, fortitude, courage, obedience, modesty, and temperance, excites the brave man's patriotism, and is a chastening correction of the rich man's pride."

Alas! in the existing relations of nations, the infidel philosopher, and the rhetorical soldier find too much support for a theory which slanders human nature, and insults the goodness of God. It is true that there are impulses in us which unhappily tend to strife. There are propensities that we have in common with the beasts, which, if not kept in subordination to what in man is human, or perhaps divine — if not directed to labors of justice and beneficence — will break forth in acts of outrage. In all these we discern the predominance of the animal qualities. Hence come wars and fightings and the false glory which crowns such barbarism. But the Christian elevation of nations, as of individuals, may well be determined by the extent to which these evil dispositions are restrained. Nor does the Christian teacher ever perform his high office more truly than when, recognizing the supremacy of the moral and intellectual faculties, he calls upon nations, as upon individuals, to declare independence of the bestial propensities, to abolish or abandon all those practices and customs which are founded on these propensities, and in every way to beat down the profane spirit which provokes to strife. But in making this appeal he will be startled by the fact, as discreditable as it is important, that, while the municipal law of each Christian state — discarding the arbitrament of force — provides a judicial tribunal for the determination of controversies between individuals, the international law expressly establishes the arbitrament of war for the determination of controversies between nations.

Here, then, in unfolding the true grandeur of nations, we encounter a practice or custom, sanctioned by the law of nations, and constituting a part of that law, which exists in defiance of all those principles of morals and religion which regulate the conduct of individuals. If it is wrong and inglorious in individuals to consent and agree to determine their petty controversies by combat, it must be equally wrong and inglorious for nations to consent and agree to determine their vaster controversies by combat. Here is a positive, precise, and specific evil, of gigantic proportions — inconsistent with all that is truly honorable — making within the sphere of its influence all true grandeur impossible — which does not proceed from any uncontrollable impulses of our nature, but is expressly established and organized by law. To this evil I ask your best attention.

As all citizens are parties to the municipal law, and are responsible for its institutions, so are all the Christian nations parties to the international law, and responsible for its provisions. By recognizing these provisions, nations consent and agree beforehand to the arbitrament of war, precisely as citizens, by recognizing the trial by jury, consent and agree beforehand to this tribunal. And as to understand the true nature of the trial by jury, we first repair to the municipal law by which it is established; so to understand the true nature of the arbitrament of war, we must first repair to the law of nations.

Writers of transcendent genius and learning have defined this arbitrament, and laid down the rules by which it is gov-

erned, constituting a complex code with innumerable subtle
provisions, regulating the resort to it, and the manner in
which it shall be conducted,— called the " Laws of War."
In these quarters let us catch our first authentic glimpse of
its folly and wickedness. War is called by Lord Bacon,
" One of the highest trials of right, when princes and states
that acknowledge no superior upon earth, shall put themselves
upon the justice of God for the deciding of their controversies
by such success as it shall please him to give on either side."
[Works, Vol. III, p. 40.] This definition of the English
philosopher has been adopted by the American jurist, Chan-
cellor Kent, in his authoritative " Commentaries on American
Law." [Vol. I, p. 46.] The Swiss professor Vattel, whose
work is regarded as an important depository of the law of
nations, defines war as " that state in which we prosecute our
rights by force." [Book III, ch. 1, § 1.] In this he very
nearly follows the eminent Dutch authority Bynkershoek, who
says: " Bellum est eorum, qui suæ potestatis sunt, juris sui
persequendi ergo, concertatio per vim vel dolum." [Quæst.
Jur. Pub. Lib. I, ch. 6.] Mr. Whewell, who has done so
much to illustrate philosophy in all its departments, says, in
his recent work on the elements of morality and polity,
" Though war is appealed to, because there is no other ultimate tribunal to which states can have recourse, it is appealed
to for justice." [Vol. II, § 1146.] And in our country,
Mr. Lieber says, in a work abounding in learning and
sagacious thought [" Political Ethics," Vol. II, 643], that
war is a mode of obtaining rights,— a definition which hardly
differs in form from that of Vattel and Bynkershoek.

In harmony with these definitions, let me define the evil
which I now arraign. War is a public armed contest between
nations, under the sanction of international law, in order to

establish justice between them; as, for instance, to determine a disputed boundary line, or the title to territory.

This definition, it will be at once perceived, is confined to contests between nations. It is restrained to international war. It carefully excludes the question, so often agitated, of the right of revolution, and that other question, on which the friends of peace sometimes differ, the right of personal self-defence. It does not in any way involve the question, of the right to employ force in the administration of justice, or in the conservation of domestic quiet.

It is true that the term defensive is always applied to wars in our day. And it is creditable to the moral sense of nations that they feel constrained to allege this seeming excuse, although its absurdity is openly attested by the fact that it is advanced equally by each belligerent party. But it is unreasonable and impossible to suppose that any war can arise in the present age, under the sanctions of international law, except to determine an asserted right. Whatever may have been its character in periods of barbarism, or when invoked to repel an incursion of robbers or pirates — the enemies of the human race — war becomes in our day, among all the nations who are parties to the existing international law, simply a mode of litigation, or of deciding a *lis pendens*, between these nations. It is a mere trial of right. It is an appeal for justice to force. The wars that now lower from Mexico and from England are of this character. On the one side we assert a title to Texas, which is disputed; and on the other side, we assert a title to Oregon, which is disputed. Surely it is only according to " martial logic," or the " flash language " of a dishonest patriotism, that the ordeal by battle in these causes can be regarded, on either side, as defensive war. Nor did the threatened war with France in 1834, promise to assume any different character. Its professed object was to secure the payment of five millions of dollars — in other words, to determine by this ultimate tribunal a simple question of justice. And, going back still further in our history, the avowed purpose of the war declared by the United States against Great Britain in 1812, was to obtain from the latter power an abandonment of her claim to search American vessels. Unrighteous as was this claim, it seems clear that war was here invoked only as a trial of right.

But it forms no part of my purpose to consider individual wars in the past, except so far as necessary by way of example. My aim is above this. I wish to expose the irrational, cruel, and impious enormity of the whole custom of war, as sanctioned by the law of nations. On this account I resort to that supreme law, for the true definition of the evil. And let me be understood here as planting myself on this definition. This is the main foundation of the argument which I now venture to submit.

When we have considered, in succession, first, the character of war; secondly, the miseries it produces; and thirdly, its utter and shameful insufficiency, as a mode of determining justice, we may be able to decide, strictly and logically, whether it must not be ranked with crimes from which no true honor can spring, to individuals or nations, but rather condemnation and shame. It will then be important, in order fully to appreciate the character of this evil, and the necessity for its overthrow, to pass in review the various prejudices by which war is sustained, and especially that most pernicious prejudice, in obedience to which uncounted sums are diverted from the blessed purposes of peace to preparations for war.

I. And first, as to the character of war, or that part of our nature in which it has its origin.   Listen to the voice of the ancient poet of Bœotian Ascra:

> " This is the law for mortals ordained by the Ruler of Heaven;
> Fishes and beasts and birds of the air devour each other;
> Justice dwells not among them; only to man has he given
> Justice the highest and best."

The first idea that rises to the mind, in regarding war, is, that it is a resort to brute force, whereby each nation strives to overpower the other. Reason, and the divine part of our nature, in which alone we differ from the beasts, in which alone we approach the Divinity, in which alone are the elements of justice, the professed object of war, are dethroned. It is, in short, a temporary adoption, by men, of the character of wild beasts, emulating their ferocity, rejoicing like them in blood, and seeking, as with a lion's paw, to hold an asserted right.   This character of war is somewhat disguised, in more recent days, by the skill and knowledge which it employs; it is, however, still the same, made more destructive by the genius and intellect which have been degraded to be its servants. The early poets, in the unconscious simplicity of the world's childhood, make this boldly apparent. All the heroes of Homer are likened in their rage to the ungovernable fury of animals, or things devoid of human reason or human affection. Menelaus presses his way through the crowd, "like a beast." Sarpedon was aroused against the Argives, " as a lion against the crooked-horned oxen;" and afterwards rushes forward, "like a lion nourished on the mountains for a long time famished for want of flesh, but whose courage compels him to go even to the well-guarded sheepfold."   The Great Telamonian Ajax in one and the same passage is likened to " a beast," " a tawny lion," and "an obstinate ass;" and all the Greek chiefs, the flower of the camp, are described as ranged about Diomed, "like raw-eating lions or wild boars whose strength is irresistible." Even Hector, the hero in whom cluster the highest virtues of polished war, is called by the characteristic term, "the tamer of horses," and one of his renowned feats in battle, indicating only brute strength, is where he takes up and hurls a stone which two of the strongest men could not easily put into a wagon; and he drives over dead bodies and shields, while the axle is defiled by gore, and the guard about the seat, sprinkled from the horse's hoofs and from the tires of the wheels; and, in that most admired passage of ancient literature, before returning his child, the young Astyanax, to the arms of his wife, he invokes the gods for a single blessing on the boy's head, "that he may excel his father, and bring home bloody spoils, his enemy being slain, and so make glad the heart of his mother!"

Similar illustrations might be gathered, also, from the early fields of modern literature, as from those of antiquity, all showing the unconscious degradation of the soldier, who, in the pursuit of justice, renounces the human character to assume that of the beast. Henry V, in our own Shakespeare, in the spirit-stirring appeal to his troops, says:

> "When the blast of war blows in our ears,
> Then imitate the action of the tiger."

This is plain and frank, and reveals the true character of war.

I need not dwell on the moral debasement of man that must ensue. The passions of his nature are unleashed like so many bloodhounds, and suffered to rage. All the crimes which fill our prisons stalk abroad, plaited with the soldier's garb, and unwhipped of justice. Murder, robbery, rape, arson, theft, are the sports of this fiendish Saturnalia, when

> " The gates of mercy shall be all shut up,
> And the fleshed soldier, rough and hard of heart,
> In the liberty of bloody hand shall range
> With conscience wide as hell."

Such is the foul disfigurement which war produces in man; man, of whom it has been said, "How noble in reason, how infinite in faculties! in form and moving, how express and admirable! in action, how like an angel! in apprehension, how like a God!"

II. Let us now consider more particularly the effects or consequences of this resort to brute force, in the pursuit of justice.

The immediate effect of war is to sever all relations of friendship and commerce between the belligerent nations, and every individual thereof, impressing upon each citizen or subject the character of enemy. Imagine this change between England and the United States. The innumerable ships of the two countries, the white doves of commerce, bearing the olive of peace, would be driven from the sea, or turned from their proper purposes to be ministers of destruction; the threads of social and business intercourse which have become woven into a thick web would be suddenly snapped asunder; friend could no longer communicate with friend; the twenty thousand letters, which each fortnight are speeded, from this port alone, across the sea, could no longer be sent, and the human affections and desires, of which these are the precious expression, would seek in vain for utterance. Tell me, you, who have friends and kindred abroad, or who are bound to foreigners by more worldly relations of commerce, are you prepared for this rude separation?

This, however, is little compared with what must follow. It is but the first portentous shadow of the disastrous eclipse, the twilight usher of thick darkness, that is to cover the whole heavens, as with a pall, to be broken only by the blazing lightnings of the battle and the siege.

These horrors redden every page of history; while to the scandal of humanity, they have never wanted historians to describe them with feelings kindred to those by which they were inspired. The demon that has drawn the sword has also guided the pen. The favorite chronicler of modern Europe, Froissart — while according his admiration equally to bravery and cunning, to the courtesy which pardoned as to the rage which caused the flow of torrents of blood — dwells with especial delight on "beautiful captures," "beautiful rescues," "beautiful prowesses," and "beautiful feats of arms," and he wantons in picturing the assaults of cities, "which, being soon gained by force, were robbed, and put to the sword without mercy, men and women and children, while the churches were burnt." This was in a barbarous age. But popular writers, in our own day, dazzled by those false ideas of greatness, at which reason and Christianity blush, do not hesitate to dwell on similar scenes with terms of rapture and eulogy. Even the beautiful soul of Wilberforce, which sighed "that the bloody laws of his country sent many unprepared into another world," by capital punishment, could hail the slaughter of Waterloo, on the Sabbath that he held so holy, by which thousands were hurried into eternity, as "a splendid victory."

But my present purpose is less to judge the writer than to expose the horrors on horrors which he applauds. At Tarragona, above six thousand human beings, almost all defenceless, men and women, gray hairs and infant innocence, attract-

ive youth and wrinkled age, were butchered by the infu-
riated troops in one night, and the morning sun rose upon
a city whose streets and houses were inundated with blood.
And yet this is called "a glorious exploit." This was a
conquest by the French. At a later day, Ciudad Rodrigo
was stormed by the British, when in the license of victory,
there ensued a savage scene of plunder and violence, while
shouts and screams on all sides mingled fearfully with the
groans of the wounded. The churches were desecrated, the
cellars of wine and spirits were pillaged; fire was wantonly
applied to different parts of the city; and brutal intoxication
spread in every direction. It was only when the drunken
men dropped from excess, or fell asleep, that any degree of
order was restored, and yet the storming of Ciudad Rodrigo
is pronounced "one of the most brilliant exploits of the British army." This "beautiful feat of arms" was followed by
the storming of Badajoz, in which the same scenes were again
enacted with added atrocities. Let the story be told in the
words of a partial historian: "Shameless rapacity, brutal
intemperance, savage lust, cruelty and murder, shrieks, and
piteous lamentations, groans, shouts, imprecations, the hissing
of fire bursting from the houses, the crashing of doors and
windows, and the report of muskets used in violence,
resounded for two days and nights in the streets of Badajoz!
On the third, when the city was sacked, when the soldiers
were exhausted by their excesses, the tumult rather subsided
than was quelled! The wounded were then looked to, the
dead disposed of."

The same terrible war affords another instance of the atrocities of a siege, which cries to heaven for judgment. For
weeks before the surrender of Saragossa, the deaths were
from four to five hundred daily; the living were unable to

bury the dead, and thousands of carcasses, scattered about the streets and court-yards or piled in heaps at the doors of churches, were left to dissolve in their own corruption, or to be licked up by the flames of the burning houses. The city was shaken to its foundation by sixteen thousand shells thrown during the bombardment, and the explosion of forty-five thousand pounds of powder in the mines, while the bones of forty thousand persons of every age and both sexes bore dreadful testimony to the unutterable cruelty of war.

These might seem to be pictures from the age of Alaric, Scourge of God, or of Attila, whose boast was that the grass did not grow where his horse had set his foot: but no; they belong to our own times. They are portions of the wonderful but wicked career of him, who stands forth as the foremost representative of worldly grandeur. The heart aches, as we follow him and his marshals from field to field of Satanic glory. At Albuera, in Spain, we see the horrid piles of carcasses, while all the night the rain pours down, and the river and the hills and the woods on each side resound with the dismal clamors and groans of dying men. At Salamanca, long after the battle, we behold the ground strewn with the fragments of casques and cuirasses, and still blanched by the skeletons of those who fell. We follow in the dismal traces of his Russian campaign; at Valentina, we see the soldiers black with powder, their bayonets bent with the violence of the encounter; the earth ploughed with cannon shot, the trees torn and mutilated, the field covered with broken carriages, wounded horses, and mangled bodies, while disease, sad attendant on military suffering, sweeps thousands from the great hospitals of the army, and the multitude of amputated limbs, which there is not time to destroy, accumulate in bloody heaps, filling the air with corruption. What tongue, what pen, can describe the horrors of the field of Borodino, where between the rise and set of a single sun, more than one hundred thousand of our fellow men, equalling in number the population of this whole city, sank to the earth dead or wounded? Fifty days after the battle, no less than twenty thousand are found lying where they have fallen, and the whole plain is strewn with half-buried carcasses of men and horses, intermingled with garments dyed in blood, and bones gnawed by dogs and vultures. Who can follow the French army, in their dismal retreat, avoiding the pursuing spear of the Cossack, only to sink beneath the sharper frost and ice, in a temperature below zero, on foot, without a shelter for their bodies, and famishing on horse-flesh and a miserable compound of rye and snow-water? Still later, we behold him with a fresh array, contending against new forces under the walls of Dresden; and as the Emperor — having indulged the night before in royal supper with the King of Saxony — now rides over the field of battle, ghastly traces of the recent slaughter are seen on all sides; out of the newly made graves hands and arms are projecting, stark and stiff above the earth. And shortly afterward, when shelter is needed for the troops, direction is given to occupy the hospitals for the insane, with the order, " turn out the mad."

But why follow further in this career of blood? There is, however, one other picture of the atrocious, though natural consequences of war, occurring almost within our own day, that I would not omit. Let me bring to your mind Genoa, called the Suburb, City of Palaces, dear to the memory of American childhood as the birthplace of Christopher Columbus, and one of the spots first enlightened by the morning beams of civilization, whose merchants were princes, and whose rich argosies, in those early days, introduced to

Europe the choicest products of the East, the linen of Egypt, the spices of Arabia, and the silks of Samarcand. She still sits in queenly pride, as she sat then,—her mural crown studded with towers,—her churches rich with marble floors and rarest pictures,—her palaces of ancient doges and admirals yet spared by the hand of Time,—her close streets, thronged by one hundred thousand inhabitants,—at the feet of the maritime Alps, as they descend to the blue and tideless waters of the Mediterranean Sea,—leaning with her back against their strong mountain sides, overshadowed by the foliage of the fig-tree and the olive, while the orange and lemon fill with their perfume the air where reigns perpetual spring. Who can contemplate such a city without delight? Who can listen to the story of her sorrows without a pang?

In the last autumn of the last century the armies of the French Republic, which had dominated over Italy, were driven from their conquests, and compelled with shrunk forces, under Massena, to seek shelter within the walls of Genoa. After various efforts by the Austrian general on the land, aided by a bombardment from the British fleet in the harbor, to force the strong defences by assault, the city is invested by a strict blockade. All communication with the country is cut off on the one side, while the harbor is closed by the ever-wakeful British watch-dogs of war. Besides the French troops, within the beleaguered and unfortunate city, are the peaceful unoffending inhabitants, more than those of Boston in number. Provisions soon become scarce; scarcity sharpens into want, till fell famine, bringing blindness and madness in her train, rages like an Erinnys. Picture to yourself this large population, not pouring out their lives in the exulting rush of battle, but wasting at noon-day, the daughter by the side of the mother, the husband by the side of the wife. When grain and rice fail, flax-seed, millet, cocoas and almonds are ground by hand-mills into flour, and even bran, baked with honey, is eaten not to satisfy, but to deaden hunger. During the siege, but before the last extremities, a pound of horse-flesh is sold for thirty-two cents; a pound of bran for thirty cents; a pound of flour for $1.75. A single bean is soon sold for four cents, and a biscuit of three ounces for $2.25, and none are finally to be had. The miserable soldiers, after devouring all the horses in the city, are reduced to the degradation of feeding on dogs, cats, rats, and worms, which are eagerly hunted in the cellars and common sewers. Happy were now, exclaims an Italian historian, not those who lived, but those who died! The day is dreary from hunger; the night more dreary still from hunger accompanied by delirious fancies. Recourse is now had to herbs; monk's rhubarb, sorrel, mallows, wild succory. People of every condition, women of noble birth and beauty, seek on the slope of the mountain inclosed within the defences, those aliments which nature destined solely for the beast. A little cheese and a few vegetables are all that can be afforded to the sick and wounded, those sacred stipendiaries upon human charity. Men and women, in the last anguish of despair, now fill the air with their groans and shrieks; some in spasms, convulsions and contortions, gasping their last breath on the unpitying stones of the streets; alas! not more unpitying than man. Children, whom a dying mother's arms had ceased to protect, the orphans of an hour, with piercing cries, seek in vain the compassion of the passing stranger; but none pity or aid them. The sweet fountains of sympathy are all closed by the selfishness of individual distress. In the general agony, the more impetuous rush from the gates, and impale themselves on the Austrian bayonets, while others precipitate themselves into the sea. Others still (pardon the dire recital!) are driven to devour their shoes and the leather of their pouches, and the horror of human flesh so far abates that numbers feed like cannibals on the bodies of the dead.

At this stage the French general capitulated, claiming and receiving what are called "the honors of war;" but not before twenty thousand innocent persons, old and young, women and children, having no part or interest in the war, had died the most horrible of deaths. The Austrian flag floated over the captured Genoa but a brief span of time; for Bonaparte had already descended, like an eagle, from the Alps, and in less than a fortnight afterwards, on the plains of Marengo, shattered, as with an iron mace, the Austrian empire in Italy.

But wasted lands, ruined and famished cities, and slaughtered armies are only a part of "the purple testament of bleeding war." Every soldier is connected with others, as all of you, by dear ties of kindred, love, and friendship. He has been sternly summoned from the embraces of family. To him there is, perhaps, an aged mother, who has fondly hoped to lean her decaying frame upon his more youthful form; perhaps a wife, whose life has been just entwined inseparably with his, now condemned to wasting despair; perhaps brothers, sisters. As he falls on the field of battle, must not all these rush with his blood? But who can measure the distress that radiates as from a bloody sun, penetrating innumerable homes? Who can give the gauge and dimensions of this incalculable sorrow? Tell me, ye who feel the bitterness of parting with dear friends and kindred, whom you watch tenderly till the last golden sands are run out, and the great hour-glass is turned, what is the measure of your anguish? Your friend departs, soothed by kindness and in the arms of love; the soldier gasps out his life with no friend

DEAN STANLEY

near, while the scowl of hate darkens all that he beholds, darkens his own departing soul.   Who can forget the anguish that fills the bosom and crazes the brain of Leonora, in the matchless ballad of Burger, when seeking in vain among the returning squadrons for her lover left dead on Prague's ensanguined plain?   But every field of blood has many Leonoras. From a master-poet of antiquity we draw a vivid image of homes made desolate by battle:

> " But through the bounds of Grecia's land,
> Who sent her sons for Troy to part,
> See mourning, with much suffering heart,
> On each man's threshold stand,
> On each sad hearth in Grecia's land.
> Well may her soul with grief be rent;
> She well remembers whom she sent,
> She sees them not return;
> Instead of men, to each man's home,
> Urns and ashes only come,
> And the armor which they wore;
> Sad relics to their native shore.
> For Mars, the barterer of the lifeless clay,
> Who sells for gold the slain,
> And holds the scale in battle's doubtful day,
> High balanced o'er the plain,
> From Ilium's walls for men returns
> Ashes and sepulchral urns;
> Ashes wet with many a tear,
> Sad relics of the fiery bier.
> Round the full urns the general groan
> Goes, as each their kindred own.
> One they mourn in battle strong,
> And one, that 'mid the armed throng,
> He sunk in glory's slaughtering tide,
> And for another's consort died.
>
> .   .   .   .   .   .
>
> Others they mourn whose monuments stand
> By Ilium's walls on foreign strand;
> Where they fell in beauty's bloom,
> There they lie in hated tomb;
> Sunk beneath the massy mound,
> In eternal chambers bound,"

III. From this dreary picture of the miseries of war, I turn to another branch of the subject.

War is utterly ineffectual to secure or advance the object at which it professes to aim.   The misery which it excites, contributes to no end, helps to establish no right, and therefore in no respect determines justice between the contending nations.

The fruitlessness and vanity of war appear in the results of the great wars by which the world has been lacerated. After long struggles, in which each nation has inflicted and received incalculable injury, peace has been gladly obtained on the basis of the condition of things before the war — *Status ante bellum.* I cannot better illustrate this point than by the familiar example — humiliating to both countries, in the light of true glory — of the last war with Great Britain, the professed object of which was to obtain from the latter power a renunciation of her claim to impress our seamen. The greatest number of American seamen ever officially alleged to be compulsorily serving in the British navy was about eight hundred. To overturn this injustice, the arbitrament of war was invoked; and the whole country was doomed, for more than three years, to its accursed blight. Our commerce was driven from the seas; the resources of the land were drained by taxation; villages on the Canadian frontier were laid in ashes; the metropolis of the Republic was captured, while gaunt distress raged everywhere within our borders. Weary at last with this rude trial, our government appointed commissioners to treat for peace, under these specific instructions: "Your first duty will be to conclude peace with Great Britain, and you are authorized to do it in case you obtain a satisfactory stipulation against impressment, one which shall secure under our flag protection to the crew. If this encroachment of Great Britain is not provided against, the United States have appealed to arms in vain." Afterward, despairing of extorting from Great Britain a relinquishment of the unrighteous claim, and foreseeing only an accumulation of calamities from an inveterate prosecution of the war, our government directed their negotiators, in concluding a treaty of peace, "to omit any stipulation on the subject of impressment. The instructions were obeyed, and the treaty that once more restored to us the blessings of peace, which we had rashly cast away, and which the country hailed with an intoxication of joy, contained no allusion to the subject of impressment, nor did it provide for the surrender of a single American sailor detained in the service of the British navy, and thus, by the confession of our own government, "the United States had appealed to arms in vain."

All this is the natural result of an appeal to war, in order to establish justice. Justice implies the exercise of the judgment in the determination of right. Now war not only supersedes the judgment, but delivers over the results to superiority of force or to chance.

Superior force may end in conquest; indeed, this is its natural consequence; but it cannot adjudicate any right. We expose the absurdity of its arbitrament, when, by a familiar phrase of sarcasm, we speak of the right of the strongest — excluding, of course, all idea of right, except the right of the lion as he springs upon a weaker beast, of the wolf as he tears in pieces the lamb, of the vulture as he gorges upon the dove. The grossest spirits will admit that this is not justice.

But the battle is not always to the strong, and even the superiority of force is often checked by the proverbial contingencies of war. Especially are such contingencies revealed in rankest absurdity, where nations, as is their acknowledged custom, without regard to their respective forces, whether weaker or stronger, voluntarily appeal to this mad umpirage. Who can measure beforehand the currents of the heady

fight? In common language we speak of the chances of battle; and soldiers whose lives are devoted to this harsh vocation, yet call it a game. The Great Captain of our age, who
seemed to chain victory to his chariot wheels, in a formal
address to his officers, on entering Russia, says: "In war,
fortune has an equal share with ability in procuring success."
The mighty victory of Marengo, the accident of an accident,
wrested unexpectedly at the close of the day from a foe, who
at an earlier hour was successful, had taught him the uncertainty of war. Afterwards, in the bitterness of his spirit,
when his immense forces had been shivered, and his triumphant eagles driven back with broken wing, he exclaimed, in
that remarkable conversation recorded by the Abbé de Pradt:
"Well! this is war. High in the morning — low enough at
night. From a triumph to a fall is often but a step." The
same sentiment is uttered by the military historian of the
Peninsular campaigns, when he says: "Fortune always
asserts her supremacy in war, and often from a slight mistake, such disastrous consequences flow, that, in every age
and in every nation, the uncertainty of wars has been proverbial;" and again, in another place, in considering the
conduct of Wellington, he confesses: "A few hours' delay,
an accident, a turn of fortune, and he would have been foiled!
ay! but this is war, always dangerous and uncertain, an ever-
rolling wheel and armed with scythes." And can intelligent
man look for justice to an ever-rolling wheel armed with
scythes?

Chance is written on every battle-field. It may be less
discerned, in the conflict of large masses, than in the conflict of individuals, though equally present in both. How
capriciously the wheel turned when the fortunes of Rome
were staked on the combat between the Horatii and Curiatii!

— and who, at one time, could have augured that the single Horatius, with his two slain brothers on the field, would overpower the three living enemies? But this is not alone. In all the combats of history, involving the fate of individuals or nations, we learn to revolt at the frenzy which carried questions of property, of freedom, or of life to a judgment so uncertain and senseless.

During the early modern centuries, and especially in the moral night of the dark ages, the practice extensively prevailed throughout Europe, of submitting controversies, whether of individuals or communities, to this adjudication. I pass over the custom of private war, though it aptly illustrates the subject, stopping merely to join in that delight, which,— in a period of ignorance, before this mode of determining justice had gradually yielded to the ordinances of monarchs, and an advancing civilization,— hailed its temporary suspension, as the truce of God; and I come at once to the judicial combat, or trial by battle. In this custom, as in a mirror, we may behold the hideousness of war.

The trial by battle was a formal and legitimate mode of deciding controversies, principally between individuals. Like the other ordeals, by burning ploughshares, by holding hot iron, by dipping the hand in hot water or hot oil — and like the great ordeal of war — it was a presumptuous appeal to Providence, under an apprehension and hope that Heaven would give the victory to him who had the right. Its object was precisely the professed object of war,— the determination of justice. It was sanctioned by municipal law as an arbitrament for individuals, as war — to the scandal of civilization — is still sanctioned by international law as an arbitrament for nations. Men, says the brilliant Frenchman, Montesquieu, subject to rules even their prejudices; and the trial by

battle was surrounded by artificial regulations of multifarious
detail, constituting an extensive system, determining how and
when it should be waged; as war is surrounded by a complex
code, known as the laws of war.

No question was too sacred, grave, or recondite for this
tribunal. The title of an abbey to a neighboring church, in
France, was decided by it; and an emperor of Germany,
according to a faithful ecclesiastic, "desirous of dealing honor-
ably with his people and nobles," (mark here the standard of
honor!) waived the judgment of the court on a grave question
of law, as to the descent of property, and referred it to champions. Human folly did not stop here. In Spain a subtle
point of theology was submitted to the same determination.
But the trial by battle was not confined to particular countries or to rare occasions. It prevailed everywhere in Europe,
while in many places it superseded all other ordeals and even
trial by proofs, and was extended alike to criminal matters,
and to questions of property. But like war in our day, its
justice and fitness as an arbitrament were early doubted or
condemned. Luitprand, a king of the Lombards, in Italy,
during that middle period which belongs neither to ancient
nor to modern times, in a law bearing date 713, expresses
his distrust of it as a mode of determining justice; but the
monarch is obliged to add that, on account of the custom of
his Lombard people, he cannot forbid the impious law. His
words deserve emphatic mention: "Propter consuetudinem
gentis nostræ Longobardorum legem impiam vetare non pos-
sumus." The appropriate epithet by which he has branded
the trial by battle is the important bequest of the royal Lombard law-giver to a distant posterity. For this his name will
be cherished, with grateful regard, in the annals of civilization.

This custom received another blow from Rome. At the

latter part of the thirteenth century, Don Pedro, of Aragon, and Charles, of Anjou, having exchanged letters of defiance, the former proposed a personal combat, which was accepted by the latter, on condition that Sicily should be the prize of success.   Each called down upon himself all the vengeance of heaven, and the last dishonor, if he failed to appear at the appointed time before the Seneschal of Acquitaine, or, in case of defeat, if he refused to consign Sicily undisturbed to the victor.   While the two champions were preparing for the lists, the Pope, Martin IV, protested with all his power against this new trial by battle, which staked the sovereignty of a kingdom, a feudatory of the Holy See, on a wild stroke of chance.   By a papal bull, dated at Civita Vecchia, April 5, 1283, he threatened excommunication to either of the princes who proceeded to a combat which he pronounced criminal and abominable.   And, by a letter of the same date, he announced to Edward I of England, Duke of Acquitaine, the agreement of the two princes, which he most earnestly declared to be full of indecency and rashness, hostile to the concord of Christendom, and careless of Christian blood; and he urged upon the English monarch to spare no effort to prevent the combat— menacing him with excommunication, and his territories with interdict, if it should take place.   Edward refusing to guaranty the safety of the combatants in Acquitaine, the parties retired without consummating their duel. And the judgment of the Holy See, which thus accomplished its immediate object, though not in terms directed to the suppression of the custom of trial by battle, remains, nevertheless, from its peculiar energy of language, in perpetual testimony against it.

To a monarch of France belongs the honor of first interposing the royal authority, for the entire suppression within his jurisdiction of this impious custom, so universally adopted, so dear to the nobility, and so profoundly rooted in the institutions of the Feudal Age. And here, let me pause with reverence, as I mention the name of St. Louis, a prince, whose unenlightened errors may find easy condemnation in our age of larger toleration and wider knowledge, but whose firm and upright soul, whose exalted sense of justice, whose fatherly regard for the happiness of his people, whose respect for the rights of others, whose conscience void of offence before God and man, make him foremost among Christian rulers, the highest example for a Christian prince or a Christian people,— a model of true greatness. He was of conscience all-compact, subjecting all that he did to the single and exclusive test of moral rectitude, disregarding all considerations of worldly advantage, all fear of worldly consequences.

His soul, thus tremblingly sensitive to questions of right, was shocked by the judicial combat. It was a sin, in his sight, thus to tempt God, by demanding of him a miracle, whenever judgment was pronounced. From these intimate convictions sprung a royal ordinance, first promulgated at a parliament assembled in 1260, in these words: "We forbid to all persons throughout our dominions the trial by battle; and, instead of battles, we establish proofs by witnesses; and we do not take away the other good and loyal proofs which have been used in lay courts to this day. . . . And these battles we abolish in our dominions forever."

Such were the restraints on the royal authority, that this ordinance did not extend to the demesnes of the barons and feudatories of the realm, being confined in its operation to those of the king. But where the power of St. Louis did not reach, there he labored by his example, his influence, and his express intercession. He treated with many of the great vassals of the crown, and induced them to renounce this unnatural usage. Though for many years later, France in some parts continued to be vexed by it, still its overthrow commenced with the Ordinance of St. Louis.

Honor and blessings attend the name of this truly Christian king; who submitted all his actions to the heaven-descended sentiment of duty; who began a long and illustrious reign by renouncing and restoring a portion of the conquests of his predecessor, saying to those about him, whose souls did not ascend to the height of his morality, "I know that the predecessors of the King of England have lost by the right of conquest the land which I hold; and the land which I give him, I do not give because I am bound to him or his heirs, but to put love between my children and his children, who are cousins-german; and it seems to me that what I thus give, I employ to good purpose!" Honor to him who never grasped by force or cunning any new acquisition; who never sought advantage from the turmoils and dissensions of his neighbors, but studied to allay them; who, first of Christian princes, rebuked the spirit of war, saying to those who would have him profit by the dissensions of his neighbors, "Blessed are the peacemakers;" who, by an immortal ordinance, abolished trial by battle throughout his dominions; who aimed to do justice to all his people, and to all neighbors, and in the extremity of his last illness on the sickening sands of Tunis, among the bequests of his spirit, enjoined on his son and successor, "in maintaining justice to be inflexible and loyal, turning neither to the right hand nor to the left!"

To condemn the trial by battle no longer requires the sagacity above his age of the Lombard monarch — the intrepid judgment of the sovereign Pontiff, or the ecstatic soul of St.

Louis. An incident of history, as curious as it is authentic, illustrates this point, and shows the certain progress of opinion. This custom, as a part of the common law of England, was partially restrained by Henry II, and rebuked at a later day by Elizabeth. But though it fell into desuetude, quietly overruled by the enlightened sense of successive generations, yet, to the disgrace of English jurisprudence, it was not legislatively abolished till almost in our own day,— as late as 1817,— when the right to it had been openly claimed in Westminster Hall. An ignorant man charged with murder, —whose name, Abraham Thornton, is necessarily connected with the history of this monstrous usage,— being proceeded against by the ancient process of appeal, pleaded, when brought into court, as follows "Not guilty, and I am ready to defend the same by my body;" and thereupon, taking off his glove, he threw it upon the floor. The appellant, not choosing to respond to this challenge, abandoned his proceedings. The bench, the bar, and the whole country were startled by the outrage; and at the next session of Parliament trial by battle was abolished in England. On introducing a bill for this purpose, the attorney-general remarked in appropriate words, that "if the party had persevered, he had no doubt the legislature would have felt it their imperious duty to interfere, and pass an *ex post facto* law to prevent so degrading a spectacle from taking place."

These words aptly portray the impression which the trial by battle excites in our day. Its folly and wickedness are apparent to all. As we revert to those early periods in which it prevailed, our minds are impressed by the general barbarism; we recoil, with horror, from the awful subjection of justice to brute force; from the impious profanation of God in deeming him present in these outrages; from the moral

degradation out of which they sprang, and which they perpetuated; we involve ourselves in self-complacent virtue, and
thank God that we are not as these men, that ours is, indeed,
an age of light, while theirs was an age of darkness!

But do not forget, fellow citizens, that this criminal and
impious custom, which we all condemn in the case of individuals, is openly avowed by our own country, and by the
other countries of the great Christian federation — nay, that
it is expressly established by international law — as a proper
mode of determining justice between nations; while the feats
of hardihood by which it is waged, and the triumphs of its
fields, are exalted beyond all other labors, whether of learning, of industry, or of benevolence, as a well-spring of glory.
Alas! upon our own heads and upon our own age, be the
judgment of barbarism, which we pronounce upon those that
have gone before! At this moment, in this period of light,
while the noon-day sun of civilization, to the contented souls
of many, seems to be standing still in the heavens, as upon
Gibeon, the relations between nations continue to be governed by the odious rules of brute violence, which once pre-
dominated between individuals. The dark ages have not yet
passed away; Erebus and black Night, born of Chaos, still
brood over the earth; nor can we hail the clear day, until the
mighty hearts of the nations have been touched, as the hearts
of individual men, and all shall acknowledge one and the
same law of right.

Who has told you, fond man! thus to find glory in an act
— when performed by a nation — which you condemn as a
crime or a barbarism when committed by an individual! In
what vain conceit of wisdom and virtue do you find this
incongruous morality? Where is it declared that God, who
is no respecter of persons, is a respecter of multitudes?

Whence do you draw these partial laws of a powerful and impartial God? Man is immortal; but states are mortal. He has a higher destiny than states. Can states be less amenable to the supreme moral law? Each individual is an atom of the mass. Must not the mass, in its conscience, be like the individuals of which it is composed? Shall the mass, in its relations with other masses, do what individuals in their relations with each other may not do? Clearly not. As in the physical creation, so in morals, there is but one law for individuals and masses. It was the lofty discovery of Newton, that the simple law, which determines the fall of an apple, prevails everywhere throughout the universe — ruling each particle in reference to every other particle, whether large or small — reaching from the earth to the heavens, and controlling the infinite motions of the spheres; so, with equal scope, another simple law, the law of right, which binds the individual, binds also two or three when gathered together — binds conventions and congregations of men — binds villages, towns, and cities — binds states, nations, and empires — clasps the whole human family in its seven-fold embrace; nay more,

> " Beyond the flaming bounds of place and time,
> The living throne, the sapphire blaze,"

it binds the angels of heaven, the Seraphim, full of love, the Cherubim, full of knowledge; above all, it binds, in self-imposed bonds, a just and omnipotent God. This is the law, of which the ancient poet sings, as queen alike of mortals and immortals. It is of this, and not of any earthly law, that Hooker speaks in that magnificent period which sounds like an anthem; " Of law no less can be said, than that her seat is the bosom of God, her voice the harmony of the world; all things in heaven and earth do her homage, the very least as feeling her care, the greatest as not exempted from her power; both angels and men, and creatures of what condition soever, though each in different sort and manner, yet all with uniform consent admiring her as the mother of their peace and joy."

Stripped of all delusive apologies, and tried by this comprehensive law — under which nations are set to the bar like common men — war falls from glory into barbarous guilt. It takes its place among bloody transgressions, while its flaming honors are turned into ignominy and shame. Painful as it may be to existing prejudices, we must learn to abhor it, as we abhor similar transgressions by a vulgar offender. Every word of reprobation, which the enlightened conscience now fastens upon the savage combatant in the trial by battle, or which it applies to the unhappy being, who, in murderous duel, takes the life of his fellow man, belongs also to the nation that appeals to war. Amidst the thunders which made Sinai tremble, God declared, " Thou shalt not kill; " and the voice of these thunders, with this commandment, has been prolonged to our own day in the echoes of Christian churches. What mortal shall restrain the application of these words? Who on earth is empowered to vary or abridge the commandments of God? Who shall presume to declare that this injunction was directed, not to nations, but to individuals only; not to many, but to one only; that one man may not kill, but that many may; that it is forbidden to each individual to destroy the life of a single human being, but that it is not forbidden to a nation to cut off by the sword a whole people? We are struck with horror and our hair stands on end, at the report of a single murder; we think of the soul that has been hurried to its final account; we seek the murderer; and the state puts forth all its energies to secure his

punishment. Viewed in the unclouded light of truth, what
is war but organized murder; murder of malice aforethought;
in cold blood; under the sanctions of an impious law; through
the operation of an extensive machinery of crime; with
innumerable hands; at incalculable cost of money; by subtle
contrivances of cunning and skill; or amidst the fiendish
atrocities of the savage brutal assault?

The Scythian, undisturbed by the illusion of military
glory, snatched a phrase of justice from an acknowledged
criminal, when he called Alexander "the greatest robber in
the world." And the Roman satirist, filled with similar
truth, in pungent words, touched to the quick that flagrant
unblushing injustice which dooms to condign punishment the
very guilt, that in another sphere, and on a grander scale,
under the auspices of a nation, is hailed with acclamation.

"Ille crucem sceleris pretium tulit, hic diadema."

Mankind, blind to the real character of war, while condemn-
ing the ordinary malefactor, may continue yet a little longer
to crown its giant actors with glory. A generous posterity
may pardon to unconscious barbarism the atrocities which
they have waged; but the whole custom — and it is of this
that I speak — though sanctioned by existing law, cannot
escape the unerring judgment of reason and religion. The
outrages, which it madly permits and invokes for professed
purposes of justice, cannot be authorized by any human
power; and they must rise in overwhelming judgment, not
only against those who wield the weapons of battle, but
against all who uphold its monstrous arbitrament.

When, oh! when shall the St. Louis of the nations arise —
the Christian ruler, or Christian people, who, in the spirit of
true greatness, shall proclaim, that henceforward forever the
great trial by battle shall cease; that "these battles" shall

be abolished throughout the commonwealth of civilization; that a spectacle so degrading shall never be allowed again to take place; and that it is the duty of nations, involving of course the highest policy, to establish love between each other, and, in all respects, at all times, with all persons, whether their own people or the people of other lands, to be governed by the sacred law of right, as between man and man. May God speed the coming of that day!

I have already alluded, in the early part of this address, to some of the obstacles encountered by the advocate of peace. One of these is the warlike tone of the literature, by which our minds are formed. The world has supped so full with battles, that all its inner modes of thought, and many of its rules of conduct seem to be incarnadined with blood; as the bones of swine, fed on madder, are said to become red. But I now pass this by, though a fruitful theme, and hasten to other topics. I propose to consider in succession, very briefly, some of those prejudices, which are most powerful in keeping alive the custom of war.

1. One of the most important of these is the prejudice in its favor founded on the belief in its necessity. When war is called a necessity, it is meant, of course, that its object cannot be attained in any other way. Now I think that it has already appeared with distinctness, approaching demonstration, that the professed object of war, which is justice between nations, is in no respect promoted by war; that force is not justice, nor in any way conducive to justice; that the eagles of victory can be the emblems only of successful force, and not of established right. Justice can be obtained only by the exercise of the reason and judgment; but these are silent in the din of arms. Justice is without passion; but war lets loose all the worst passions of our nature, while

" Chance, high arbiter, more embroils the fray." The age has passed in which a nation, within the enchanted circle of civilization, can make war upon its neighbor, for any professed purpose of booty or vengeance. It does " naught in hate, but all in honor." There are professions of tenderness even which mingle with the first mutterings of the dismal strife. As if conscience-struck at the criminal abyss into which they are madly plunging, each of the great litigants seeks to fix on the other the charge of hostile aggression, and to assume to itself the ground of defending some right; some stolen Texas; some distant, worthless Oregon. Like Pontius Pilate, it vainly washes its hands of innocent blood, and straightway allows a crime at which the whole heavens are darkened, and two kindred countries are severed, as the veil of the Temple was rent in twain.

The various modes, proposed for the determination of international disputes, are negotiation, mediation, arbitration, and a congress of nations — all of them practicable and calculated to secure peaceful justice. These may be employed at any time under the existing law of nations. But the very law itself, which sanctions war, may be changed — as regards two or more nations by treaty between them, and as regards all the Christian nations by general consent. If nations can agree together, in the solemn provisions of international law, to establish war as an arbiter of justice between them, they can also agree together to abolish this arbitrament, and to establish peaceful substitutes; precisely as similar substitutes have been established by the municipal law in order to determine controversies among individuals. A system of arbitration may be instituted by treaties, or a congress of nations may be charged with the high duty of organizing an ultimate tribunal instead of " these battles "

3 for the decision of international controversies. The will only
is required in order to succeed in this work.

Let it not be said, then, that war is a necessity; and may
our country aim at the true glory of taking the lead in disowning the revolting system of international lynch law, and
in proclaiming peaceful substitutes therefor, as the only
proper modes of determining justice between nations! Such
a glory, unlike the earthly fame of battles, shall be immortal
as the stars, dropping perpetual light upon the souls of men!

2. Another prejudice in favor of war is founded on the
practice of nations, past and present. There is no crime or
enormity in morals which may not find the support of
human example, often on an extended scale. But it cannot
be urged in our day that we are to look for a standard of
duty in the conduct of vain, mistaken, fallible man. It is
not in the power of man, by any subtle alchemy, to transmute
wrong into right. Because war is according to the practice
of the world, it cannot follow that it is right. For ages the
world worshipped false gods; but these gods were not less
false, because all bowed before them. At this moment the
larger portion of mankind are heathen; but heathenism is
not true. It was once the practice of nations to slaughter
prisoners of war; but even the spirit of war recoils now from
this bloody sacrifice. In Sparta, theft, instead of being
judged as a crime, was, by a perverse morality, like war itself
dignified into an art and an accomplishment; like war, it was
admitted into the system of youthful education; and it was
enlightened, like war also, by an instance of unconquerable
firmness, which is a barbaric counterfeit of virtue. The
Spartan youth, who allowed the stolen fox beneath his robe
to eat into his heart, is an example of mistaken fortitude,
not unlike that which we are asked to admire in the soldier.

Other illustrations of this character crowd upon the mind; but I will not dwell upon them. We turn with disgust from Spartan cruelty and the wolves of Taygetus; from the awful cannibalism of the Fiji Islands; from the profane rites of innumerable savages; from the crushing Juggernaut; from the Hindoo widow lighting her funeral pyre; from the Indian dancing at the stake. But had not all these, in their respective places and days, like war, the sanction of established usage?

But it is often said, "Let us not be wiser than our fathers." Rather let us try to excel our fathers in wisdom. Let us imitate what in them was good, but not bind ourselves, as in the chains of fate, by their imperfect example. Principles are higher than human examples. Examples may be followed when they accord with the admonitions of duty. But he is unwise and wicked who attempts to lean upon these, rather than upon those truths, which, like the everlasting arm, cannot fail!

In all modesty be it said, we have lived to little purpose, if we are not wiser than the generations that have gone before us. It is the grand distinction of man that he is a progressive being; that his reason at the present day is not merely the reason of a single human being, but that of the whole human race, in all ages from which knowledge has descended, in all lands from which it has been borne away. We are the heirs to an inheritance of truth, grandly accumulating from generation to generation. The child at his mother's knee is now taught the orbits of the heavenly bodies,

        "Where worlds on worlds compose one universe,"

the nature of this globe, the character of the tribes of men by which it is covered, and the geography of nations, to an extent far beyond the ken of the most learned of other days. It is, therefore, true, as has been said, that antiquity is the real infancy of man; it is then that he is immature, ignorant, wayward, childish, selfish, finding his chief happiness in pleasures of sense, unconscious of the higher delights of knowledge, of justice, and of love. The animal part of his nature reigns supreme, and he is driven on by the gross impulses of force. He seeks contests, war and blood. But we are advanced from the childhood of man; reason and the kindlier virtues of age, repudiating and abhorring force, now bear sway. We are the true Ancients. The single lock on the battered forehead of Old Time is thinner now than when our fathers attempted to grasp it; the hour-glass has been turned often since; the scythe is heavier laden with the work of death.

Let us cease, then, to look for a lamp to our feet, in the feeble tapers that glimmer in the sepulchres of the Past. Rather let us hail those ever-burning lights above, in whose beams is the brightness of noon-day!

3. There is a topic which I approach with diffidence; but in the spirit of frankness. It is the influence which war, though condemned by Christ, has derived from the Christian Church. When Constantine on one of his marches, at the head of his army, beheld the luminous trophy of the cross in the sky right above the meridian sun, inscribed with these words, " By this conquer," had his soul been penetrated by the true spirit of Him whose precious symbol it was, he would have found in it no inspiration to the spear and the sword. He would have received the lesson of self-sacrifice, as from the lips of the Saviour, and would have learned that by no earthly weapons of battle can any true victory be won. The pride of conquest would have been rebuked, and the bauble

sceptre of empire would have fallen from his hands. By this conquer; that is, by patience, suffering, forgiveness of evil, by all those virtues of which the cross is the affecting token, conquer; and the victory shall be greater than any in the annals of Roman conquest; it may not find a place in the records of man; but it shall appear in the register of everlasting life.

The Christian Church, after the first centuries of its existence, failed to discern the peculiar spiritual beauty of the faith which it professed. Like Constantine, it found new incentives to war in the religion of peace; and such has been its character, let it be said fearlessly, even to our own day. The Pope of Rome, the asserted head of the church, the Vicegerent of Christ on earth, whose seal is a fisherman, on whose banner is a Lamb before the holy Cross, assumed the command of armies, often mingling the thunders of battle with the thunders of the Vatican. The dagger which projected from the sacred vestments of the Archbishop de Retz, as he appeared in the streets of Paris, was called by the crowd "the Archbishop's Missal." We read of mitred prelates in armor of proof, and seem still to catch the jingle of the golden spurs of the bishops in the streets of Cologne. The sword of knighthood was consecrated by the Church; and priests were often the expert masters in military exercises. I have seen at the gates of the Papal palace in Rome a constant guard of Swiss soldiers; I have seen, too, in our own streets a show, as incongruous and as inconsistent, a pastor of a Christian church swelling by his presence the pomp of a military parade! Ay! more than this; some of us have heard, within a few short weeks, in a Christian pulpit, from the lips of an eminent Christian divine, a sermon in which we are encouraged to serve the God of battles, and, as citizen soldiers, to fight for peace; — a sentiment in unhappy harmony with the profane language of the British peer, when, in addressing the House of Lords, he said, " The best road to peace, my Lords, is war; war carried on in the same manner in which we are taught to worship our Creator, namely, with all our souls, with all our minds, with all our hearts, and with all our strength; " but which surely can find no support in the religion of him who has expressly enjoined, when one cheek is smitten to turn the other, and to which we listen with pain and mortification from the lips of one who has voluntarily become a minister of Christian truth; alas! in his mind inferior to that of the heathen, who declared that he preferred the unjustest peace to the justest war.

Well may we be astonished, that now in an age of civilization the god of battles should be invoked. *Deo imperante, quem adesse bellantibus credunt,* are the appropriate words of surprise, by which Tacitus describes a similar savage superstition of the ancient Germans. The polite Roman did not think God present, to cheer those who fight in battle. And this heathen superstition must at last have lost something of its hold even in Germany; for, at a recent period, her most renowned captain — whose false glory procured for him from flattering courtiers and a barbarous world the title of Great — Frederick of Prussia said, with a commendable frankness, that he always found the god of battles on the side of the strongest regiments; and when it was proposed to him to adopt as an inscription for his banner, soon to flout the sky of Silesia, " For God and Country," he rejected the first word, declaring that it was not proper to introduce the name of the Deity in the quarrels of men. By this Christian sentiment the war-worn monarch may be remembered, when the fame of his battles has passed away.

The sanctions of religion are now thrown about the very arbitrament of war. By sermon and prayer, the name of Christ
is pressed into the retinue of this wicked custom; and the
chosen ministers of the Prince of Peace, careless of his example and of his precepts, continue to mingle in all its pomps,
its observances and its battles. When alas! will they learn
to look for their faith,— not to human examples, not to the
ideas, prejudices and practices of the crowd by which they
are surrounded,— but to the Master whom they vainly
acknowledge, and to the sacred written Word from which
they imperfectly preach!

One of the beautiful pictures, adorning the dome of a
church in Rome, by that master of art, whose immortal colors
breathe as with the voice of a poet, the divine Raphael, represents Mars, in the attitude of war, with a drawn sword
uplifted and ready to strike, while an unarmed angel from
behind, with gentle but irresistible force, arrests and holds
the descending arm. Such is the true image of Christian
duty; nor can I readily perceive the difference in principle
between those ministers of the Gospel, who themselves gird
on the sword, as in the olden time, and those others, who,
unarmed, and in customary suit of solemn black, lend the
sanction of their presence to the martial array, or to any form
of preparation for war. The drummer, who pleaded that he
did not fight, was held more responsible for the battle than
the mere soldier; for it was the sound of his drum that
inflamed the flagging courage of the troops.

4. From the prejudices engendered by the Church, I pass
to the prejudices engendered by the army itself; prejudices
having their immediate origin more particularly in military
life, but unfortunately diffusing themselves, in widening
though less apparent circles, throughout the community. I

allude directly to what is called the point of honor, early child of chivalry, the living representative in our day of an age of barbarism. It is difficult to define what is so evanescent, so impalpable, so chimerical, so unreal; and yet which exercises such fiendish power over many men, and controls the relations of states. As a little water, fallen into the crevice of a rock, under the congelation of winter, swells till it bursts the thick and stony fibres, so a word, or a slender act, dropping into the heart of man, under the hardening influence of this pernicious sentiment, dilates till it rends in pieces the sacred depository of human affections, while the demons hate and strife, no longer restrained, are let loose abroad. The musing Hamlet saw the strange and unnatural potency of this sentiment, when his soul pictured to his contemplations—

> —" the army of such mass and charge,
> Led by a delicate and tender prince,
> Exposing what is mortal and unsure
> To all that fortune, death, and danger dare
> Even for an egg-shell;"

and when he says, with a point which has given to the sentiment its strongest and most popular expression,

> —" rightly to be great
> Is not to stir without great argument;
> But greatly to find quarrel in a straw
> When honor's at the stake."

And when is honor at stake? This question opens again the views with which I commenced, and with which I hope to close this discourse. Honor can be at stake only where justice and beneficence are at stake; it can never depend on an egg-shell, or a straw; it can never depend on an impotent word of anger or folly, not even if that word be followed by a blow. In fine, true honor is to be found in the highest moral and intellectual excellence, in the dignity of the human soul, in the nearest approach to those qualities which we reverence as the attributes of God. Our community frowns with indignation upon the profaneness of the duel, which has its rise in this irrational point of honor. But are they aware that they themselves indulge the sentiment, on a gigantic scale, when they recognize what is called the honor of the country as a proper ground for war? We have already seen that justice is in no respect promoted by war. Is true honor promoted where justice is not?

But the very word honor, as used by the world, fails to express any elevated sentiment. How infinitely below the sentiment of duty! It is a word of easy virtue, that has been prostituted to the most opposite characters and transactions. From the field of Pavia, where France suffered one of the greatest reverses in her annals, Francis writes to his mother: "All is lost except honor." At a later day, the renowned cook, the grand Vatel, in a paroxysm of grief and mortification at the failure of two dishes expected on the table, exclaims, "I have lost my honor." Montesquieu, whose writings are a constellation of epigrams, places it in direct contrast with virtue. He represents what he calls the prejudice of honor as the animating principle of monarchy, while virtue is the animating principle of a republic; saying that in well-governed monarchies almost everybody will be a good citizen, but it will be rare to meet with a really good man. By an instinct that points to the truth, we do not apply this term to the high columnar virtues which sustain and decorate life, to parental affection, to justice, to the attributes of God. He would seem to borrow a worldly phrase, showing a slight appreciation of the distinctive qualities for which they are reverenced, who should speak of a father, a mother, a judge, an angel or of God, as persons of honor. In such sacred connections we feel, beyond the force of any argument, the unworthy character of the sentiment to which this term refers.

The degrading rule of honor is founded in the imagined necessity of resenting by force a supposed injury, whether by word or act. But admit that such an injury is received, falsely seeming to sully the character; is it wiped away by a resort to force, and thus descending to the brutal level of its author? "Could I have wiped your blood from my conscience as easily as I can this insult from my face," said a marshal of France, greater on this occasion than on any field of fame, "I would have laid you dead at my feet." It is Plato, reporting the angelic wisdom of Socrates, who declares in one of those beautiful dialogues, which shine with stellar light across the ages, that it is more shameful to do a wrong than to receive a wrong. And this benign sentiment commends itself, alike to the Christian who is told to render good for evil, and to the universal heart of man. But who that confesses its truth can vindicate a resort to force for the sake of honor? Better far to receive the blow that a false morality has thought degrading, than that it should be revenged by force. Better that a nation, like an individual, should submit to what is wrong, rather than vainly seek to maintain its honor by the crime of war.

It seems that in ancient Athens, as in unchristianized Christian lands, there were sophists who urged that to suffer was unbecoming a man, and would draw down upon him incalculable evils. The following passage will show the manner in which the moral cowardice of these persons of little faith was rebuked by him whom the Gods pronounced wisest of men: "These things being so, let us inquire what it is you reproach me with; whether it is well said, or not, that I, forsooth, am not able to assist either myself, or any of my

friends or my relations, or to save them from the greatest
dangers, but that, like the outlaws, I am at the mercy of
any one who may choose to smite me on the temple — and
this was the strong point in your argument — or to take
away my property, or to drive me out of the city, or (to take
the extreme case) to kill me; now, according to your argument, to be so situated is the most shameful thing of all. But
my view is — a view many times expressed already, but there
is no objection to its being stated again,— my view, I say,
is, O Callicles, that to be struck unjustly on the temple is not
most shameful, nor to have my body mutilated, nor my purse
cut; but to strike me and mine unjustly, and to mutilate me
and to cut my purse is more shameful and worse; and stealing
too, and enslaving, and housebreaking, and in general, doing
any wrong whatever to me and mine is more shameful and
worse for him who does the wrong, than for me who suffer it.
These things thus established in the former arguments, as I
maintain, are secured and bound, even if the expression be
somewhat too rustical, with iron and adamantine arguments,
and unless you, or some one more vigorous than you, can
break them, it is impossible for any one, speaking otherwise
than I now speak, to speak well: since for my part, I always
have the same thing to say, that I know not how these things
are, but that of all whom I have ever discoursed with as now,
not one is able to say otherwise without being ridiculous."
Such is the wisdom of Socrates; and it has found a beautiful
expression in the verse of an English poet, who says:

> " Dear as freedom is and in my heart's just
> Esteem prized above all price, myself
> Had rather be the slave, and wear the chains,
> Than fasten them on him."

But the modern point of honor does not find a place in
warlike antiquity. Themistocles at Salamis did not send a

cartel to the Spartan commander, when threatened by a blow. "Strike, but hear," was the response of that firm nature, which felt that true honor was gained only in the performance of duty. It was in the depths of modern barbarism, in the age of chivalry, that this sentiment shot up in the wildest and most exuberant fancies; not a step was taken without reference to it; no act was done which had not some point tending to the "bewitching duel;" and every stage in the combat, from the ceremonies of its beginning, to its deadly close, were measured by this fantastic law. Nobody can forget the humorous picture of the progress of a quarrel to a duel, through the seven degrees of Touchstone, in "As You Like It." But the degradation, in which the law of honor has its origin, may be best illustrated by an authentic incident from the life of its most brilliant representative. The Chevalier Bayard, the cynosure of chivalry, the knight without fear and without reproach, in a contest with the Spaniard Don Alonzo de Soto Mayor, by a feint struck him such a blow in the throat that despite the gorget the weapon penetrated four fingers deep. The wounded Spaniard, gasping and struggling with his adversary, they both rolled on the ground, when Bayard, drawing his dagger, and thrusting its point in the nostrils of his foe, exclaimed, "Señor Alonzo, surrender, or you are a dead man;" a speech which appeared superfluous, as his second cried out, "Señor Bayard, he is dead; you have conquered." Bayard would have given one hundred thousand crowns for the opportunity to spare that life; but he now fell upon his knees, kissed the ground three times, and then dragged his dead enemy out of the camp, saying to the second, "Señor Don Diego, have I done enough?" To which the other piteously replied, "Too much, Señor, for the honor of Spain!" when Bayard very generously presented him with the corpse, although it was his right, by the laws of honor, to dispose of it as he thought proper; an act which is highly commended by the chivalrous Brantome, who thinks it difficult to say which did most honor to the faultless knight — not having ignominiously dragged the body like the carcass of a dog by a leg out of the field, or having condescended to fight while laboring under an ague!

If such a transaction conferred honor on the brightest son of chivalry, we may understand therefrom something of the real character of that age, the departure of which has been lamented with such touching but inappropriate eloquence. Do not condescend to draw a comprehensive rule of conduct from a period like this. Let the fanaticism of honor stay with the daggers, the swords and the weapons of combat by which it was guarded; let it appear only with its inseparable American companions, the bowie-knife and the pistol!

Be our standard of conduct derived, not from the degradation of our nature, though it affect the semblance of sensibility and refinement, but let it find its sources in the loftiest attributes of man, in truth, in justice, in duty; and may this standard, while governing our relations to each other, be recognized also among the nations! Alas! when shall we behold the dawning of that happy day, harbinger of infinite happiness beyond, in which nations, like individuals, shall feel that it is better to receive a wrong than to do a wrong.

Apply this principle to our relations at this moment with England. Suppose that proud monarchy, refusing all submission to negotiation or arbitration, should absorb the whole territory of Oregon into her own overgrown dominions, and add, at the mouth of the Columbia River, a new morning drum-beat to the national airs with which she has encircled the earth; who, then, is in the attitude of truest honor, England appropriating, by an unjust act, what is not her own, or the United States, the victim of the injustice?

5. There is still another influence which stimulates war, and interferes with the natural attractions of peace; I refer to a selfish and exaggerated love of country, leading to its physical aggrandizement, and political exaltation, at the expense of other countries, and in disregard of the principles of true greatness. Our minds, nursed by the literature of antiquity, have imbibed the narrow sentiment of heathen patriotism. Exclusive love for the land of birth was a part of the religion of Greece and Rome. It is an indication of the lowness of their moral nature that this sentiment was so material as well as exclusive in its character. The oracle directed the returning Roman to kiss his mother, and he kissed the mother earth. Agamemnon, according to Æschylus, on regaining his home, after a perilous separation of more than ten years, at the siege of Troy, before addressing his family, his friends, his countrymen, first salutes Argos:

" By your leave, Lords, first Argos I salute."

The school-boy cannot forget the cry of the victim of Verres, which was to stay the descending fasces of the lictor, " I am a Roman citizen; " nor those other words echoing through the dark past, " How sweet it is to die for one's country! " The Christian cry did not rise, " I am a man; " the Christian ejaculation did not swell the soul, "How sweet it is to die for duty! " The beautiful genius of Cicero, at times instinct with truth almost divine, did not ascend to that highest heaven, where is taught that all mankind are neighbors and kindred, and that the relations of fellow countryman are less holy than those of fellow man. To the love of universal man may be applied those words by which the great Roman elevated his selfish patriotism to a virtue when he said that country alone embraced all the charities of all. Attach this admired phrase for a moment to the single idea of country, and you will see how contracted are its charities, compared with the world-wide circle of Christian love, whose neighbor is the suffering man, though at the farthest pole. Such a sentiment would dry up those fountains of benevolence, which now diffuse themselves in precious waters in distant unenlightened lands, bearing the blessings of truth to the icy mountains of Greenland, and the coral islands of the Pacific sea.

It has been a part of the policy of rulers to encourage this exclusive patriotism; and the people of modern times have all been quickened by the feeling of antiquity. I do not know than any one nation is in a condition to reproach another with this patriotic selfishness. All are selfish. Men are taught to live, not for mankind, but only for a small portion of mankind. The pride, vanity, ambition, brutality even, which we rebuke in individuals, are accounted virtues when displayed in the name of country. Among us, the sentiment is active, while it derives new force from the point with which it has been expressed. An officer of our navy, one of the so-called heroes nurtured by war, whose name has been praised in churches, has gone beyond all Greek, all Roman example. "Our country, be she right or wrong," was his exclamation; a sentiment dethroning God and enthroning the devil, whose flagitious character should be rebuked by every honest heart. Unlike this officer was the virtuous Andrew Fletcher of Saltoun, in the days of the English Revolution, of whom it was said that he "would lose his life to serve his country, but would not do a base thing to save it." "Our country, our whole country, and nothing but our country," are other words which, falling first from the lips of an eminent American, have often been painted on banners, and echoed by the voices of innumerable multitudes. Cold and dreary, narrow and selfish, would be this life, if nothing but our country occupied our souls; if the thoughts that wander through eternity, if the infinite affections of our nature, were restrained to that spot of earth where we have been placed by the accident of birth.

I do not inculcate indifference to country. We incline by a natural sentiment to the spot where we were born, to the fields that witnessed the sports of childhood, to the seat of youthful studies, and to the institutions under which we have been trained. The finger of God writes all these things in indelible colors upon the heart of man, so that in the anxious extremities of death he reverts in fondness to early associations, and longs for a draught of cold water from the bucket in his father's well. This sentiment is independent of reflection, for it begins before reflection, grows with our growth, and strengthens with our strength. It is blind in its nature; and it is the duty of each of us to take care that it does not absorb and pervert the whole character. In the moral night which has enveloped the world, nations have lived ignorant and careless of the interests of others, which they imperfectly saw; but the thick darkness is now scattered, and we begin to discern, all gilded by the beams of morning, the distant mountain-peaks of other lands. We find that God has not placed us on this earth alone; that there are others, equally with us, children of his protecting care.

The curious spirit goes further, and while recognizing an inborn sentiment of attachment to the place of birth, inquires into the nature of the allegiance due to the State. According to the old idea, still too much received, man is made for the

State, and not the State for man. Far otherwise is the truth.
The State is an artificial body, intended for the security of
the people. How constantly do we find, in human history,
that the people have been sacrificed for the State; to build the
Roman name, to secure to England the trident of the sea.
This is to sacrifice the greater for the less; for the false
grandeur of earth to barter life and the soul itself. Is it not
clear that no dominion of the State — not even the State
itself — is worth preserving at the cost of the lives and happiness of the people?

It is not that I love country less, but humanity more, that
now, on this national anniversary, I plead the cause of a
higher and truer patriotism. Remember that you are men,
by a more sacred bond than you are citizens; that you are
children of a common father more than you are Americans.

Recognizing God as a common father, the seeming diversi-
ties of nations — separated only by the accident of mountains,
rivers, and seas, into those distinctions around which cluster
the associations of country — all disappear, and the various
people of the globe stand forth as brothers — members of one
great human family. Discord in this family is treason to
God; while all war is nothing else than civil war. In vain
do we restrain this odious term, importing so much of horror,
to the petty dissensions of a single State. It belongs as justly
to the feuds between nations, when referred to the umpirage
of battle. The soul trembles aghast, as we contemplate fields
drenched in fraternal gore, where the happiness of homes has
been shivered by the unfriendly arms of neighbors, and kins-
men have sunk beneath the steel nerved by a kinsman's hand.
This is civil war, which stands accursed forever in the calendar of time. But the muse of history, in the faithful record
of the future transactions of nations, inspired by a new and

loftier justice, and touched to finer sensibilities, shall extend to the general sorrows of universal man the sympathy still profusely shed for the selfish sorrow of country, and shall pronounce international war to be civil war, and the partakers in it as traitors to God and enemies to man.

6. I might here pause, feeling that those of my hearers who have kindly accompanied me to this stage would be ready to join in the condemnation of war and hail peace as the only condition becoming the dignity of human nature, and in which true greatness can be achieved. But there is still one other consideration, which yields to none of the rest in importance; perhaps it is more important than all. It is at once cause and effect; the cause of much of the feeling in favor of war, and the effect of this feeling. I refer to the costly preparations for war in time of peace. And here is one of the great practical evils which requires an immediate remedy. Too much time cannot be taken in exposing its character.

I do not propose to dwell upon the immense cost of war itself. That will be present to the minds of all, in the mountainous accumulations of debt, piled like Ossa upon Pelion, with which Europe is pressed to the earth. According to the most recent tables to which I have had access, the public debt of the different European states, so far as it is known, amounts to the terrific sum of $6,387,000,000, all of this the growth of war! It is said that there are throughout these states 17,900,000 paupers, or persons subsisting at the expense of the country, without contributing to its resources. If these millions of the public debt, forming only a part of what has been wasted in war, could be apportioned among these poor, it would give to each of them $375, a sum which would place all above want, and which is about equal to the average value of the property of each inhabitant of Massachusetts.

The public debt of Great Britain reached in 1839 to $4,265,000,000, the growth of war since 1688! This amount is nearly equal to the sum-total, according to the calculations of Humboldt, of all the treasures which have been reaped from the harvest of gold and silver in the mines of Spanish America, including Mexico and Peru, since the first discovery of our hemisphere by Christopher Columbus! It is much larger than the mass of all the precious metals, which at this moment form the circulating medium of the world! It is sometimes rashly said by those who have given little attention to this subject that all this expenditure was widely distributed, and therefore beneficial to the people; but this apology does not bear in mind that it was not bestowed in any productive industry or on any useful object. The magnitude of this waste will appear by a contrast with other expenditures; the aggregate capital of all the joint stock companies in England, of which there was any known record in 1842, embracing canals, docks, bridges, insurance companies, banks, gas-lights, water, mines, railways, and other miscellaneous objects, was about $835,000,000; a sum which has been devoted to the welfare of the people, but how much less in amount than the war debt! For the six years ending in 1836 the average payment for the interest on this debt was about $140,000,000 annually. If we add to this sum $60,000,000 during this same period paid annually to the army, navy and ordnance, we shall have $200,000,000 as the annual tax of the English people, to pay for former wars and to prepare for new. During this same period there was an annual appropriation of only $20,000,000 for all the civil purposes of the government. It thus appears that war absorbed

ninety cents of every dollar that was pressed by heavy taxation from the English people, who almost seem to sweat
blood! What fabulous monster or chimera dire ever raged
with a maw so ravenous! The remaining ten cents sufficed
to maintain the splendor of the throne, the administration
of justice, and the diplomatic relations with foreign powers,
in short, all the proper objects of a Christian state.

Thus much for the general cost of war. Let us now look
exclusively at the preparations for war in time of peace. It
is one of the miseries of war, that, even in peace, its evils
continue to be felt by the world, beyond any other evils by
which poor suffering humanity is oppressed. If Bellona
withdraws from the field, we only lose the sight of her flaming torches; the bay of her dogs is heard on the mountains,
and civilized man thinks to find protection from their sudden
fury, only by enclosing himself in the barbarous armor of
battle. At this moment the Christian nations, worshipping
a symbol of common brotherhood, live as in entrenched
camps, in which they keep armed watch to prevent surprise
from each other. Recognizing the custom of war as a proper
arbiter of justice, they hold themselves perpetually ready for
the bloody umpirage.

It is difficult, if not impossible, to arrive at any exact estimate of the cost of these preparations, ranging under four
different heads; the standing army; the navy; the fortifications and arsenals; and the militia or irregular troops.

The number of soldiers now affecting to keep the peace of
European Christendom, as a standing army, without count-
ing the navy, is upwards of two millions. Some estimates
place it as high as three millions. The army of Great Britain
exceeds 300,000 men; that of France 350,000; that of Russia
730,000, and is reckoned by some as high as 1,000,000; that

of Austria 275,000; that of Prussia 150,000. Taking the smaller number, suppose these two millions to require for their annual support an average sum of only $150 each, the result would be $300,000,000 for their sustenance alone; and reckoning one officer to ten soldiers, and allowing to each of the latter an English shilling a day, or $87 a year, for wages, and to the former an average salary of $500 a year, we should have for the pay of the whole no less than $256,000,000, or an appalling sum-total for both sustenance and pay of $556,000,000. If the same calculation be made, supposing the forces to amount to three millions, the sum-total will be $835,000,000! But to this enormous sum another still more enormous must be added on account of the loss sustained by the withdrawal of two millions of hardy, healthy men, in the bloom of life, from useful, productive labor. It is supposed that it costs an average sum of $500 to rear a soldier; and that the value of his labor, if devoted to useful objects, would be $150 a year. The Christian powers, therefore, in setting apart two millions of men as soldiers sustain a loss of $1,000,000,000 on account of their training; and $300,000,000 annually on account of their labor, in addition to the millions already mentioned as annually expended for sustenance and pay. So much for the cost of the standing army of European Christendom in time of peace.

Glance now at the navy of European Christendom. The royal navy of Great Britain consists at present of 557 ships of all classes; but deducting such as are used for convict ships, floating chapels, coal depots, the efficient navy consists of 88 sail of the line; 109 frigates; 190 small frigates, corvettes, brigs and cutters, including packets; 65 steamers of various sizes; 3 troopships and yachts; in all 455 ships. Of these there were in commission in 1839, 190 ships, carrying in all 4,202 guns. The number of hands employed was 34,465. The navy of France, though not comparable in size with that of England, is of vast force. By royal ordinance of January 1, 1837, it was fixed in time of peace at 40 ships of the line, 50 frigates, 40 steamers, and 190 smaller vessels; and the amount of crews in 1839 was 20,317 men. The Russian navy consists of two large fleets in the Gulf of Finland and the Black Sea; but the exact amount of their force and their available resources has been a subject of dispute among naval men and politicians. Some idea of the size of the navy may be derived from the number of hands employed. The crews of the Baltic fleet amounted in 1837 to not less than 30,800 men; and those of the fleet in the Black Sea to 19,800, or altogether 50,600. The Austrian navy consisted in 1837 of 8 ships of the line, 8 frigates, 4 sloops, 6 brigs, 7 schooners or galleys, and a number of smaller vessels; the number of men in its service in 1839 was 4,547. The navy of Denmark consisted at the close of 1837, of 7 ships of the line, 7 frigates, 5 sloops, 6 brigs, 3 schooners, 5 cutters, 58 gunboats, 6 gun-rafts, and 3 bomb vessels, requiring about 6,500 men to man them. The navy of Sweden and Norway consisted recently of 238 gun-boats, 11 ships of the line, 8 frigates, 4 corvettes, 6 brigs, with several smaller vessels. The navy of Greece consists of 32 ships of war, carrying 190 guns, and 2,400 men. The navy of Holland in 1830 consisted of 8 ships of the line, 21 frigates, 15 corvettes, 21 brigs, and 95 gun-boats. Of the immense cost of all these mighty preparations for war it is impossible to give any accurate idea. But we may lament that means so gigantic should be applied by European Christendom to the erection, in time of peace, of such superfluous wooden walls!

In the fortifications and arsenals of Europe, crowning every height, commanding every valley, and frowning over every plain and every sea, wealth beyond calculation has been sunk. Who can tell the immense sums that have been expended in hollowing out for the purposes of war the living rock of Gibraltar? Who can calculate the cost of all the preparations at Woolwich, its 27,000 cannons, and its hundreds of thousands of small arms? France alone contains upwards of one hundred and twenty fortified places. And it is supposed that the yet unfinished fortifications of Paris have cost upward of $50,000,000!

The cost of the militia or irregular troops, the yeomanry of England, the national guards of Paris, and the landwehr and landsturm of Prussia, must add other incalculable sums to these enormous amounts.

Turn now to the United States, separated by a broad ocean from immediate contact with the great powers of Christendom, bound by treaties of amity and commerce with all the nations of the earth; connected with all by the strong ties of mutual interest; and professing a devotion to the principles of peace. Are the treaties of amity mere words? Are the relations of commerce and mutual interest mere things of a day? Are the professions of peace vain? Else why not repose in quiet, unvexed by preparations for war?

Enormous as are the expenses of this character in Europe, those in our own country are still greater in proportion to the other expenditures of the federal government.

It appears that the average annual expenditures of the federal government for the six years ending with 1840, exclusive of payments on account of debt, were $26,474,892. Of this sum, the average appropriation each year for military and naval purposes amounted to $21,328,903, being eighty per cent of the whole amount! Yes; of all the annual appropriations by the federal government, eighty cents in every dollar were applied in this irrational and unproductive manner. The remaining twenty cents sufficed to maintain the government in all its branches, executive, legislative and judicial, the administration of justice, our relations with foreign nations, the post office and all the light-houses which, in happy useful contrast with any forts, shed their cheerful signals over the rough waves beating upon our long and indented coast, from the Bay of Fundy to the mouth of the Mississippi. A table of the relative expenditures of nations for military preparations in time of peace, exclusive of payments on account of the debts, presents results which will surprise the advocates of economy in our country. These are in proportion to the whole expenditure of government:

In Austria, as 33 per cent,

In France, as 38 per cent,

In Prussia, as 44 per cent,

In Great Britain, as 74 per cent,

In the United States as 80 per cent!

To this magnificent waste by the federal government may be added the still larger and equally superfluous expenses of the militia throughout the country, placed recently by a candid and able writer at $50,000,000 a year!

By a table of the expenditures of the United States, exclusive of payments on account of the public debt, it appears that in the fifty-three years from the formation of our present government, from 1789 down to 1843, $246,620,055 have been expended for civil purposes, comprehending the executive, the legislative, the judiciary, the post office, light-houses, and intercourse with foreign governments. During this same period $368,626,594 have been devoted to the military establishment, and $170,437,684 to the naval establishment; the two forming an aggregate of $538,964,278. Deducting from this sum the appropriations during three years of war, and we shall find that more than $400,000,000 were absorbed by vain preparations in time of peace for war. Add to this amount a moderate sum for the expenses of the militia during the same period, which, as we have already seen, have been placed recently at $50,000,000 a year; for the past years we may take an average of $25,000,000; and we shall have the enormous sum of $1,335,000,000 to be added to the $400,000,000; the whole amounting to $1,735,000,000, a sum beyond the conception of human faculties, sunk under the sanction of the government of the United States in mere peaceful preparations for war; more than seven times as much as was dedicated by the government, during the same period, to all other purposes whatsoever!

From this serried array of figures the mind instinctively retreats. If we examine them from a nearer point of view, and, selecting some particular part, compare it with the figures representing other interests in the community, they will present a front still more dread. Let us attempt the comparison.

Within a short distance of this city stands an institution of learning, which was one of the earliest cares of the early forefathers of the country, the conscientious Puritans. Favored child of an age of trial and struggle, carefully nursed through a period of hardship and anxiety, endowed at that time by the oblations of men like Harvard, sustained from its first foundation by the paternal arm of the Commonwealth, by a constant succession of munificent bequests and by the prayers of all good men, the university at Cambridge now invites our homage as the most ancient, the most interesting, and the most important seat of learning in the land; possess-

ing the oldest and most valuable library, one of the largest
museums of mineralogy and natural history,—a school of
law, which annually receives into its bosom more than one
hundred and fifty sons from all parts of the Union, where
they listen to instruction from professors whose names have
become among the most valuable possessions of the land—a
school of divinity, the nurse of true learning and piety—one
of the largest and most flourishing schools of medicine in the
country—besides these, a general body of teachers, twenty-
seven in number, many of whose names help to keep the name
of the country respectable in every part of the globe, where
science, learning and taste are cherished—the whole, presided over at this moment by a gentleman, early distinguished
in public life by his unconquerable energies and his mascu-
line eloquence, at a later period, by the unsurpassed ability
with which he administered the affairs of our city, and now
in a green old age, full of years and honors, preparing to lay
down his present high trust. Such is Harvard University;
and as one of the humblest of her children, happy in the
recollection of a youth nurtured in her classic retreats, I
cannot allude to her without an expression of filial affection
and respect.

It appears from the last report of the treasurer that the
whole available property of the university, the various accumulations of more than two centuries of generosity, amounts
to $703,175.

Change the scene, and cast your eyes upon another object.
There now swings idly at her moorings, in this harbor, a ship
of the line, the "Ohio," carrying ninety guns, finished as late
as 1836 for $547,888; repaired only two years afterwards in
1838 for $223,012; with an armament which has cost
$53,945; making an amount of $834,845 as the actual cost

at this moment of that single ship; more than $100,000 beyond all the available accumulations of the richest and most ancient seat of learning in the land! Choose ye, my fellow citizens of a Christian State, between the two caskets — that wherein is the loveliness of knowledge and truth, or that which contains the carrion death.

I refer thus particularly to the "Ohio," because she happens to be in our waters. But in so doing I do not take the strongest case afforded by our navy. Other ships have absorbed still larger sums. The expense of the "Delaware" in 1842 had been $1,051,000.

Pursue the comparison still further. The expenditures of the university during the last year, for the general purposes of the college, the instruction of the under-graduates, and for the schools of law and divinity, amount to $46,949. The cost of the "Ohio" for one year in service, in salaries, wages and provisions, is $220,000; being $175,000 more than the annual expenditures of the university; more than four times as much. In other words, for the annual sum which is lavished on one ship of the line, four institutions like Harvard University might be sustained throughout the country!

Still further let us pursue the comparison. The pay of the captain of a ship like the "Ohio" is $4,500 when in service; $3,500 when on leave of absence or off duty. The salary of the president of the Harvard University is $2,205 without leave of absence and never being off duty!

If the large endowments of Harvard University are dwarfed by a comparison with the expense of a single ship of the line, how much more must it be so with those of other institutions of learning and beneficence, less favored by the bounty of many generations. The average cost of a sloop of war is $315,000; more, probably, than all the endowments of those twin stars of learning in the western part of Massachusetts, the colleges at Williamstown and Amherst, and of that single star in the east, the guide to many ingenuous youth, the seminary at Andover. The yearly cost of a sloop of war in service is about $50,000; more than the annual expenditures of these three institutions combined.

I might press the comparison with other institutions of beneficence, with the annual expenditures for the blind — that noble and successful charity, which has shed true lustre upon our Commonwealth — amounting to $12,000; and the annual expenditures for the insane of the Common-wealth, another charity dear to humanity, amounting to $27,844.

Take all the institutions of learning and beneficence, the precious jewels of the Commonwealth, the schools, colleges, hospitals and asylums, and the sums by which they have been purchased and preserved are trivial and beggarly com-pared with the treasures squandered within the borders of Massachusetts in vain preparations for war. There is the navy yard at Charlestown, with its stores on hand, all costing $4,741,000; the fortifications in the harbors of Massachusetts, in which incalculable sums have been already sunk, and in which it is now proposed to sink $3,853,000 more; and besides, the arsenal at Springfield, containing in 1842, 175,118 muskets, valued at $2,999,998, and which is fed by an annual appropriation of about $200,000; but whose highest value will ever be, in the judgment of all lovers of truth, that it inspired a poem, which in its influence shall be mightier than a battle, and shall endure when arsenals and fortifications have crumbled to the earth. Some of the verses of this Psalm of Peace may happily relieve the detail of statistics, while they blend with my argument.

" ' re half the power that fills the world with terror,
      Were half the wealth bestowed on camp and courts,
   Given to redeem the human mind from error,
      There were no need of arsenals and forts.

   The warrior's name would be a name abhorred!
      And every nation that should lift again
   Its hand against its brother, on its forehead
      Would wear forevermore the curse of Cain!"

Look now for one moment at a high and peculiar interest
of the nation, the administration of justice. Perhaps no
part of our system is regarded, by the enlightened sense of
the country, with more pride and confidence. To this,
indeed, all the other concerns of government, all its compli-
cations of machinery, are in a manner subordinate, since it
is for the sake of justice that men come together in States and
establish laws. What part of the government can compare
in importance with the federal judiciary, that great balance
wheel of the constitution, controlling the relations of the
States to each other, the legislation of Congress and of the
States, besides private interests to an incalculable amount?
Nor can the citizen who discerns the true glory of his country fail to recognize in the judicial labors of Marshall, now
departed, and in the immortal judgments of Story who is still
spared to us,— *serus in cœlum redeat* — a higher claim to
admiration and gratitude than can be found in any triumph
of battle. The expenses of the administration of justice,
throughout the United States, under the federal government,
in 1842, embracing the salaries of the judges, the cost of
juries, court-houses and all officers thereof, in short all the
outlay by which justice, according to the requirements of
Magna Charta, is carried to every man's door, amounted to
$560,990, a larger sum than is usually appropriated for this
purpose, but how insignificant compared with the cormorant
demands of the army and navy!

Let me allude to one more curiosity of waste. It appears, by a calculation founded on the expenses of the navy, that the average cost of each gun, carried over the ocean, for one year, amounts to about fifteen thousand dollars; a sum sufficient to sustain ten or even twenty professors of colleges, and equal to the salaries of all the judges of the supreme court of Massachusetts and the governor combined!

Such are a few brief illustrations of the tax which the nations, constituting the great federation of civilization, and particularly our own country, impose on the people, in time of profound peace, for no permanent productive work, for no institution of learning, for no gentle charity, for no purpose of good. As we wearily climb, in this survey, from expenditure to expenditure, from waste to waste, we seem to pass beyond the region of ordinary calculation; Alps on Alps arise, on whose crowning heights of everlasting ice, far above the habitations of man, where no green thing lives, where no creature draws its breath, we behold the cold, sharp, flashing glacier of war.

In the contemplation of this spectacle the soul swells with alternate despair and hope; with despair, at the thought of such wealth, capable of rendering such service to humanity, not merely wasted but given to perpetuate hate; with hope, as the blessed vision arises of the devotion of all these incalculable means to the purposes of peace. The whole world labors at this moment with poverty and distress; and the painful question occurs to every observer, in Europe more than here at home — what shall become of the poor — the increasing standing army of the poor. Could the humble voice that now addresses you, penetrate those distant counsels, or counsels nearer home, it would say, disband your standing armies of soldiers, apply your navies to purposes of peaceful and enriching commerce, abandon your fortifications and arsenals, or dedicate them to works of beneficence, as the statue of Jupiter Capitolinus was changed to the image of a Christian saint; in fine, utterly forsake the present incongruous system of armed peace.

That I may not seem to press to this conclusion with too much haste, at least as regards our own country, I shall consider briefly, as becomes the occasion, the asserted usefulness of the national armaments, which it is proposed to abandon, and shall next expose the outrageous fallacy, at least in the present age, and among the Christian nations, of the maxim by which alone they are vindicated, that in time of peace we must prepare for war.

What is the use of the standing army of the United States? It has been a principle of freedom, during many generations, to avoid a standing army; and one of the complaints, in the Declaration of Independence, was that George III had quartered large bodies of troops in the colonies. For the first years after the adoption of the federal constitution, during our weakness, before our power was assured, before our name had become respected in the family of nations, under the administration of Washington, a small sum was deemed ample for the military establishment of the United States. It was only when the country, at a later day, had been touched by martial insanity, that, in unworthy imitation of monarchical states, it abandoned the true economy of a republic, and lavished the means, which it begrudged to the purposes of peace, in vain preparation for war. It may now be said of our army, as Dunning said of the influence of the crown, it has increased, is increasing, and ought to be diminished. At this moment there are, in the country, more than fifty-five military posts. It would be difficult to assign a reasonable

4 apology for any of these — unless, perhaps, on some distant Indian frontier. Of what use is the detachment of the second regiment of artillery in the quiet town of New London in Connecticut? Of what use is the detachment of the first regiment of artillery in that pleasant resort of fashion, Newport? By their exhilarating music and showy parade they may serve to amuse an idle hour; but it is doubtful if emotions of a different character will not be aroused in generous bosoms. Surely, he must have lost something of his sensibility to the true dignity of human nature, who, without regret and mortification, can observe the discipline, the drill, the unprofitable marching and counter-marching — the putting guns to the shoulder and then dropping them to the earth — which fills the lives of the poor soldiers, and prepare them to become the rude inanimate parts of that machine, to which an army has been likened by the great living master of the art of war. And this sensibility must be more offended by the spectacle of a chosen body of ingenuous youth, under the auspices of the government, amidst the bewitching scenery of West Point, painfully trained to these same fantastic and humiliating exercises — at a cost to the country, since the establishment of this academy, of upwards of $4,000,000.

In Europe standing armies are supposed to be needed to sustain the power of governments; but this excuse cannot prevail here. The monarchs of the Old World, like the chiefs of the ancient German tribes, are upborne by the shields of the soldiery. Happily with us the government springs from the hearts of the people, and needs no janizaries for its support.

But I hear the voice of some defender of this abuse, some upholder of this "rotten borough" of our constitution, crying, the army is needed for the defence of the country! As

well might you say that the shadow is needed for the defence
of the body; for what is the army of the United States but
the feeble shadow of the power of the American people?
In placing the army on its present footing, so small in numbers compared with the forces of the great European states,
our government has tacitly admitted its superfluousness for
defence. It only remains to declare distinctly that the country will repose, in the consciousness of right, without the
wanton excess of supporting soldiers, lazy consumers of the
fruits of the earth, who might do the state good service in the
various departments of useful industry.

What is the use of the navy of the United States? The
annual expense of our navy, during recent years, has been
upwards of $6,000,000. For what purpose is this paid?
Not for the apprehension of pirates; for frigates and ships
of the line are of too great bulk to be of service for this purpose. Not for the suppression of the slave trade; for under
the stipulations with Great Britain we employ only eighty
guns in this holy alliance. Not to protect our coasts; for all
agree that our few ships would form an unavailing defence
against any serious attack. Not for these purposes, you will
admit; but for the protection of our navigation. This is not
the occasion for minute calculations. Suffice it to say that an
intelligent merchant who has been extensively engaged in
commerce for the last twenty years, and who speaks, therefore, with the authority of knowledge, has demonstrated in
a tract of perfect clearness that the annual profits of the
whole mercantile marine of the country do not equal the
annual expenditure of our navy. Admitting the profit of a
merchant ship to be $4,000 a year, which is a large allow-
ance, it will take the earnings of one hundred ships to build
and employ for one year a single sloop of war — one hun-

'dred and fifty ships to build and employ a frigate, and nearly three hundred ships to build and employ a ship of the line. Thus more than five hundred ships must do a profitable business in order to earn a sufficient sum to sustain this little fleet. Still further, taking a received estimate of the value of the mercantile marine of the United States at $40,000,000, we find that it is only a little more than six times the annual cost of the navy; so that this interest is protected at a charge of more than fifteen per cent of its whole value! Protection at such price is more ruinous than one of Pyrrhus's victories!

But it is to the navy, as an unnecessary arm of national defence, and as part of the war establishment, that I confine my objection. So far as it may be required for purposes of science and for the police of the seas — to scour them of pirates, and, above all, to defeat the hateful traffic in human flesh,— it is an expedient instrument of government, and does not seem obnoxious as a portion of the machinery of war. But surely a navy, supported at immense cost in time of peace, to protect our navigation against the piracies of civilized nations is absurdly superfluous. The free cities of Hamburgh and Bremen, survivors of the great Hanseatic league, with a commerce that whitens the most distant seas, are without a single ship of war. Let the United States be willing to follow their prudent example, and abandon an institution which has already become a vain and most expensive toy!

What is the use of the fortifications of the United States? We have already seen the enormous sums which have been locked in the dead hands — in the odious mortmain — of their everlasting masonry. Like the pyramids, they seem by their mass and solidity to defy time. Nor can I doubt that hereafter, like these same monuments, they will be looked upon with wonder as the types of an extinct superstition, not less degrading than that of ancient Egypt — I mean the super- stition of war. It is in the hope of saving the country from the horrors of conquest and bloodshed that they are reared. But whence is the danger? On what side is it to come? Of what people is there any just cause of fear? No Christian nation threatens our borders with piracy or rapine. None will. Nor is it possible to suppose any war with such a nation, in the existing state of civilization, and under the existing international law, unless we voluntarily renounce the peaceful tribunal of arbitration, and consent to appeal to the trial by battle. The fortifications might be of service in waging this impious appeal. But let it also be borne in mind that they alone would invite the attack, which they might be inadequate to defeat. It is a rule now recognized, even in the barbarous code of war, one branch of which has been illustrated with admirable ability in the diplomatic corre- spondence of Mr. Webster, that non-combatants on land shall not in any way be molested, and that the property of private persons on land shall in all cases be held sacred. So firmly did the Duke of Wellington act upon this rule, that, through- out the revengeful campaigns of Spain, and afterwards when he entered France, flushed with the victory of Waterloo, he directed his army to pay for all provisions, and even for the forage of their horses. War is carried on against public prop- erty, — against fortifications, navy yards and arsenals. But if these do not exist, where is the aliment, where is the fuel for the flame? Paradoxical as it may seem, and disparaging to the whole trade of war, it may be proper to inquire, whether, according to the acknowledged laws, which now govern this bloody arbitrament, every new fortification and 'every additional gun in our harbor is not less a safeguard than a source of danger to the city? Better throw them in the sea than madly allow them to draw the lightning of battle upon our homes, without, alas, any conductor to hurry its terrors innocently beneath the concealing bosom of the earth!

What is the use of the militia of the United States? This immense system spreads, with innumerable suckers, over the whole country, draining its best life-blood, the unbought energies of the youth. The same fantastic discipline, which we have observed in the soldier, absorbs their time, though, of course, to a less degree than in the regular army. Theirs also is the savage pomp of war. We read with astonishment of the painted flesh and uncouth vestments of our progenitors, the ancient Britons. But the generation must soon come that will regard with equal wonder the pictures of their ancestors of our day, closely dressed in padded and well-buttoned coats of blue, "besmeared with gold," surmounted by a huge mountain-cap of shaggy bear-skin, and with a barbarous device, typical of brute force, a tiger, painted on oil-skin, tied with leather to their backs! In the streets of Pisa the galley-slaves are compelled to wear dresses stamped with the name of the crime for which they are suffering punishment; as theft, robbery, murder. It is not a little strange that Christians, living in a land "where bells have tolled to church," should voluntarily adopt devices, which, if they have any meaning, recognize the example of beasts as worthy of imitation by man.

The general considerations which belong to the subject of preparations for war will illustrate the inanity of the militia for the purposes of national defence. I do not know, indeed, that it is now strongly advocated on this ground. It is oftener spoken of as an important part of the police of the country. I would not undervalue the blessings derived from an active, efficient, ever-wakeful police; and I believe that such a police has been long required in our country. But the militia, composed of youth of undoubted character, though of untried courage and little experience, is clearly inadequate for this purpose. No person, who has seen this arm of the police in an actual riot, can hesitate in this judgment. A very small portion of the means which are absorbed by the militia would provide a substantial police, competent to all the emergencies of domestic disorder and violence. The city of Boston has long been convinced of the inexpediency of a fire department composed of mere volunteers. A similar conviction with regard to the police, it is hoped, may soon pervade the country.

I am well aware, however, that efforts to abolish the militia will be encountered by some of the dearest prejudices of the common mind; not only by the war spirit; but by that other spirit, which first animates childhood, and at a later day, "children of a larger growth," inviting to finery of dress and parade,— the same spirit which fantastically bedecks the dusky feather-cinctured chiefs of the soft regions warmed by the tropical sun; which inserts rings in the noses of the North American Indians; which slits the ears of the Australian savages; and tattoos the New Zealand cannibals.

Such is a review of the true character and value of the national armaments of the United States! It will be observed that I have thus far regarded them in the plainest light of ordinary worldly economy, without reference to those higher considerations, founded on the nature and history of man, and the truths of Christianity, which pronounce them to be vain. It is grateful to know, that, though they may yet have the support of what Jeremy Taylor calls the "popular noises," still the more economical, more humane, more wise, more Christian system is daily commending itself to wide circles of the good people of the land. On its side are all the virtues that truly elevate a State. Economy, sick of the pigmy efforts to staunch the smallest fountains and rills of exuberant expenditure, pleads that here is an endless, boundless, fathomless river, an Amazon of waste, rolling its prodigal waters turbidly, hatefully, ruinously to the sea. It chides us with an unnatural inconsistency when we strain at a little twine and red tape, and swallow the monstrous cables and armaments of war. Humanity pleads for the great interests of knowledge and benevolence, from which such mighty means are withdrawn. Wisdom frowns on these preparations as calculated to nurse sentiments inconsistent with peace. Christianity calmly rebukes the spirit in which they have their origin, as being of little faith, and treacherous to her high behests; while history, exhibiting the sure, though gradual, progress of man, points with unerring finger to that destiny of true grandeur, when nations, like individuals — disowning war as a proper arbiter of justice — shall abandon the oppressive apparatus of armies, navies and fortifications by which it is impiously waged.

And now, before considering the sentiment that in time of peace we must prepare for war, I hope I shall not seem to descend from the proper sphere of this discussion, if I refer to the parade of barbarous mottoes, and of emblems of brute force, as furnishing another impediment to the proper appreciation of these preparations. These mottoes and emblems, prompting to war, are obtruded on the very ensigns of power and honor; and men, careless of their discreditable import, learn to regard them with patriotic pride. Beasts and birds of prey, in the armorial bearings of nations and individuals, are selected as the exemplars of true grandeur. The lion is rampant on the flag of England — the leopard on the flag of Scotland — a double-headed eagle spreads its wings on the imperial standard of Austria. After exhausting the known kingdom of nature, the pennons of knights, like the knapsacks of our militia, were disfigured by imaginary and impossible monsters, griffins, hippogriffs, unicorns, all intended to represent the excess of brute force. The people of Massachusetts have unconsciously adopted this degrading standard. In the escutcheon which is used as the seal of the State there is an unfortunate combination of disagreeable and unworthy suggestions, to which I shall refer briefly by way of example. On that part which, in the language of heraldry, is termed the shield, is an Indian, with a bow in his hand — certainly, no agreeable memento, except to those who find honor in the disgraceful wars in which our fathers robbed and murdered King Philip, of Pokanoket, and his tribe, the rightful possessors of the soil. The crest is a raised arm, holding, in a threatening attitude, a drawn sabre — being precisely the emblem once borne on the flag of Algiers. The scroll, or legend, consists of the last of those two lines, in bad Latin, from an unknown source, which we first encounter, as they were inscribed by Algernon Sydney, in the album at the university of Copenhagen, in Denmark:

> — "Manus hæc, inimica tyrannis,
> Ense petit placidam sub libertate quietem."

The legislature of Massachusetts, with singular unanimity, has adopted resolutions expressing an earnest desire for the establishment of a high court of nations to adjudge international controversies, and thus supersede the arbitrament of war. It would be an act of moral dignity, consistent with these professions of peace, and becoming the character which it vaunts before the world, to abandon its bellicose escutcheon — at least, to erase that Algerine emblem, fit only for Corsairs, and those words of barbarous Latin, which can awaken only the idea of ignorance and brute force. If a Latin motto be needed, it might be those words of Virgil, "*Pacisque imponere morem*," or that sentence of noble truth from Cicero, "*Sine summa justitia rempublicam geri nullo modo posse.*" Where the spirit of these words prevailed, there would be little occasion to consider the question of preparations for war.

The sentiment that in time of peace we must prepare for war has been transmitted from distant ages when brute force prevailed. It is the terrible inheritance, *damnosa hæreditas*, which painfully reminds the people of our day of their relations with the past. It belongs to the rejected dogmas of barbarism. It is the companion of those harsh rules of tyranny, by which the happiness of the many has been offered up to the propensities of the few. It is the child of suspicion and the forerunner of violence. Having in its favor the almost uninterrupted usage of the world, it possesses a hold on popular opinion which is not easily unloosed. And yet the conscientious soul cannot fail, on careful observation, to detect its mischievous fallacy — at least among Christian States in the present age — a fallacy the most costly the world has witnessed, which dooms nations to annual tributes, in comparison with which all that have been extorted by conquests are as the widow's mite by the side of Pharisaical contributions. So true is what Rousseau said, and Guizot has since repeated, "that a bad principle is far worse than a bad fact;" for the operations of the one are finite, while those of the other are infinite.

I speak of this principle with earnestness: for I believe it to be erroneous and false, founded in ignorance and barbarism, unworthy of an age of light, and disgraceful to Christians. I have called it a principle; but it is a mere prejudice —sustained by vulgar example only, and not by lofty truth— in obeying which we imitate the early mariners, who steered from headland to headland and hugged the shore, unwilling to venture upon the broad ocean, where their guide was the luminaries of heaven.

Dismissing from our minds the actual usage of nations on the one side, and the considerations of economy on the other, let us regard these preparations for war in the unclouded light of reason, in a just appreciation of the nature of man, and in the injunctions of the highest truth, and we cannot hesitate to brand them as pernicious. They are pernicious on two grounds; and whoso would vindicate them must satisfactorily answer these objections; first, because they inflame the people who make them, exciting them to deeds of violence, otherwise alien to their minds; and secondly, because, having their origin in the low motive of distrust and hate, they inevitably, by a sure law of the human mind, excite a corresponding feeling in other nations. Thus they are, in fact, not the preservers of peace, but the provokers of war.

In illustration of the first of these objections it will occur to every inquirer that the possession of power is always in itself dangerous, that it tempts the purest and highest natures to self-indulgence, that it can rarely be enjoyed without abuse; nor is the power to employ force in war an exception to this law. History teaches that the nations possessing the greatest armaments have always been the most belligerent; while the feebler powers have enjoyed, for a longer period, the blessings of peace. The din of war resounds throughout more than seven hundred years of Roman history, with only two short lulls of repose; while smaller states, less potent in arms, and without the excitement to quarrels on this account, have enjoyed long eras of peace. It is not in the history of nations only that we find proofs of this law. Like every moral principle it applies equally to individuals. The experience of private life, in all ages, confirms it. The wearing of arms has always been a provocative to combat. It has excited the spirit and furnished the implements of strife. Reverting to the progress of society in modern Europe, we find that the odious system of private quarrels, of hostile meetings even in the street, continued so long as men persevered in the habit of wearing arms. Innumerable families were thinned by death received in these hasty and unpremeditated encounters; and the lives of scholars and poets were often exposed to their rude chances. Marlowe, "with all his rare learning and wit," perished ignominiously under the weapon of an unknown adversary; and Savage, whose genius and misfortune inspired the friendship and the eulogies of Johnson, was tried for murder committed in a sudden broil. "The expert swordsman," says Mr. Jay, "the practised marksman, is ever more ready to engage in personal combats than the man who is unaccustomed to the use of deadly weapons. In those portions of our country where it is supposed essential to personal safety to go armed with pistols and bowie-knives, mortal affrays are so frequent as to excite but little attention, and to secure, with rare exceptions, impunity to the murderer; whereas, at the North and East, where we are unprovided with such facilities for taking life, comparatively few murders of the kind are perpetrated. We might, indeed, safely submit the decision of the principle we are discussing to the calculations of pecuniary interest. Let two men, equal in age and health, apply for an insurance on their lives; one known to be ever

armed to defend his honor and his life against every assailant;
and the other a meek, unresisting Quaker; can we doubt for
a moment which of these men would be deemed by the insurance company most likely to reach a good old age?"

The second objection is founded on that law of the human
mind, in obedience to which the sentiment of distrust or hate,
— of which these preparations are the representatives,—must
excite a corresponding sentiment in others.   This law is a
part of the unalterable nature of man, recognized in early
ages, though unhappily too rarely made the guide to peaceful intercourse among nations.   It is an expansion of the old
Horatian adage, *Si vis me flere, dolendum est primum ipsi
tibi;* if you wish me to weep, you must yourself first weep.
Nobody can question its force or its applicability; nor is
it too much to say that it distinctly declares that military
preparations by one nation, in time of professed peace, must
naturally prompt similar preparations by other nations, and
quicken everywhere, within the circle of their influence, the
spirit of war.   So are we all knit together that the feelings
in our own bosoms awaken corresponding feelings in the
bosoms of others; as harp answers to harp in its softest vibra-
tions; as deep responds to deep in the might of its passions.
What within us is good invites the good in our brother; generosity begets generosity; love wins love; peace secures peace;
while all within us that is bad challenges the bad in our
brother; distrust engenders distrust; hate provokes hate; war
arouses war.

Life is full of illustrations of this beautiful law.   Even
the miserable maniac, in whose mind the common rules of
conduct are overthrown, confesses its overruling power; and
the vacant stare of madness may be illumined by a word of
love.   The wild beasts confess it; and what is the story of

Orpheus, whose music drew, in listening rapture, the lions and panthers of the forest, but an expression of its prevailing influence? It speaks also in the examples of literature. And here, at the risk of protracting this discussion, I am tempted to glance at some of these instructive instances — hoping, however, not to seem to attach undue meaning to them, and especially disclaiming any conclusions from them beyond the simple law which they illustrate.

Looking back to the early dawn of the world, one of the most touching scenes which we behold, illumined by that Auroral light, is the peaceful visit of the aged Priam to the tent of Achilles to entreat the body of his son. The fierce combat has ended in the death of Hector, whose unhonored corse the bloody Greek has already trailed behind his chariot. The venerable father, after twelve days of grief, is moved to efforts to regain the remains of the Hector he had so dearly loved. He leaves his lofty cedarn chamber, and with a single aged attendant, unarmed, repairs to the Grecian camp, by the side of the distant sounding sea. Entering alone, he finds Achilles within his tent, in the company of two of his chiefs. Grasping his knees, he kisses those terrible homicidal hands which had taken the life of his son. The heart of the inflexible, the angry, the inflamed Achilles, touched by the sight which he beholds, responds to the feelings of Priam. He takes the suppliant by the hand, seats him by his side, consoles his grief, refreshes his weary body, and concedes to the prayers of a weak, unarmed old man what all Troy in arms could not win. In this scene, which fills a large part of a book of the Iliad, the poet, with unconscious power, has presented a picture of the omnipotence of that law of our nature, making all mankind of kin, in obedience to which no word of kindness, no act of confidence, falls idly to the earth.

Among the legendary passages of Roman history, perhaps none makes a deeper impression than that scene, after the Roman youth had been consumed at Allia, and the invading Gauls under Brennus had entered the city, where we behold the venerable senators of the republic, too old to flee, and careless of surviving the Roman name, seated each on his curule chair, in a temple, unarmed, looking, as Livy says, more august than mortal, and with the majesty of the gods. The Gauls gaze on them, as upon sacred images, and the hand of slaughter, which had raged through the streets of Rome, is stayed by the sight of an assembly of unarmed men. At length a Gaul approaches, and with his hands gently strokes the silver beard of a senator, who, indignant at the license, smites the barbarian with his ivory staff; which was the signal for general vengeance. Think you, that a band of savages could have slain these senators, if the appeal to force had not first been made by one of their own number? This story, though recounted by Livy, and also by Plutarch, is properly repudiated by Niebuhr as a legend; but it is none the less interesting, as showing the law by which hostile feelings are necessarily aroused or subdued. The heart of man confesses that the Roman senator provoked death for himself and his associates.

Other instances present themselves. An admired picture by Virgil, in his melodious epic, represents a person, venerable for piety and deserts, assuaging by words alone a furious populace,. which had just broken into sedition and outrage. Guizot, in his "History of French Civilization," has preserved a similar instructive example of the effect produced by an unarmed man, in an illiterate epoch, who, employing the word instead of the sword, subdued an angry multitude. And surely no reader of that noble historical romance, the

"Promessi Sposi," can forget that finest scene, where Fra
Christofero, in an age of violence, after slaying a comrade
in a broil, in unarmed penitence seeks the presence of the
family and retainers of his victim, and, by his dignified gentleness, awakens the admiration of those already mad with
the desire of vengeance. Another example, made familiar
by recent translations of Frithjof's "Saga," the Swedish epic,
is more emphatic. The scene is a battle. Frithjof is in
deadly combat with Atlé, when the falchion of the latter
breaks. Throwing away his own weapon, he says:

> — "swordless foeman's life
> Ne'er dyed this gallant blade."

The two champions now close in mutual clutch; they hug like
bears, says the poet:

> " 'Tis o'er: for Frithjof's matchless strength
> Has felled his ponderous size;
> And 'neath that knee, at giant length,
> Supine the Viking lies.
> ' But fails my sword, thou Berserk swart! '
> The voice rang far and wide,
> ' Its point should pierce thy inmost heart,
> Its hilt should drink the tide.'
> ' Be free to lift the weaponed hand,'
> Undaunted Atlé spoke,
> ' Hence, fearless, quest thy distant brand!
> Thus abide the stroke.' "

Frithjof regains his sword, intent to close the dread debate,
while his adversary awaits the stroke; but his heart responds
to the generous courage of his foe; he cannot injure one who
has shown such confidence in him; —

> " This quelled his ire, this checked his arm,
> Outstretched the hand of peace."

I cannot leave these illustrations, without alluding particularly to the history of the treatment of the insane, which
teaches, by conclusive example, how strong in nature must

be the principle that leads us to respond to the conduct and
feelings of others. When Pinel first proposed to remove the
heavy chains from the raving maniacs of the hospitals of
Paris, he was regarded as one who saw visions, or dreamed
dreams. At last his wishes were gratified. The change in
the conduct of his patients was immediate; the wrinkled front
of evil passions was smoothed into the serene countenance of
peace. The old treatment by force is now universally abandoned; the law of love has taken its place; and all these
unfortunates mingle together, unvexed by those restraints,
which implied suspicion, and, therefore, aroused opposition.
The warring propensities, which, while the hospitals for the
insane were controlled by force, filled them with confusion
and strife, are a dark but feeble type of the present relations
of nations, on whose hands are the heavy chains of military
preparations, assimilating the world to one great mad-house;
while the peace and good will, which now abound in these
retreats, are the happy emblems of what awaits mankind when
they shall recognize the supremacy of the higher sentiments
of our nature; of gentleness, of confidence, of love;

> — " making their future might
> Magnetic o'er the fixed untrembling heart."

I might also dwell on the recent experience, so full of
delightful wisdom, in the treatment of the distant, degraded
convicts of New South Wales, showing how confidence and
kindness, on the part of their overseers, awaken a corresponding sentiment even in these outcasts, from whose souls virtue,
at first view, seems to be wholly blotted out.

Thus from all quarters, from the far-off past, from the far-
away Pacific, from the verse of the poet, from the legend of
history, from the cell of the mad-house, from the assembly of
transported criminals, from the experience of daily life, from

the universal heart of man, ascends the spontaneous tribute to that law, according to which we respond to the feelings by which we are addressed, whether of love or hate, of confidence or distrust.

It may be urged that these instances are exceptions to the general laws by which mankind are governed. It is not so. They are the unanswerable evidence of the real nature of man. They reveal the divinity of humanity, out of which all goodness, all happiness, all true greatness can alone proceed. They disclose susceptibilities which are general, which are confined to no particular race of men, to no period of time, to no narrow circle of knowledge and refinement — but which are present wherever two or more human beings come together, and which are strong in proportion to their virtue and intelligence. It is, then, on the impregnable ground of the nature of man, that I place the fallacy of that prejudice, in obedience to which, now, in an age of civilization, among Christian nations, in time of peace we prepare for war.

But this prejudice is not only founded on a misconception of the nature of man; it is abhorrent to Christianity, which teaches that love is more puissant than force. To the reflecting mind the Omnipotence of God himself is less discernible in the earthquake and the storm than in the gentle but quickening rays of the sun and the sweet descending dews. And he is a careless observer who does not recognize the superiority of gentleness and kindness as a mode of exercising influence or securing rights among men. As the winds of violence beat about them, they hug those mantles, which are gladly thrown to the earth under the warmth of a kindly sun. Thus far, nations have drawn their weapons from the earthly armories of force, unmindful of those others of celestial temper from the house of love.

to about $11,000,000, while those during a recent similar period of eight years stretch to upwards of $164,000,000 — an increase of fifteen hundred per cent! To him who quotes the precept of Washington I commend the example. He must be strongly possessed by the military mania who is not ready to confess that in this age, when the whole world is at peace, and when our national power is assured, there is less need of these preparations than in an age convulsed with war, when our national power was little respected. The only semblance of an argument in their favor is founded in the increased wealth of the country; but the capacity to endure taxation is no criterion of its justice, or even its expediency.

The fallacy that whatever is is right is also invoked as an apology. Our barbarous practice is exalted above all those principles by which these preparations are condemned. We are made to count principles as nothing, because they have not yet been recognized by nations. But they have been practically applied to the relations of individuals, of towns, of counties. All these have disarmed. It remains only that they should be extended to the grander sphere of nations. Be it our duty to proclaim the principles, whatever may be the practice! Through us let truth speak. The bigots of the past, and all who are selfishly concerned in the existing system, may close their minds and hearts to her message. Thus it has been in all ages. Nay more; there is often an irritation excited by her presence; and men, who are kind and charitable, forget their kindness and lose their charity towards the unaccustomed stranger. Harshness, neglect, intolerance, ensue. It was this spirit which awarded a dungeon to Galileo, when he declared that the earth moved round the sun — which neglected the great discovery by Harvey of the circulation of the blood — which bitterly opposed the divine philanthropy of Clarkson, when first denouncing the wickedness of the slave-trade. But truth, rejected and dishonored in our day, shall become the household companion of the next generation.

Auspicious omens from the past and the present cheer us for the future. The terrible wars of the French Revolution were the violent rending of the body which preceded the exorcism of the fiend. Since the morning stars first sang together the world has not witnessed a peace so harmonious and enduring as that which now blesses the Christian nations. Great questions between them, fraught with strife, and in another age sure heralds of war, are now determined by mediation or arbitration. Great political movements, which, only a few short years ago, must have led to forcible rebellion, are now conducted by peaceful discussion. Literature, the press, and various societies all join in the holy work of inculcating good will to man. The spirit of humanity now pervades the best writings, whether the elevated philosophical inquiries of the "Vestiges of Creation," the ingenious but melancholy moralizings of the "Story of a Feather," or the overflowing raillery of "Punch." Nor can the breathing thought and burning word of poet or orator have a higher inspiration. Genius is never so Promethean as when it bears the heavenly fire of love to the hearths of men.

In the last age Dr. Johnson uttered the detestable sentiment that he liked "a good hater." The man of this age must say that he likes "a good lover." Thus reversing the objects of regard, he follows a higher wisdom and a purer religion than the renowned moralist knew. He recognizes that peculiar Christian sentiment, the brotherhood of mankind, destined soon to become the decisive touchstone of all human institutions. He confesses the power of love, des-

tined to enter, more and more, into all the concerns of life.
And as love is more heavenly than hate, so must its influence
redound more to the true glory of man, and to his acceptance
with God.   A Christian poet — whose few verses bear him
with unflagging wing on his immortal flight — has joined
this sentiment with prayer.   Thus he speaks in words of
uncommon pathos and power:

> "He prayeth well who loveth well
> All things both great and small.

> "He prayeth best who loveth best
> Both man and bird and beast,
> For the dear God, who loveth us,
> He made and loveth all."

Surely the ancient law of hate is yielding to the law of
love.   It is seen in the manifold labors of philanthropy and
in the voyages of charity.   It is seen in the institutions for
the insane, for the blind, for the deaf and dumb, for the
poor, for the outcast — in the generous efforts to relieve those
who are in prison — in the public schools, opening the gates
of knowledge to all the children of the land.   It is seen in the
diffusive amenities of social life, and in the increasing fellowship of nations.   It is seen in the rising opposition to slavery
and to war.

There are yet other special auguries of this great change,
auspicating, in the natural progress of man, the abandonment
of all international preparations for war.   To these I allude
briefly, but with a deep conviction of their significance.

Look at the past; and observe the change in dress.   Down
to a period quite recent the sword was the indispensable companion of the gentleman wherever he appeared, whether in
the street or in society; but he would be thought a madman
or a bully who should wear it now.   At an earlier period
the armor of complete steel was the habiliment of the knight.

From the picturesque sketch by Sir Walter Scott, in the "Lay
of the Last Minstrel," we may learn the barbarous constraint
of this costume.

> "Ten of them were sheathed in steel,
> With belted sword, and spur on heel;
> They quitted not the harness bright,
> Neither by day, nor yet by night;
> They lay down to rest,
> With corselet laced,
> Pillowed on buckler cold and hard;
> They carved at the meal
> With gloves of steel,
> And they drunk the red wine through the helmet barred."

But this is all changed now. Observe also the change in
architecture and in domestic life. The places once chosen
for castles, or houses, were in savage, inaccessible retreats,
where the massive structure was reared, destined to repel
attacks and to enclose its inhabitants. Even monasteries
and churches were fortified, and girdled by towers, ramparts
and ditches, while a child was often stationed as a watchman,
to observe what passed at a distance, and announce the
approach of an enemy. The homes of peaceful citizens in
towns were castellated, often without so much as an aperture
for light near the ground, but with loop-holes through which
the shafts of the cross-bow might be aimed. From a letter
of Margaret Paston, in the time of Henry VII of England,
I draw a curious and authentic illustration of the armed life
of that period. Addressing in dutiful phrase her "right wor-
shipful husband," she asks him to procure for her "some
cross-bows and wyndnacs [grappling irons] to bind them
with, and quarrels" [arrows with a square head], — also
"two or three short pole-axes to keep within doors;" and she
tells her absent lord of the preparations made apparently by
a neighbor — "great ordnance within the house" — "bars to
bar the door crosswise, and wickets in every quarter of the

house to shoot out at, both with bows and hand-guns." Savages could hardly live in greater distrust of each other. Let now the poet of chivalry describe another scene:

> " Ten squires, ten yeomen, mail-clad men,
> Waited the beck of the warders ten;
> Thirty steeds, both fleet and wight,
> Stood saddled in stable day and night,
> Barbed with frontlet of steel I trow,
> And with Jedwood axe at saddle bow;
> A hundred more fed free in stall:
> Such was the custom at Branksome Hall."

This also is all changed now. But the principles which have caused this change are not only active still but increasing in activity. They cannot be restrained to individuals. Nations also must soon confess them, and, like individuals, abandoning martial habiliments and fortifications, enter upon a peaceful unarmed life. With shame let it be said, that they continue to live in the very relations of distrust towards their neighbors which shocks us in the knights of Branksome Hall and in the house of Margaret Paston. They seem to pillow themselves on "buckler cold and hard;" and their highest anxiety and largest expenditure are for the accumulation of new munitions of war. The barbarism which individuals have renounced nations continue to cherish. So doing, they take counsel of the wild boar in the fable, who whetted his tusks on a tree of the forest, when no enemy was near, saying that in time of peace he must prepare for war. But has not the time now come, when man, whom God created in his own image, and to whom he gave the heaven-directed countenance, shall cease to look down to the beasts for examples of conduct? Nay; let me not dishonor the beasts by the comparison. Man alone of the animal creation preys upon his own species. The kingly lion turns from his brother lion —the ferocious tiger will not raven upon his kindred tiger —

the wild boar of the forest does not glut his sharpened tusks upon a kindred boar!

> " Sed jam serpentum major concordia; parcit
> Cognatis maculis similis fera. Quando leoni
> Fortior eripuit vitam leo? quo nemore unquam
> Exspiravit aper majoris dentibus apri?
> Indica tigris agit rabida cum tigride Pacem
> Perpetuam."

To an early monarch of France homage has already been offered for his efforts in the cause of peace, particularly in abolishing the trial by battle. To another monarch of France, in our own day, a descendant of St. Louis, worthy of the illustrious lineage, Louis Philippe, belongs the honest fame of first, from the throne, publishing the truth, that Peace was endangered by preparations for war. "The sentiment, or rather the principle," he says, in reply to an address from the London Peace Convention in 1843, "that in peace you must prepare for war, is one of difficulty and danger; for while we keep armies on land to preserve peace, they are, at the same time, incentives and instruments of war. He rejoiced in all efforts to preserve peace, for that was what all need. He thought the time was coming when we shall get rid entirely of war in all civilized countries." This time has been hailed by a generous voice from the army itself, by a marshal of France,— Bugeaud, the Governor of Algiers,— who gave, as a toast at a public dinner in Paris, the following words of salutation to a new and approaching era of happiness: "To the pacific union of the great human family, by the association of individuals, nations, and races! To the annihilation of war! To the transformation of destructive armies into corps of industrious laborers, who will consecrate their lives to the cultivation and embellishment of the world!" Be it our duty to speed this consummation! And

let us dare to pursue it. Let us now, in this age of civilization, surrounded by Christian nations, be willing to follow the successful example of William Penn, surrounded by savages. Let us, while recognizing those transcendent ordinances of God, the law of right and the law of love,— the double suns which illumine the moral universe,— aspire to the true glory, and, what is higher than glory, the great good of taking the lead in the disarming of the nations. Let us abandon the system of preparations for war in time of peace, as irrational, unchristian, vainly prodigal of expense, and having a direct tendency to excite the very evil against which it professes to guard. Let the enormous means, thus released from iron hands, be devoted to labors of beneficence. Our battlements shall be schools, hospitals, colleges, and churches; our arsenals shall be libraries; our navy shall be peaceful ships, on errands of perpetual commerce; our army shall be the teachers of youth, and the ministers of religion. This is indeed the cheap defence of nations. In such entrenchments what Christian soul can be touched with fear? Angels of the Lord shall throw over the land an invisible, but impenetrable panoply.

> " Or if virtue feeble were,
> Heaven itself would stoop to her."

At the thought of such a change in policy, the imagination loses itself in the vain effort to follow the various streams of happiness, which gush forth as from a thousand hills. Then shall the naked be clothed and the hungry fed. Institutions of science and learning shall crown every hill-top; hospitals for the sick and other retreats for the unfortunate children of the world, for all who suffer in any way, in mind, body or estate, shall nestle in every valley; while the spires of new churches shall leap exulting to the skies. The whole land shall testify to the change; art shall confess it in the new inspiration of the canvas and the marble; the harp of the poet shall proclaim it in a loftier rhyme. Above all, the heart of man shall bear witness to it, in the elevation of his sentiments, in the expansion of his affections, in his devotion to the highest truth, in his appreciation of true greatness. The eagle of our country, without the terror of his beak, and dropping the forceful thunderbolt from his pounces, shall soar, with the olive of peace, into untried realms of ether, nearer to the sun.

And here let us review the field over which we have passed. We have beheld war, sanctioned by international law, as a mode of determining justice between nations, elevated into an established custom, defined and guarded by a complex code, known as the laws of war; we have detected its origin in an appeal, not to the moral and intellectual part of man's nature, in which alone is justice, but in an appeal to that low part of his nature, which he has in common with the beasts; we have contemplated its infinite miseries to the human race; we have weighed its sufficiency as a mode of determining justice between nations, and found that it is a rude appeal to force, or a gigantic game of chance, in which God's children are profanely dealt with as a pack of cards, while, in its unnatural wickedness, it is justly likened to the monstrous and impious custom of trial by battle, which disgraced the dark ages; thus showing that, in this period of boastful civilization, justice between nations is determined by the same rules of barbarous, brutal violence which once controlled the relations between individuals. We have next considered the various prejudices by which war is sustained; founded on a false belief in its necessity; on the practice of nations, past and present; on the infidelity of the Christian

Church; on a false idea of honor; on an exaggerated idea of the duties of patriotism; and finally, that monster prejudice, which draws its vampire life from the vast preparations in time of peace for war; especially dwelling, at this stage, upon the thriftless, irrational, and unchristian character of these preparations; hailing also the augeries of their overthrow, and catching a vision of the surpassing good that will be achieved, when the boundless means, thus barbarously employed, shall be dedicated by our Republic to the works of peace, opening the serene path to that righteousness which exalteth a nation.

And now, if it be asked why, on this national anniversary, in considering the true grandeur of nations, I have dwelt, thus singly and exclusively, on war, it is, because war is utterly and irreconcilably inconsistent with true greatness. Thus far mankind have worshipped, in military glory, a phantom idol, compared with which the colossal images of ancient Babylon or modern Hindostan are but toys; and we, in this blessed land of freedom, in this blessed day of light, are among the idolators. The heaven-descended injunction, "Know thyself," still speaks to an unheeding world from the distant letters of gold at Delphi "know thyself; know that the moral nature is the most noble part of man," transcending far that part which is the seat of passion, strife, and war; nobler than the intellect itself. And the human heart, by its untutored judgments,— rendering spontaneous homage to the virtues of peace,— points to the same truth. It admonishes the military idolator that it is not the bloody combats, even of the bravest chiefs, even of the gods themselves,— as they echo from the resounding lines of the great poet of war,— which have received the warmest admiration; but those two scenes, in which he has painted the gentle, unwarlike affections of our nature, the parting of Hector and Andromache, and the supplication of Priam. In this definitive election of the peaceful pictures of Homer, the soul of man, inspired by a better wisdom than that of books, and drawn unconsciously by the heavenly attractions of what is truly great, has acknowledged, by a touching instance, the vanity of military glory. The Beatitudes of Christ, which shrink from saying "Blessed are the war-makers," inculcate the same lesson. Reason affirms and repeats what the heart has prompted, and Christianity declared. Suppose war to be decided by force, where is the glory? Suppose it to be decided by chance, where is the glory? Surely, in other ways true greatness lies. Nor is it difficult to tell where.

True greatness consists in imitating, as near as is possible for finite man, the perfections of an infinite Creator; above all, in cultivating those highest perfections, justice and love, justice, which, like that of St. Louis, shall not serve to the right hand or to the left; love, which, like that of William Penn, shall regard all mankind of kin. "God is angry," says Plato, "when any one censures a man like himself, or praises a man of an opposite character. And the God-like man is the good man." And again, in another of those lovely dialogues, vocal with immortal truth, "Nothing resembles God more than that man among us who has arrived at the highest degree of justice." The true greatness of nations is in those qualities which constitute the true greatness of the individual. It is not in extent of territory, or in vastness of population, or in wealth; not in fortifications, or armies, or navies; not in the phosphorescent glare of fields of battle; not in Golgothas, though covered by monuments that kiss the clouds; for all these are the creatures and representa-

tives of those qualities in our nature, which are unlike anything in God's nature. Nor is it to be found in triumphs of
the intellect alone,— in literature, learning, science, or art.
The polished Greeks, our masters in the delights of language
and in range of thought, and the commanding Romans, over-
awing the earth with their power, were little more than splendid savages. And the age of Louis XIV of France, spanning
so long a period of ordinary worldly magnificence; thronged
by marshals bending under military laurels; enlivened by
the unsurpassed comedy of Molière; dignified by the tragic
genius of Corneille; illumined by the splendors of Bossuet;
is degraded by immoralities that cannot be mentioned without a blush; by a heartlessness, in comparison with which
the ice of Nova Zembla is warm; and by a succession of deeds
of injustice, not to be washed out by the tears of all the
recording angels of heaven.

The true greatness of a nation cannot be in triumphs of
the intellect alone. Literature and art may enlarge the
sphere of its influence; they may adorn it; but they are in
their nature but accessaries. The true grandeur of humanity is in moral elevation, sustained, enlightened, and deco-
rated by the intellect of man. The surest tokens of this
grandeur, in a state, are that Christian beneficence, which
diffuses the greatest happiness among the greatest number,
and that passionless, God-like justice, which controls the relations of the state to other states, and to all the people committed to its charge.

But war crushes, with bloody heel, all beneficence, all happiness, all justice, all that is God-like in man. It suspends
every commandment of the Decalogue. It sets at naught
every principle of the Gospel. It silences all law, human
as well as divine, except only that blasphemous code of its

5 own, the laws of war. If, in its dismal annals, there is any
cheerful passage, be assured that it is not inspired by a martial fury. Let it not be forgotten,— let it ever be borne in
mind, as you ponder this theme,— that the virtues, which
shed their charm over its horrors, are all borrowed of peace;
they are emanations of the spirit of love, which is so strong
in the heart of man that it survives the rudest assaults. The
flowers of gentleness, of kindliness, of fidelity, of humanity,
which flourish, in unregarded luxuriance, in the rich meadows
of peace, receive unwonted admiration when we discern them
in war, like violets, shedding their perfume on the perilous
edges of the precipice, beyond the smiling borders of civilization. God be praised for all the examples of magnan-
imous virtue which he has vouchsafed to mankind! God be
praised that the Roman emperor, about to start on a distant expedition of war, encompassed by squadrons of cav-
alry, and by golden eagles which swayed in the winds, stooped
from his saddle to listen to the prayer of the humble widow,
demanding justice for the death of her son! God be praised
that Sidney, on the field of battle, gave, with dying hand,
the cup of cold water to the dying soldier! That single act
of self-forgetful sacrifice has consecrated the fenny field of
Zutphen, far, O, far beyond its battle; it has consecrated thy
name, gallant Sidney, beyond any feat of thy sword, beyond
any triumph of thy pen! But there are humble suppliants
for justice, in other places than the camp; there are hands out-
stretched, elsewhere than on fields of blood, for so little as
a cup of cold water; the world constantly affords opportunities for deeds of like greatness. But, remember well, that
these are not the product of war. They do not spring from
enmity, hatred, and strife; but from those benign sentiments,
whose natural and ripened fruit, of joy and blessing, can be

found only in peace. If, at any time, they appear in the soldier, it is not because, but notwithstanding, he is the hireling of battle. Let me not be told, then, of the virtues of war. Let not the acts of generosity and sacrifice, which have blossomed on its fields, be invoked in its defence. From such a giant root of bitterness no true good can spring. The poisonous tree, in oriental imagery, though watered by nectar, and covered with roses, can produce only the fruit of death!

Casting our eyes over the history of nations, with horror we discern the succession of murderous slaughters by which their progress has been marked. Even as the hunter traces the wild beast, when pursued to his lair, by the drops of blood on the earth, so we follow man, faint, weary, staggering with wounds, through the black forest of the past, which he has reddened with his gore. O, let it not be in the future ages, as in those which we now contemplate! Let the grandeur of man be discerned, not in bloody victories, or in ravenous conquests, but in the blessings which he has secured; in the good he has accomplished; in the triumphs of beneficence and justice; in the establishment of perpetual peace.

As the ocean washes every shore, and, with all-embracing arms, clasps every land, while, on its heaving bosom, it bears the products of various climes; so peace surrounds, protects, and upholds all other blessings. Without it commerce is vain, the ardor of industry is restrained, justice is arrested, happiness is blasted, virtue sickens and dies.

And peace has its own peculiar victories, in comparison with which Marathon and Bannockburn and Bunker Hill, fields held sacred in the history of human freedom, shall lose their lustre. Our own Washington rises to a truly heavenly stature,— not when we follow him over the ice of the Delaware to the capture of Trenton,— not when we behold him victorious over Cornwallis at Yorktown,—but when we regard him, in noble deference to justice, refusing the kingly crown which a faithless soldiery proffered, and, at a later day, upholding the peaceful neutrality of the country, while he received unmoved the clamor of the people wickedly crying for war. What glory of battle in England's annals will not fade by the side of that great act of justice, by which her Parliament, at a cost of $100,000,000, gave freedom to 800,-000 slaves! And when the day shall come (may these eyes be gladdened by its beams!) that shall witness an act of greater justice still, the peaceful emancipation of 3,000,000 of our fellow men, "guilty of a skin not colored as our own," now, in this land of jubilant freedom, held in gloomy bondage, then shall there be a victory, in comparison with which that of Bunker Hill shall be as a farthing candle held up to the sun. That victory shall need no monument of stone. It shall be written on the grateful hearts of uncounted multitudes, that shall proclaim it to the latest generation. It shall be one of the famed land-marks of civilization; nay, more, it shall be one of the links in the golden chain by which humanity shall connect itself with the throne of God.

As man is higher than the beasts of the field; as the angels are higher than man; as Christ is higher than Mars; as he that ruleth his spirit is higher than he that taketh a city, so are the victories of peace higher than the victories of war.

Far be from us, fellow citizens, on this festival, the pride of national victory, and the illusions of national freedom, in which we are too prone to indulge. None of you make rude boasts of individual prosperity, individual possessions, individual power, or individual bravery. But there can be only one and the same rule, whether in morals or in conduct, for nations and individuals; and our country will act wisely, and in the spirit of true greatness, by emulating, in its public behavior, the reserve and modesty which are universally commended in private life. Let it cease to vaunt itself and to be puffed up; but rather brace itself, by firm resolves and generous aspirations, to the duties before it. We have but half done, when we have made ourselves free. Let not the scornful taunt, wrung from the bitter experience of the early French Revolution, be directed at us: "They wish to be free; but know not how to be just." Freedom is not an end in itself, but a means only,—a means of securing justice and beneficence, in which alone is happiness, the real end and aim of nations, as of every human heart. It becomes us to inquire earnestly, if there is not much to be done by which these can be advanced. If I have succeeded in impressing on your minds the truths, which I have endeavored to uphold to-day, you will be ready, as faithful citizens, alike of our own republic, and of the universal Christian commonwealth, to join in efforts to abolish the arbitrament of war, to suppress international lynch law, and to induce the disarming of the nations, as measures indispensable to the establishment of permanent peace — that grand, comprehensive blessing, at once the child and parent of all those guardian virtues, without which there can be no national honor, no national glory, no true grandeur of nations!

To this great work let me summon you. That future, which filled the lofty visions of the sages and bards of Greece and Rome, which was foretold by the prophets and heralded by the evangelists, when man, in Happy Isles, or in a new Paradise, shall confess the loveliness of peace, may be secured by your care, if not for yourselves, at least for your children. Believe that you can do it, and you can do it. The true golden age is before you, not behind you. If man has been driven once from Paradise, while an angel, with a flaming sword, forbade his return, there is another Paradise, even on earth, which he may form for himself, by the cultivation of knowledge, religion, and the kindly virtues of life; where the confusion of tongues shall be dissolved in the union of hearts; and joyous nature, borrowing prolific charms from the prevailing harmony, shall spread her lap with unimagined bounty, and there shall be a perpetual jocund spring, and sweet strains borne on "the odoriferous wing of gentle gales," through valleys of delight, more pleasant than the vale of Tempe, richer than the garden of the Hesperides, with no dragon to guard its golden fruit.

Let it not be said that the age does not demand this work. The robber conquerors of the past, from their fiery sepulchres, demand it; the precious blood of millions unjustly shed in war, crying from the ground, demands it; the voices of all good men demand it; the conscience, even of the soldier, whispers "peace." There are considerations, springing from our situation and condition, which fervently invite us to take the lead in this work. Here should bend the patriotic ardor of the land; the ambition of the statesman; the efforts of the scholar; the pervasive influence of the press; the mild persuasion of the sanctuary; the early teachings of the school. Here, in ampler ether and diviner air, are untried fields for exalted triumphs, more truly worthy the American name than any snatched from rivers of blood. War is known as the last reason of kings. Let it be no reason of our Republic. Let us renounce, and throw off forever, the yoke of a tyranny more oppressive than any in the annals of the world. As those standing on the mountain-tops first discern the coming beams of morning, let us, from the vantage-ground of liberal institutions, first recognize the ascending sun of a new

era!   Lift high the gates, and let the King of Glory in,— the
King of True Glory,— of peace.   I catch the last words of
music from the lips of innocence and beauty;

"And let the whole earth be filled with his glory!"

It is a beautiful picture in Grecian story that there was
at least one spot, the small Island of Delos, dedicated to the
gods, and kept at all times sacred from war.   No hostile foot
ever sought to press this kindly soil; and the citizens of all
countries here met, in common worship, beneath the ægis of
inviolable peace.   So let us dedicate our beloved country;
and may the blessed consecration be felt, in all its parts,
everywhere throughout its ample domain!   'The temple of
honor shall be surrounded, here at last, by the temple of concord, that it may never more be entered through any portal
of war; the horn of abundance shall overflow at its gates;
the angel of religion shall be the guide over its steps of flashing adamant; while within its enraptured courts, purged of
violence and wrong, justice, returned to the earth from her
long exile in the skies, with mighty scales for nations as for
men, shall rear her serene and majestic front; and by her side,
greatest of all, charity, sublime in meekness, hoping all and
enduring all, shall divinely temper every righteous decree
and, with words of infinite cheer, shall inspire those good
works that cannot vanish away.   And the future chiefs of
the Republic, destined to uphold the glories of a new era,
unspotted by human blood, shall be "the first in peace, and
the first in the hearts of their countrymen."

But while seeking these blissful glories for ourselves, let
us strive to extend them to other lands.   Let the bugles sound
the truce of God to the whole world forever.   Let the selfish
boast of the Spartan women become the grand chorus of

mankind, that they have never seen the smoke of an enemy's camp. Let the iron belt of martial music, which now encompasses the earth, be exchanged for the golden cestus of peace, clothing all with celestial beauty. History dwells with fondness on the reverent homage that was bestowed, by massacring soldiers, upon the spot occupied by the sepulchre of the Lord. Vain man! to restrain his regard to a few feet of sacred mould! The whole earth is the sepulchre of the Lord; nor can any righteous man profane any part thereof. Let us recognize this truth, and now, on this Sabbath of our country, lay a new stone in the grand temple of universal peace, whose dome shall be as lofty as the firmament of heaven, as broad and comprehensive as the earth itself.

GREELEY

H ORACE GREELEY, a celebrated American journalist, was born in Amherst, New Hampshire, February 3, 1811, the son of a small farmer. His earliest education was obtained at a district school and from such books as he was able to borrow. At ten years of age he removed with his parents to Westhaven, Vermont, where he assisted his father in his farm work; at fifteen he was apprenticed to a printer and learned his trade in about four years. His parents having meanwhile removed to the vicinity of Erie, Pennsylvania, he followed them and for several months worked at his trade in Erie. As his earnings were very small he went to New York city at the age of twenty, and was for two years a journeyman printer there, until in 1833 he began to publish "The Morning Post," the first daily penny paper ever issued. It was soon suspended, but was succeeded by "The New Yorker," a weekly, its editor contributing also to "The Log Cabin" and other journals. In 1841 "The New Yorker" and "The Log Cabin" were merged in "The Tribune," the first number of which was issued April 10, 1841. The paper was soon placed on a sound financial basis, Greeley having sole charge of the editorial department, and continuing for a generation to be one of the most influential leaders of public opinion in America. For a few months of 1849 he sat in Congress to fill out a vacancy in the House, at which time he was an active opponent of the abuses of the public mileage system and an advocate of the measure for establishing homesteads in the public lands. He visited Europe in 1851 and again in 1855, sending characteristic descriptive letters to "The Tribune" during his absence. In the National Republican Convention of 1860 he labored to avert civil war, but after it was once begun he advocated a vigorous prosecution of military movements. In 1864 he made an unsuccessful attempt to bring about a reconciliation between the contending parties, and at the close of the war he warmly advocated universal amnesty and impartial suffrage. He considered the imprisonment of Jefferson Davis a serious mistake and subsequently signed Mr. Davis's bail bond, an act which brought down upon him a storm of abuse. Since then his course in this matter has received juster appreciation. In 1872 he was nominated for the presidency by the Liberal Republican party and also by the Democratic party, but after an exciting canvass, characterized by great bitterness on both sides, he was defeated by a large majority. During the campaign Greeley travelled and spoke constantly, and the long strain of the canvass, to which was added the loss of his wife, seriously affected his health. He resumed his editorial chair for a short period after the election, but was soon obliged to relinquish it, his death occurring at Chappaqua, New York, November 29, 1872. He was sincerely mourned, even by many of his political opponents, for the integrity of his character commanded the entire respect of those who differed from him politically. He had many peculiarities of manner and opinion, and was often reckless in his invective, but his virtues were at least as conspicuous as his faults. His published works comprise "Hints Toward Reforms" (1850); "Glances at Europe" (1851); History of the Struggle for Slavery Extension" (1856); "Overland Journey to San Francisco" (1860); "The American Conflict" (1854-66); "Recollections of a Busy Life" (1868); "Essays in Political Economy" (1870); "What I Know of Farming" (1871).

ON THE UNION OF WORKERS

[Address delivered to the organized journeymen printers of New York, at their celebration of the birthday of Benjamin Franklin, January 17, 1850.]

THE ancient Egyptians had a custom of seating at their feasts the robed skeleton of some departed friend, whose stern silence contrasted strikingly with the mirth and hilarity of his living companions.

I believe scholars are not agreed as to the purpose and meaning of this strange custom — whether the rigid, silent guests were intended to say to the festal throng, "Enjoy and revel while you may, for time flies, man perishes; in a few years all is dust, is nothing; therefore, make haste to quaff the wine while it sparkles, to seize pleasure while the capacity of enjoyment remains to you;" or rather to impress the opposite sentiment — "Life is short; life is earnest; stupendous consequences hang suspended on your use or abuse of the speck of time allotted you; therefore, be temperate in your indulgence, moderate in you festive mirth, and, seeing in what I am what you soon must be, consider and beware!"

I shall not, of course, pretend to decide this grave question, though I shall assume for the occasion that the latter is the true rendering; and, in accordance with the elemental idea, I venture to assume among you to-night the functions of the Egyptians' silent monitor, and while others stir you with lofty eloquence or charm you with dulcet flatteries, with pie-tures of the grand achievements of our art in the past, and its brilliant prospects for the future, I shall speak to you frankly of our deficiencies, our failings, and the urgent demands upon us for new and more arduous exertions in yet unrecognized fields of duty.

It is now some four centuries since the discovery or invention of our art, fully three since our continent began to be the home of civilized men, and more than two since the Pilgrim fugitives first landed on Plymouth Rock. Since that landing, and even within the last century, what amazing strides have been made in the diffusion of knowledge and the perfection of the implements and processes of industry; in the efficiency of human labor and the facilitation of intercourse between country and country, clime and clime! The steam-engine, the spinning-jenny, the power-loom, the canal, steam-ship, power-press, railroad and lightning telegraph,— these, in their present perfection and efficiency, are a few of the trophies of human genius and labor within even the last century.

But while labor has thus doubled and quadrupled its own efficacy in the production of whatever is needful to the physical sustenance, intellectual improvement and social enjoyment of man, I do not find that there has been a corresponding melioration in the condition of the laborer. That there has been some improvement I do not deny; but has it been at all commensurate with the general progress of our race in whatever pertains to physical convenience or comfort?

I think not; and I could not help pondering this matter even while our orator's silvery tones were delighting our ears with poetical descriptions of the wonders which science and invention have achieved and are achieving. I could not help considering that, while labor builds far more sumptuous mansions in our day than of old, furnishing them far more gorgeously and luxuriously, the laborer who builds those mansions lives oftenest in a squalid lodging, than which the builders of palaces in the fifteenth century can hardly have dwelt in more wretched; and that while the demands for labor, the uses of labor, the efficiency of labor, are multiplied and extended on every side by the rush of invention and the growth of luxury around us, yet in this middle of the nineteenth century (call it the last year of the first half or the first year of the last half, as you please), labor is a drug in the market; that the temperate, efficient, upright worker often finds the comfortable maintenance and proper education of his children beyond his ability; and that, in this thriving commercial emporium of the New World, this trophy and pride of Christian civilization, there are at this day not less than forty thousand human beings anxious to earn the bread of honest industry but vainly seeking, and painfully, despairingly awaiting opportunity for so doing.

This last is the feature of our condition which seems to me most important and commanding, and it is to this, on occasions like the present, and in listening to such orations as that which has just delighted us, that my thoughts are irresistibly turned.

What can be the reason of this? Why is it that these forty thousand strong-handed, willing workers stand here thus fixed, enchained, in loathed, despairing idleness? Why are they compelled to wear out our pavements in hurrying hither and thither in anxious, heart-sick quest of something to do,— with downcast looks and trembling voice beseeching some fellow man to give them leave to labor for their bread?

I trust no one here gives any heed to the mumbling of self-styled political economists about "over-production" and the kindred phrases with which counsel is darkened. "Over-production"—of what? Where? Can there be over-production of food, when so many, even in our midst, are suffering the pangs of famine? "Over-production" of clothing and fabrics, while our streets swarm with men, women and children who are not half clad, and who shiver through the night beneath the clothing they have worn by day? "Over-production" of dwellings, when not half the families of our city have adequate and comfortable habitations, not to speak of that large class whose lodgings are utterly incompatible with decency and morality?

No, friends! there is no "over-production," save of articles pernicious and poisonous, like alcoholic liquors, lewd books, implements of gaming, etc.

Of whatever conduces to human sustenance, comfort or true education, there is not and never has been too much produced, although, owing to imperfect and vicious arrangements for distribution, there may often be a glut in the warehouses of trade, while thousands greatly need and would gladly purchase if they could.

What the world eminently requires is some wise adjustment, some remodelling of the social machinery diminishing its friction, whereby every person willing to work shall assuredly have work to do, and the just reward of that work in the articles most essential to his sustenance and comfort.

It may be that there is indeed a surplus of that particular product which some man's labor could most skilfully or rapidly produce,— pianos, watches, or gauzes, for example — and therefore it may be advisable to intermit for a season the production of these, yet the skill, the faculty, the muscular energy not required in that particular department of production might nevertheless be made available, even though in a subordinate degree, in the fabrication of some kindred product for which there is a demand among the general mass of consumers.

I maintain, then, that in our day no man should be compelled to stand idle or wander vainly in search of employment, even though that particular calling for which he is best fitted has now no place for him, but that the palpable self-interest of the community should prescribe the creation of some social providence expressly to take care that no man, woman or child shall ever stand uselessly idle when willing and anxious to work.

Even the most injudicious application of the labor now wasted through lack of opportunity could not fail to increase the national wealth to the extent of millions on millions per annum, while its effect on the condition of the laboring class, in preserving them from temptation, dissipation and crime, would be incalculably beneficent.

Now what I stand here to complain of is the indifference and inattention of the laboring mass, and especially of those entitled to a leading position in it, like the printers, to the discussion of a truth so grand and so fruitful as the right to labor. It is more discussed, more pondered, to-day, by merchants, capitalists, scholars, and men who are called aristocrats, than by the mass of those who earn their living by the sweat of the face.

It is now eighteen years since I came to this city a journeyman printer, during which years I have been intimately connected with our craft in one capacity or another, and yet I have never heard of a meeting of printers to consider and discuss the rights generally of labor, the causes of its depression, the means of its advancement.

During these eighteen years there have been hard times and good times, so called; seasons of activity and seasons of depression — in the course of which the country has been "saved"— I forget how often — our city has doubled in population and more than doubled in wealth, and yet the laboring class as a class is just where it was when I came here, or, if anything, in a worse condition, as the increased valuation of property has caused advance in rents and in some other necessaries of life. Individuals have risen out of the laboring class, becoming buyers of labor and sellers of its products, and grown rich thereby; but the condition of the laboring class, as such, has not improved, and I think is less favorable than it was twenty years ago.

Why should it not investigate, determine and develop the causes of this? Why not consider the practicability of securing work and homes to all willing to work for them? Can we imagine that inprovement is to come without effort or even inquiry? Is it the order of nature or of providence that it should? Do blessings come to other classes without foresight or calculation? I have heard complaints that machinery and invention do not work for the laboring class, but rather against them.

Concede the assumption, and is not the inquiry a fair one, What has the laboring class ever done to make machinery work in its favor? When has it planned, or sought, or calculated, to render machinery its ally and aid rather than its enemy and oppressor?

I am here to-night to tell you that you, and our trade and the laboring class of our city have been glaringly unfaithful in this respect to yourselves, your posterity, and your race, and that the workers of Paris, for example, are in advance of their brethren here in knowledge of and devotion to the interests and rights of labor. And I am here, not to find fault merely, but to exhort you to awake from your apathy and heed the summons of duty.

I stand here, friends, to urge that a new leaf be now turned over, that the laboring class, instead of idly and blindly waiting for better circumstances and better times, shall begin at once to consider and discuss the means of controlling circumstances and commanding times, by study, calculation, foresight, union. We have heard to-night of a union of printers and a printers' library, for which latter one generous donation has been proffered.

I have little faith in giving, as a remedy for the woes of mankind, and not much of any effort for the elevation or improvement of any one section of producers of wealth in our city. What I would suggest would be the union and organization of all workers for their mutual improvement and benefit, leading to the erection of a spacious edifice at some central point in our city to form a Laborers' Exchange, just as commerce now has its exchange, very properly.

Let the new exchange be erected and owned as a joint-stock property, paying a fair dividend to those whose money erected it; let it contain the best spacious hall for general meetings to be found in our city, with smaller lecture-rooms for the meetings of particular sections or callings — all to be leased or rented at fair prices to all who may choose to hire them, when not needed for the primary purpose of discussing and advancing the interests of labor.

Let us have here books opened, wherein any one wanting work may inscribe his name, residence, capacities and terms, while any one wishing to hire may do likewise, as well as meet personally those seeking employment. These are but hints toward a few of the uses which such a labor exchange

might subserve, while its reading-room and library, easily
formed and replenished, should be opened freely and gladly
to all.   Such an edifice, rightly planned and constructed,
might become, and I confidently hope would become, a most
important instrumentality in the great work of advancing the
laboring class in comfort, intelligence and independence.   I
trust we need not long await its erection.

THACKERAY

WILLIAM MAKEPEACE THACKERAY, an English novelist, by many critics considered the most eminent of the century, was born at Calcutta, July 18, 1811. His father and grandfather were both connected with the East India Company. In 1816 his father died, and, his mother having married again, the boy was sent to England and entered at the famous Charterhouse school, where he remained six years. In 1829 he went to Trinity College, Cambridge, but at the end of two years withdrew without taking his degree. He visited the Continent, intending on his return to adopt the law for his profession; but having lost most of his small patrimony he turned his attention to literature. In 1833 he became editor and proprietor of the "National Standard," a weekly journal to which he had already regularly contributed. This venture proved a failure and he went to Paris to study art. In 1835 he offered his services to illustrate the "Pickwick Papers," and the following year married the dowerless daughter of an East Indian colonel. Six months later the Constitutional Company, of which his stepfather was chairman, failed disastrously, and Thackeray was left penniless. He moved to London and engaged actively in literary work. After the birth of his third daughter, in 1840, Mrs. Thackeray became hopelessly insane and his home was broken up. In 1840 appeared his first volume, the "Paris Sketchbook," but this and the "Comic Tales and Sketches" of the following year were failures. His work in "Fraser's Magazine" and elsewhere was beginning to attract attention, and in 1842 he joined the staff of "Punch" in which he published his "Snob" papers. "Vanity Fair," completed in monthly parts in July, 1848, made the author's fame secure. "Pendennis" was begun in November of that same year, and "Henry Esmond" followed in 1852. He had been lecturing in London on the English humorists with great success and was invited to deliver them in the United States. On his return in 1853 he began "The Newcomes," which was completed in 1855. In that year he gave in America his famous lectures on "the Four Georges." After his return to England he stood for Parliament as a Radical member for Oxford, but failed of election. In 1857 "The Virginians" began and three years later he became the editor of the new "Cornhill Magazine," to which he contributed "Lovell, the Widower," "Philip," and his "Roundabout Papers," and the first chapters of his unfinished "Dennis Duval," which was interrupted by his sudden death, December 24, 1863. Thackeray's master in style was Fielding; he had the same power of natural characterization; of telling a story with epic vividness and motion, the same hatred of shams, hypocrisy, and meanness, and the same keenness of humor. He satirizes with telling irony, but beneath the mask one realizes that there is a face beaming with good nature, and that though the voice may sometimes be stern the heart within is warm and human. He is not so successful in depicting attractive feminine types as in strong, lovable men. "Becky Sharp" is his masterpiece of character-drawing, but she is true to her name. It was said that "the only faculty with which he gifted his good women was the supreme faculty of tears." But "Colonel Newcome" and "Henry Esmond" are unsurpassed in their combination of noble, lovable qualities—as true English gentlemen as ever lived. Thackeray gave a great semblance of reality to his last stories by introducing the actual characters of their times—Dick Steele, Addison, Washington, and others. Personally he was reserved and uncommunicative with strangers, but his friends found him open-hearted, generous, and sympathetic. Charlotte Brontë called him a "Titan of mind," and the impression that he made on his own day and generation has been no less deep since his death.

LECTURE: CHARITY AND HUMOR

[This lecture was first delivered in New York on behalf of a charity at the time of Mr. Thackeray's visit to America in 1852, when he had been giving his series of lectures on the English humorists. It was subsequently repeated, with slight variations, in London (once under the title of "Week-Day Preachers") for the benefit of the families of Angus B. Reach and Douglas Jerrold.]

SEVERAL charitable ladies of this city, to some of whom I am under great personal obligation, having thought that a lecture of mine would advance a benevolent end which they had in view, I have preferred, in place of delivering a discourse, which many of my hearers no doubt know already, upon a subject merely literary or biographical, to put together a few thoughts which may serve as a supplement to the former lectures, if you like, and which have this at least in common with the kind purpose which assembles you here, that they rise out of the same occasion and treat of charity.

Besides contributing to our stock of happiness, to our harmless laughter and amusement, to our scorn for falsehood and pretension, to our righteous hatred of hypocrisy, to our education in the perception of truth, our love of honesty, our knowledge of life, and shrewd guidance through the world, have not our humorous writers, our gay and kind week-day preachers, done much in support of that holy cause which has assembled you in this place; and which you are all abetting,—the cause of love and charity, the cause of the poor, the weak, and the unhappy; the sweet mission of love and tenderness, and peace and good will towards men? That same theme which is urged upon you by the eloquence and example of good men to whom you are delighted listeners on Sabbath days is taught in his way and according to his power by the humorous writer, the commentator on everyday life and manners.

And as you are here assembled for a charitable purpose, giving your contributions at the door to benefit deserving people who need them, I like to hope and think that the men of our calling have done something in aid of the cause of charity, and have helped, with kind words and kind thoughts at least, to confer happiness and to do good. If the humorous writers claim to be week-day preachers, have they conferred any benefit by their sermons? Are people happier, better, better disposed to their neighbors, more inclined to do works of kindness, to love, forbear, forgive, pity, after reading in Addison, in Steele, in Fielding, in Goldsmith, in Hood, in Dickens? I hope and believe so, and fancy that in writing they are also acting charitably, contributing with the means which Heaven supplies them to forward the end which brings you, too, together.

A love of the human species is a very vague and indefinite kind of virtue, sitting very easily on a man, not confining his actions at all, shining in print, or exploding in paragraphs, after which efforts of benevolence the philanthropist is sometimes said to go home and be no better than his neighbors. Tartuffe and Joseph Surface, Stiggins and Chadband, who are always preaching fine sentiments and are no more virtuous than hundreds of those whom they denounce and whom they cheat, are fair objects of mistrust and satire; but their hypocrisy, the homage, according to the old saying, which vice pays to virtue, has this of good in it, that its fruits are good: a man may preach good morals though he may be himself but a lax practitioner; a Pharisee may put pieces of gold into the charity-plate out of mere hypocrisy and ostentation, but the bad man's gold feeds the widow and the fatherless as well as the good man's. The butcher and baker must needs look, not to motives, but to money, in return for their wares.

I am not going to hint that we of the literary calling resemble Monsieur Tartuffe or Monsieur Stiggins, though there may be such men in our body, as there are in all.

A literary man of the humoristic turn is pretty sure to be of a philanthropic nature to have a great sensibility, to be easily moved to pain or pleasure, keenly to appreciate the varieties of temper of people round about him, and sympathize in their laughter, love, amusement, tears. Such a man is philanthropic, man-loving by nature, as another is irascible, or red-haired, or six feet high. And so I would arrogate no particular merit to literary men for the possession of this faculty of doing good which some of them enjoy. It costs a gentleman no sacrifice to be benevolent on paper; and the luxury of indulging in the most beautiful and brilliant sentiments never makes any man a penny the poorer. A literary man is no better than another, as far as my experience goes; and a man writing a book no better or no worse than one who keeps accounts in a ledger or follows any other occupation. Let us, however, give him credit for the good, at least, which he is the means of doing, as we give credit to a man with a million for the hundred which he puts into the plate at a charity-sermon. He never misses them. He has made them in a moment by a lucky speculation, and parts with them knowing that he has an almost endless balance at his bank, whence he can call for more. But in esteeming the benefaction we are grateful to the benefactor, too, somewhat; and so of men of genius, richly endowed, and lavish in parting with their mind's wealth, we may view them at least kindly and favorably, and be thankful for the bounty of which Providence has made them the dispensers.

I have said myself somewhere, I do not know with what correctness (for definitions never are complete), that humor is wit and love; I am sure, at any rate, that the best humor is that which contains most humanity, that which is flavored throughout with tenderness and kindness. This love does not demand constant utterance or actual expression, as a good father, in conversation with his children or wife, is not perpetually embracing them or making protestations of his love; as a lover in the society of his mistress is not, at least as far as I am led to believe, forever squeezing her hand or sighing in her ear, " My soul's darling, I adore you! " He shows his love by his conduct, by his fidelity, by his watchful desire to make the beloved person happy; it lightens from his eyes when she appears, though he may not speak it; it fills his heart when she is present or absent; influences all his words and actions; suffuses his whole being; it sets the father cheerily to work through the long day, supports him through the tedious labor of the weary absence or journey, and sends him happy home again, yearning towards the wife and children. This kind of love is not a spasm, but a life. It fondles and caresses at due seasons, no doubt; but the fond heart is always beating fondly and truly, though the wife is not sitting hand-in-hand with him or the children hugging at his knee. And so with a loving humor: I think, it is a genial writer's habit of being; it is the kind, gentle spirit's way of looking out on the world — that sweet friendliness which fills his heart and his style. You recognize it, even[1] though there may not be a single point of wit, or a single pathetic touch in the page; though you may not be called upon to salute his genius by a laugh or a tear. That collision of ideas, which provokes the one or the other, must be occasional. They must be like papa's embraces, which I spoke of anon, who only delivers them now and again, and cannot be expected to go on kissing the children all night. And so the writer's jokes and sentiment, his ebullitions of feeling, his outbreaks of high spirits, must not be too frequent. One tires of a page of which every sentence sparkles with points, of a sentimentalist who is always pumping the tears from his eyes or your own. One suspects the genuineness of the tear, the naturalness of the humor; these ought to be true and manly in a man, as everything else in his life should be manly and true; and he loses his dignity by laughing or weeping out of place, or too often.

When the Reverend Laurence Sterne begins to sentimentalize over the carriage in Monsieur Dessein's courtyard, and pretends to squeeze a tear out of a rickety old shandrydan; when, presently, he encounters the dead donkey on his road to Paris, and snivels over that asinine corpse, I say: "Away you drivelling quack: do not palm off these grimaces of grief upon simple folks who know no better, and cry misled by your hypocrisy." Tears are sacred. The tributes of kind hearts to misfortune, the mites which gentle souls drop into the collections made for God's poor and unhappy, are not to be tricked out of them by a whimpering hypocrite, handing round a begging-box for your compassion, and asking your pity for a lie. When that same man tells me of Lefevre's illness and Uncle Toby's charity; of the noble at Rennes coming home and reclaiming his sword, I thank him for the generous emotion which, springing genuinely from his own heart, has caused mine to admire benevolence and sympathize with honor; and to feel love, and kindness, and pity.

If I do not love Swift, as, thank God, I do not, however immensely I may admire him, it is because I revolt from the man who placards himself as a professional hater of his own kind; because he chisels his savage indignation on his tombstone, as if to perpetuate his protest against being born of our race — the suffering, the weak, the erring, the wicked, if you will, but still the friendly, the loving children of God our Father: it is because, as I read through Swift's dark volumes, I never find the aspect of nature seems to delight him; the smiles of children to please him; the sight of wedded love to s othe him. I do not remember in any line of his writing a passing allusion to a natural scene of beauty. When he speaks about the families of his comrades and brother clergymen, it is to assail them with gibes and scorn, and to laugh at them brutally for being fathers and for being poor. He does mention, in the Journal to Stella, a sick child, to be sure — a child of Lady Masham, that was ill of the smallpox — but then it is to confound the brat for being ill and the mother for attending to it when she should have been busy about a court intrigue, in which the Dean was deeply engaged. And he alludes to a suitor of Stella's, and a match she might have made, and would have made, very likely, with an honorable and faithful and attached man, Tisdall, who loved her, and of whom Swift speaks, in a letter to this lady, in language so foul that you would not bear to hear it. In treating of the good the humorists have done, of the love and kindness they have taught and left behind them, it is not of this one I dare speak. Heaven help the lonely misanthrope! be kind to that multitude of sins, with so little charity to cover them!

Of Mr. Congreve's contributions to the English stock of benevolence, I do not speak; for, of any moral legacy to posterity, I doubt whether that brilliant man ever thought at all. He had some money, as I have told; every shilling of which he left to his friend the Duchess of Marlborough, a lady of great fortune and the highest fashion. He gave the gold of his brains to persons of fortune and fashion, too. There is no more feeling in his comedies than in as many books of Euclid. He no more pretends to teach love for the poor, and good will for the unfortunate, than a dancing master does; he teaches pirouettes and flic-flacs; and how to bow to a lady, and to walk a minuet. In his private life Congreve was immensely liked — more so than any man of his age, almost; and, to have been so liked, must have been kind and good natured. His good nature bore him through extreme bodily ills and pain, with uncommon cheerfulness and courage. Being so gay, so bright, so popular, such a grand seigneur, be sure he was kind to those about him, generous to his dependents, serviceable to his friends. Society does not like a man so long as it liked Congreve, unless he is likable; it finds out a quack very soon; it scorns a poltroon or a curmudgeon; we may be certain that this man was brave, good tempered, and liberal; so, very likely, is Monsieur Pirouette, of whom we spoke; he cuts his capers, he grins, bows, and dances to his fiddle. In private he may have a hundred virtues; in public, he teaches dancing. His business is cotillions, not ethics.

As much may be said of those charming and lazy Epicureans, Gay and Prior, sweet lyric singers, comrades of Anacreon, and disciples of love and the bottle. "Is there any moral shut within the bosom of a rose?" sings our great Tennyson. Does a nightingale preach from a bough, or the lark from his cloud? Not knowingly; yet we may be grateful, and love larks and roses, and the flower-crowned minstrels, too, who laugh and who sing.

Of Addison's contributions to the charity of the world I have spoken before, in trying to depict that noble figure; and say now, as then, that we should thank him as one of the greatest benefactors of that vast and immeasurably spreading family which speaks our common tongue. Wherever it is spoken, there is no man that does not feel, and understand, and use the noble English word "gentleman." And there is no man that teaches us to be gentlemen better than Joseph Addison. Gentle in our bearing through life; gentle and courteous to our neighbor; gentle in dealing with his follies and weaknesses; gentle in treating his opposition; deferential to the old; kindly to the poor, and those below us in degree; for people above us and below us we must find, in whatever hemisphere we dwell, whether kings or presidents govern us; and in no republic or monarchy that I know of, is a citizen exempt from the tax of befriending poverty and weakness, of respecting age, and of honoring his father and mother. It has just been whispered to me — I have not been three months in the country, and, of course, cannot venture to express an opinion of my own — that, in regard to paying this latter tax of respect and honor to age, some very few of the Republican youths are occasionally a little remiss. I have heard of young Sons of Freedom publishing their Declaration of Independence before they could well spell it; and cutting the connection with father and mother before they had learned to shave. My own time of life having been stated by various enlightened organs of public opinion, at almost any figure from forty-five to sixty, I cheerfully own that I belong to the fogy interest, and ask leave to rank in,

and plead for that respectable class. Now a gentleman can
but be a gentleman, in Broadway or the backwoods, in Pall
Mall or California; and where and whenever he lives, thousands of miles away in the wilderness, or hundreds of years
hence, I am sure that reading the writings of this true gentleman, this true Christian, this noble Joseph Addison, must do
him good. He may take Sir Roger de Coverley to the Dig-
gings with him, and learn to be gentle and good-humored, and
urbane, and friendly in the midst of that struggle in which
his life is engaged. I take leave to say that the most brilliant
youth of this city may read over this delightful memorial
of a bygone age, of fashions long passed away; of manners
long since changed and modified; of noble gentlemen, and
a great, and a brilliant and polished society; and find in it
much to charm and polish, to refine and instruct him, a
courteousness, which can be out of place at no time, and under
no flag, a politeness and simplicity, a truthful manhood, a
gentle respect and deference, which may be kept as the
unbought grace of life, and cheap defence of mankind, long
after its old artificial distinctions, after periwigs, and small-
swords, and ruffles, and red-heeled shoes, and titles, and stars
and garters have passed away. I will tell you when I have
been put in mind of two of the finest gentlemen books bring
us any mention of. I mean our books (not books of history,
but books of humor). I will tell you when I have been
put in mind of the courteous gallantry of the noble knight,
Sir Roger de Coverley of Coverley Manor, of the noble
Hidalgo Don Quixote of La Mancha: here in your own
omnibus carriages and railway cars, when I have seen a
woman step in, handsome or not, well dressed or not, and a
workman in hobnail shoes, or a dandy in the height of the
fashion, rise up and give her his place. I think Mr. Spectator,

with his short face, if he had seen such a deed of courtesy, would have smiled a sweet smile to the doer of that gentleman-like action, and have made him a low bow from under his great periwig, and have gone home and written a pretty paper about him.

I am sure Dick Steele would have hailed him, were he dandy or mechanic, and asked him to a tavern to share a bottle, or perhaps half a dozen. Mind, I do not set down the five last flasks to Dick's score for virtue, and look upon them as works of the most questionable supererogation.

Steele, as a literary benefactor to the world's charity, must rank very high, indeed, not merely from his givings, which were abundant, but because his endowments are prodigiously increased in value since he bequeathed them, as the revenues of the lands, bequeathed to our Foundling Hospital at London, by honest Captain Coram, its founder, are immensely enhanced by the houses since built upon them. Steele was the founder of sentimental writing in English, and how the land has been since occupied, and what hundreds of us have laid out gardens and built up tenements on Steele's ground! Before his time, readers or hearers were never called upon to cry except at a tragedy, and compassion was not expected to express itself otherwise than in blank verse, or for personages much lower in rank than a dethroned monarch, or a widowed or a jilted empress. He stepped off the high-heeled cothurnus, and came down into common life; he held out his great hearty arms, and embraced us all; he had a bow for all women; a kiss for all children; a shake of the hand for all men, high or low; he showed us Heaven's sun shining every day on quiet homes; not gilded palace roofs only, or court processions, or heroic warriors fighting for princesses and pitched battles. He took away comedy from behind the fine lady's alcove, or the screen where the libertine was watching her. He ended all that wretched business of wives jeering at their husbands, of rakes laughing wives, and husbands too, to scorn. That miserable, rouged, tawdry, sparkling, hollow-hearted comedy of the Restoration fled before him, and, like the wicked spirit in the fairy-books, shrank, as Steele let the daylight in, and shrieked, and shuddered, and vanished. The stage of humorists has been common life ever since Steele's and Addison's time; the joys and griefs, the aversions and sympathies, the laughter and tears of nature.

And here, coming off the stage, and throwing aside the motley habit, or satiric disguise, in which he had before entertained you, mingling with the world, and wearing the same coat as his neighbor, the humorist's service became straightway immensely more available; his means of doing good infinitely multiplied; his success, and the esteem in which he was held, proportionately increased. It requires an effort, of which all minds are not capable, to understand "Don Quixote;" children and common people still read "Gulliver" for the story merely. Many more persons are sickened by "Jonathan Wild" than can comprehend the satire of it. Each of the great men who wrote those books was speaking from behind the satiric mask I anon mentioned. Its distortions appal many simple spectators; its settled sneer or laugh is unintelligible to thousands, who have not the wit to interpret the meaning of the vizored satirist preaching from within. Many a man was at fault about Jonathan Wild's greatness, who could feel and relish Allworthy's goodness in "Tom Jones," and Doctor Harrison's in "Amelia," and dear Parson Adams, and Joseph Andrews. We love to read; we may grow ever so old, but we love to read of them still — of love and beauty, of frankness, and bravery, and generosity. We hate hypocrites and cowards; we long to defend oppressed innocence, and to soothe and succor gentle women and children. We are glad when vice is foiled and rascals punished; we lend a foot to kick Blifil down stairs; and as we attend the brave bridegroom to his wedding on the happy marriage day, we ask the groom's-man's privilege to salute the blushing cheek of Sophia. A lax morality in many a vital point I own in Fielding, but a great hearty sympathy and benevolence; a great kindness for the poor; a great gentleness and pity for the unfortunate; a great love for the pure and good; these are among the contributions to the charity of the world with which this erring but noble creature endowed it.

As for Goldsmith, if the youngest and most unlettered person here has not been happy with the family at Wake-field; has not rejoiced when Olivia returned, and been thankful for her forgiveness and restoration; has not laughed with delighted good humor over Moses's gross of green spectacles; has not loved with all his heart the good vicar, and that kind spirit which created these charming figures, and devised the beneficent fiction which speaks to us so tenderly — what call is there for me to speak? In this place, and on this occasion, remembering these men, I claim from you your sympathy for the good they have done, and for the sweet charity which they have bestowed on the world.

When humor joins with rhythm and music, and appears in song, its influence is irresistible, its charities are countless, it stirs the feelings to love, peace, friendship, as scarce any moral agent can. The songs of Béranger are hymns of love and tenderness; I have seen great whiskered Frenchmen warbling the "Bonne Vieille," the "Soldats, au pas, au pas;" with tears rolling down their moustachios. At a Burns's festival I have seen Scotchmen singing Burns while the drops twinkled on their furrowed cheeks; while each rough hand was flung out to grasp its neighbor's; while early scenes and sacred recollections, and dear and delightful memories of the past came rushing back at the sound of the familiar words and music, and the softened heart was full of love, and friendship, and home. Humor! if tears are the alms of gentle spirits, and may be counted, as sure they may, among the sweetest of life's charities,— of that kindly sensibility, and sweet sudden emotion, which exhibits itself at the eyes, I know no such provocative as humor. It is an irresistible sympathizer; it surprises you into compassion: you are laughing and disarmed, and suddenly forced into tears. I heard a humorous balladist not long since, a minstrel with wool on his head, and an ultra-Ethiopian complexion, who performed a negro ballad that I confess moistened these spectacles in the most unexpected manner. They have gazed at dozens of tragedy queens, dying on the stage, and expiring in appropriate blank verse, and I never wanted to wipe them. They have looked up, with deep respect be it said, at many scores of clergymen in pulpits, and without being dimmed; and behold a vagabond with a corked face and a banjo sings a little song, strikes a wild note which sets the whole heart thrilling with happy pity. Humor! humor is the mistress of tears; she knows the way to the *fons lachrymarum,* strikes in dry and rugged places with her enchanting wand, and bids the fountain gush and sparkle. She has refreshed myriads more from her natural springs, than ever tragedy has watered from her pompous old urn.

Popular humor, and especially modern popular humor, and the writers, its exponents, are always kind and chivalrous, taking the side of the weak against the strong. In our plays, and books, and entertainments for the lower classes in England, I scarce remember a story or theatrical piece in which a wicked aristocrat is not bepummelled by a dashing young champion of the people. There was a book which had an immense popularity in England, and I believe has been greatly read here, in which the mysteries of the Court of London were said to be unveiled by a gentleman who, I suspect, knows about as much about the Court of London as he does of that of Pekin. Years ago I treated myself to sixpennyworth of this performance at a railway station, and found poor dear George IV, our late most religious and gracious king, occupied in the most flagitious designs against the tradesmen's families in his metropolitan city. A couple of years after I took sixpennyworth more of the same delectable history: George IV was still at work, still ruining the peace of tradesmen's families; he had been at it for two whole years, and a bookseller at the Brighton station told me that this book was by many many times the most popular of all periodical tales then published, because, says he, " it lashes the aristocracy!" Not long since I went to two penny theatres in London; immense eager crowds of people thronged the buildings, and the vast masses thrilled and vibrated with the emotion produced by the piece represented on the stage and burst into applause or laughter such as many a polite actor would sigh for in vain. In both these pieces there was a wicked Lord kicked out of the window — there is always a wicked Lord kicked out of the window. First piece: — " Domestic drama — Thrilling interest!— Weaver's family in distress! — Fanny gives away her bread to little Jacky, and starves! — Enter wicked Lord: tempts Fanny with offer of Diamond Necklace, Champagne Suppers, and Coach to ride in! — Enter sturdy Blacksmith.— Scuffle between Blacksmith and Aristocratic minion: exit wicked Lord out of the window." Fanny, of course, becomes Mrs. Blacksmith.

The second piece was a nautical drama, also of thrilling interest, consisting chiefly of hornpipes, and acts of most tremendous oppression on the part of certain Earls and Magistrates towards the people. Two wicked Lords were in this piece the atrocious scoundrels: one Aristocrat, a deep-dyed villain, in short duck trousers and Berlin cotton gloves; while the other minion of wealth enjoyed an eyeglass with a blue ribbon, and whisked about the stage with a penny cane. Having made away with Fanny Forester's lover, Tom Bowling, by means of a press-gang, they meet her all alone on a common and subject her to the most opprobrious language and behavior: "Release me, villains!" says Fanny, pulling a brace of pistols out of her pockets and crossing them over her breast so as to cover wicked Lord to the right, wicked Lord to the left; and they might have remained in that position ever so much longer (for the aristocratic rascals had pistols too), had not Tom Bowling returned from sea at the very nick of time, armed with a great marlinespike, with which — whack! whack! down goes wicked Lord No. 1 — wicked Lord No. 2. Fanny rushes into Tom's arms with an hysterical shriek, and I dare say they marry and are very happy ever after. Popular fun is always kind: it is the champion of the humble against the great. In all popular parables it is Little Jack that conquers and the Giant that topples down. I think our popular authors are rather hard upon the great folks. Well, well! their lordships have all the money and can afford to be laughed at.

In our days, in England, the importance of the humorous

6 preacher has prodigiously increased; his audiences are enormous; every week or month his happy congregations flock to him; they never tire of such sermons. I believe my friend Mr. "Punch" is as popular to-day as he has been any day since his birth; I believe that Mr. Dickens's readers are even more numerous than they have ever been since his unrivalled pen commenced to delight the world with its humor. We have among us other literary parties; we have "Punch," as I have said, preaching from his booth; we have a Jerrold party very numerous, and faithful to that acute thinker and distinguished wit; and we have also — it must be said, and it is still to be hoped — a "Vanity Fair" party, the author of which work has lately been described by the London "Times" newspaper as a writer of considerable parts, but a dreary misanthrope, who sees no good anywhere, who sees the sky above him green, I think, instead of blue, and only miserable sinners round about him. So we are; so is every writer and every reader I ever heard of; so was every being who ever trod this earth, save One. I cannot help telling the truth as I view it, and describing what I see. To describe it otherwise than it seems to me would be falsehood in that calling in which it has pleased heaven to place me; treason to that conscience which says that men are weak; that truth must be told; that fault must be owned; that pardon must be prayed for; and that love reigns supreme over all.

I look back at the good which of late years the kind English humorists have done; and if you are pleased to rank the present speaker among that class, I own to an honest pride at thinking what benefits society has derived from men of our calling. That "Song of the Shirt" which "Punch" first published, and the noble, the suffering, the melancholy, the tender Hood sang, may surely rank as a great act of charity

ments in the northern counties. Parents were ashamed that never were ashamed before until the kind satirist laughed at them; relatives were frightened; scores of little scholars were taken away; poor schoolmasters had to shut their shops up; every pedagogue was voted a Squeers, and many suffered, no doubt unjustly; but afterwards schoolboys' backs were not so much caned; schoolboys' meat was less tough and more plentiful; and schoolboys' milk was not so sky-blue. What a kind light of benevolence it is that plays round Crummles and the Phenomenon, and all those poor theatre people in that charming book! What a humor! and what a good humor! I coincide with the youthful critic whose opinion has just been mentioned, and own to a family admiration for "Nicholas Nickleby."

One might go on, though the task would be endless and needless, chronicling the names of kind folks with whom this kind genius has made us familiar. Who does not love the Marchioness and Mr. Richard Swiveller? Who does not sympathize, not only with Oliver Twist, but his admirable young friend the Artful Dodger? Who has not the inestimable advantage of possessing a Mrs. Nickleby in his own family? Who does not bless Sairey Gamp and wonder at Mrs. Harris. Who does not venerate the chief of that illustrious family who, being stricken by misfortune, wisely and greatly turned his attention to "coals," the accomplished, the Epicurean, the dirty, the delightful Micawber?

I may quarrel with Mr. Dickens's art a thousand and a thousand times, I delight and wonder at his genius; I recognize in it — I speak with awe and reverence — a commission from that Divine Beneficence whose blessed task we know it will one day be to wipe every tear from every eye. Thankfully I take my share of the feast of love and kindness which this gentle, and generous, and charitable soul has contributed to the happiness of the world. I take and enjoy my share, and say a Benediction for the meal.

LECTURE: GEORGE THE THIRD

WE HAVE to glance over sixty years in as many minutes. To read the mere catalogue of characters who figured during that long period, would occupy our allotted time, and we should have all text and no sermon. England has to undergo the revolt of the American colonies; to submit to defeat and separation; to shake under the volcano of the French Revolution; to grapple and fight for the life with her gigantic enemy Napoleon; to gasp and rally after that tremendous struggle. The old society, with its courtly splendors, has to pass away; generations of statesmen to rise and disappear; Pitt to follow Chatham to the tomb; the memory of Rodney and Wolfe to be superseded by Nelson's and Wellington's glory; the old poets who unite us to Queen Anne's time to sink into their graves; Johnson to die, and Scott and Byron to arise; Garrick to delight the world with his dazzling dramatic genius, and Kean to leap on the stage and take possession of the astonished theatre. Steam has to be invented; kings to be beheaded, banished, deposed, restored. Napoleon to be but an episode, and George III is to be alive through all these varied changes, to accompany his people through all these revolutions of thought, government, society; to survive out of the old world into ours.

When I first saw England, she was in mourning for the young Princess Charlotte, the hope of the empire. I came

merry joke frankly spoken to the laughing fine lady. How
fine those ladies were, those ladies who heard and spoke such
coarse jokes! how grand those gentlemen!

I fancy that peculiar product of the past, the fine gentleman, has almost vanished off the face of the earth, and is
disappearing like the beaver or the Red Indian. We can't
have fine gentlemen any more, because we can't have the
society in which they lived. The people will not obey: the
parasites will not be as obsequious as formerly: children
do not go down on their knees to beg their parents' blessing:
chaplains do not say grace and retire before the pudding:
servants do not say " your honor " and " your worship " at
every moment: tradesmen do not stand hat in hand as the
gentleman passes: authors do not wait for hours in gentlemen's ante-rooms with a fulsome dedication, for which they
hope to get five guineas from his lordship. In the days
when there were fine gentlemen Mr. Secretary Pitt's under-
secretaries did not dare to sit down before him; but Mr. Pitt,
in his turn, went down on his gouty knees to George II;
and when George III spoke a few kind words to him, Lord
Chatham burst into tears of reverential joy and gratitude; so
awful was the idea of the monarch and so great the distinctions of rank. Fancy Lord John Russell or Lord
Palmerston on their knees whilst the sovereign was reading
a despatch, or beginning to cry because Prince Albert said
something civil!

At the accession of George III the patricians were yet at
the height of their good fortune. Society recognized their
superiority, which they themselves pretty calmly took for
granted. They inherited not only titles and estates, and
seats in the House of Peers, but seats in the House of
Commons. There were a multitude of government places,

and not merely these, but bribes of actual £500 notes, which members of the House took not much shame in receiving. Fox went into Parliament at twenty: Pitt when just of age: his father when not much older. It was the good time for patricians. Small blame to them if they took and enjoyed, and over-enjoyed, the prizes of politics, the pleasures of social life.

In these letters to Selwyn, we are made acquainted with a whole society of these defunct fine gentlemen: and can watch with a curious interest a life which the novel writers of that time, I think, have scarce touched upon. To Smollett, to Fielding even, a lord was a lord: a gorgeous being, with a blue ribbon, a coroneted chair, and an immense star on his bosom, to whom commoners paid reverence. Richardson, a man of humbler birth than either of the above two, owned that he was ignorant regarding the manners of the aristocracy, and besought Mrs. Donnellan, a lady who had lived in the great world, to examine a volume of "Sir Charles Grandison" and point out any errors which she might see in this particular. Mrs. Donnellan found so many faults that Richardson changed color, shut up the book, and muttered that it were best to throw it in the fire. Here, in Selwyn, we have the real original men and women of fashion of the early time of George III. We can follow them to the new club at Almack's; we can travel over Europe with them; we can accompany them not only to the public places, but to their country houses and private society. Here is a whole company of them; wits and prodigals; some persevering in their bad ways; some repentant, but relapsing; beautiful ladies, parasites, humble chaplains, led captains. Those fair creatures whom we love in Reynolds's portraits, and who still look out on us from his canvases with their 'spondents is the Earl of Carlisle, grandfather of the amiable nobleman at present viceroy in Ireland. The grandfather, too, was Irish viceroy, having previously been treasurer of the King's household; and, in 1778, the principal commissioner for treating, consulting and agreeing upon the means of quieting the divisions subsisting in his majesty's colonies, plantations and possessions in North America. You may read his lordship's manifestoes in the "Royal New York Gazette." He returned to England, having by no means quieted the colonies: and speedily afterwards the "Royal New York Gazette" somehow ceased to be published.

This good, clever, kind, highly-bred Lord Carlisle was one of the English fine gentlemen who was well-nigh ruined by the awful debauchery and extravagance which prevailed in the great English society of those days. Its dissoluteness was awful: it had swarmed over Europe after the Peace; it had danced, and raced, and gambled in all the courts. It had made its bow at Versailles; it had run its horses on the plain of Sablons, near Paris, and created the Anglomania there; it had exported vast quantities of pictures and marbles from Rome and Florence: it had ruined itself by building great galleries and palaces for the reception of the statues and pictures: it had brought over singing-women and dancing-women from all the operas of Europe, on whom my Lords lavished their thousands, whilst they left their honest wives and honest children languishing in the lonely, deserted splendors of the castle and park at home.

Besides the great London society of those days, there was another unacknowledged world, extravagant beyond measure, tearing about in the pursuit of pleasure; dancing, gambling, drinking, singing; meeting the real society in the public places (at Ranelaghs, Vauxhalls, and Ridottos, about which

our old novelists talk so constantly), and outvying the real
leaders of fashion in luxury, and splendor, and beauty. For
instance, when the famous Miss Gunning visited Paris as
Lady Coventry, where she expected that her beauty would
meet with the applause which had followed her and her sister
through England, it appears she was put to flight by an
English lady still more lovely in the eyes of the Parisians.
A certain Mrs. Pitt took a box at the opera opposite the
countess; and was so much handsomer than her ladyship
that the parterre cried out that this was the real English
angel, whereupon Lady Coventry quitted Paris in a huff.
The poor thing died presently of consumption, accelerated,
it was said, by the red and white paint with which she plastered those luckless charms of hers. (We must represent
to ourselves all fashionable female Europe, at that time,
as plastered with white and raddled with red.) She left
two daughters behind her, whom George Selwyn loved (he
was curiously fond of little children), and who are described
very drolly and pathetically in these letters, in their little
nursery, where passionate little Lady Fanny, if she had not
good cards, flung hers into Lady Mary's face; and where
they sat conspiring how they should receive a new mother-
in-law, whom their papa presently brought home. They got
on very well with their mother-in-law, who was very kind to
them; and they grew up, and they were married, and they
were both divorced afterwards, poor little souls! Poor
painted mother, poor society, ghastly in its pleasures, its
loves, its revelries!

As for my lord commissioner, we can afford to speak about
him; because, though he was a wild and weak commissioner
at one time, though he hurt his estate, though he gambled
and lost ten thousand pounds at a sitting —" five times

more," says the unlucky gentleman, "than I ever lost before;" though he swore he never would touch a card again; and yet, strange to say, went back to the table and lost still more: yet he repented of his errors, sobered down, and became a worthy peer and a good country gentleman, and returned to the good wife and the good children whom he had always loved with the best part of his heart. He had married at one-and-twenty. He found himself, in the midst of a dissolute society, at the head of a great fortune. Forced into luxury, and obliged to be a great Lord and a great idler, he yielded to some temptations, and paid for them a bitter penalty of manly remorse; from some others he fled wisely and ended by conquering them nobly. But he always had the good wife and children in his mind, and they saved him. "I am very glad you did not come to me the morning I left London," he writes to G. Selwyn, as he is embarking for America. "I can only say, I never knew till that moment of parting, what grief was." There is no parting now, where they are. The faithful wife, the kind, generous gentleman, have left a noble race behind them: an inheritor of his name and titles, who is beloved as widely as he is known; a man most kind, accomplished, gentle, friendly and pure; and female descendants occupying high stations and embellishing great names; some renowned for beauty, and all for spotless lives, and pious matronly virtues.

Another of Selwyn's correspondents is the Earl of March, afterwards Duke of Queensberry, whose life lasted into this century; and who certainly as earl or duke, young man or graybeard, was not an ornament to any possible society. The legends about Old Q. are awful. In Selwyn, in Wraxall, and contemporary chronicles, the observer of human nature may follow him, drinking, gambling, intriguing to the end of his career; when the wrinkled, palsied, toothless old Don Juan died, as wicked and unrepentant as he had been at the hottest season of youth and passion. There is a house in Piccadilly, where they used to show a certain low window at which Old Q. sat to his very last days, ogling through his senile glasses the women as they passed by.

There must have been a great deal of good about this lazy, sleepy George Selwyn, which, no doubt, is set to his present credit. "Your friendship," writes Carlisle to him, "is so different from anything I have ever met with or seen in the world, that when I recollect the extraordinary proofs of your kindness, it seems to me like a dream." "I have lost my oldest friend and acquaintance, G. Selwyn," writes Walpole to Miss Berry: "I really loved him, not only for his infinite wit, but for a thousand good qualities." I am glad, for my part, that such a lover of cakes and ale should have had a thousand good qualities — that he should have been friendly, generous, warm-hearted, trustworthy. "I rise at six," writes Carlisle to him, from Spa (a great resort of fashionable people in our ancestors' days), "play at cricket till dinner, and dance in the evening, till I can scarcely crawl to bed at eleven. There is a life for you! You get up at nine; play with Raton your dog till twelve, in your dressing-gown; then creep down to ' White's; ' are five hours at table; sleep till supper time; and then make two wretches carry you in a sedan chair, with three pints of claret in you, three miles for a shilling." Occasionally, instead of sleeping at " White's," George went down and snoozed in the House of Commons by the side of Lord North. He represented Gloucester for many years, and had a borough of his own, Ludgershall, for which, when he was too lazy to contest Gloucester, he sat himself. "I have given directions for

from lovely Sarah. She had to figure as bridesmaid at her little Mecklenburg rival's wedding, and died in our own time a quiet old lady, who had become the mother of the heroic Napiers.

They say the little Princess who had written the fine letter about the horrors of war — a beautiful letter without a single blot, for which she was to be rewarded, like the heroine of the old spelling book story — was at play one day with some of her young companions in the gardens of Strelitz, and that the young ladies' conversation was, strange to say, about husbands. "Who will take such a poor little princess as me?" Charlotte said to her friend, Ida von Bulow, and at that very moment the postman's horn sounded, and Ida said, "Princess! there is the sweetheart." As she said, so it actually turned out. The postman brought letters from the splendid young King of all England, who said, "Princess! because you have written such a beautiful letter, which does credit to your head and heart, come and be Queen of Great Britain, France and Ireland, and the true wife of your most obedient servant, George!" So she jumped for joy; and went upstairs and packed all her little trunks, and set off straightway for her kingdom in a beautiful yacht, with a harpsichord on board for her to play upon, and around her a beautiful fleet, all covered with flags and streamers: and the distinguished Madame Auerbach complimented her with an ode, a translation of which may be read in the "Gentleman's Magazine" to the present day: —

> "Her gallant navy through the main
> Now cleaves its liquid way.
> There to their queen a chosen train
> Of nymphs due reverence pay.
>
> "Europa, when conveyed by Jove
> To Crete's distinguished shore,
> Greater attention scarce could prove,
> Or be respected more."

They met, and they were married, and for years they led the happiest, simplest lives sure ever led by married couple. It is said the King winced when he first saw his homely little bride; but, however that may be, he was a true and faithful husband to her, as she was a faithful and loving wife. They had the simplest pleasures — the very mildest and simplest — little country dances, to which a dozen couple were invited, and where the honest King would stand up and dance for three hours at a time to one tune; after which delicious excitement they would go to bed without any supper (the court people grumbling sadly at that absence of supper), and get up quite early the next morning, and, perhaps the next night have another dance; or the Queen would play on the spinet — she played pretty well, Haydn said — or the King would read to her a paper out of the "Spectator," or perhaps one of Ogden's sermons. O Arcadia! what a life it must have been! There used to be Sunday drawing-rooms at court; but the young King stopped these, as he stopped all that godless gambling whereof we have made mention. Not that George was averse to any innocent pleasures, or pleasures which he thought innocent. He was a patron of the arts, after his fashion; kind and gracious to the artists whom he favored, and respectful to their calling. He wanted once to establish an Order of Minerva for literary and scientific characters; the knights were to take rank after the knights of the Bath, and to sport a straw-colored ribbon and a star of sixteen points. But there was such a row amongst the *literati* as to the persons who should be appointed, that the plan was given up, and Minerva and her star never came down amongst us.

He objected to painting St. Paul's, as Popish practice; accordingly the most clumsy heathen sculptures decorate that edifice at present. It is fortunate that the paintings, too, were spared, for painting and drawing were wofully unsound at the close of the last century; and it is far better for our eyes to contemplate whitewash (when we turn them away from the clergyman) than to look at Opie's pitchy canvases or Fuseli's livid monsters.

And yet there is one day in the year — a day when old George loved with all his heart to attend it — when I think St. Paul's presents the noblest sight in the whole world: when five thousand charity children, with cheeks like nosegays, and sweet, fresh voices, sing the hymn which makes every heart thrill with praise and happiness. I have seen a hundred grand sights in the world — coronations, Parisian splendors, Crystal Palace openings, Pope's chapels with their processions of long-tailed cardinals and quavering choirs of fat soprani — but think in all Christendom there is no such sight as Charity Children's Day. *Non Angli, sed angeli.* As one looks at that beautiful multitude of innocents: as the first note strikes: indeed, one may almost fancy that cherubs are singing.

Of church music the King was always very fond, showing skill in it both as a critic and a performer. Many stories, mirthful and affecting, are told of his behavior at the concerts which he ordered. When he was blind and ill he chose the music for the Ancient Concerts once, and the music and words which he selected were from " Samson Agonistes," and all had reference to his blindness, his captivity, and his affliction. He would beat time with his music-roll as they sang the anthem in the Chapel Royal. If the page below was talkative or inattentive, down would come the music-roll on young scapegrace's powdered head. The theatre was always his delight. His bishops and clergy used to attend it, thinking it no shame to appear where that good man was seen. He is said not to have cared for Shakespeare or tragedy much; farces and pantomimes were his joy; and especially when clown swallowed a carrot or a string of sausages he would laugh so outrageously that the lovely Princess by his side would have to say, "My gracious monarch, do compose yourself." But he continued to laugh, and at the very smallest farces, as long as his poor wits were left him.

There is something to me exceedingly touching in that simple early life of the King's. As long as his mother lived — a dozen years after his marriage with the little spinet-player — he was a great, shy, awkward boy, under the tutelage of that hard parent. She must have been a clever, domineering, cruel woman. She kept her household lonely and in gloom, mistrusting almost all people who came about her children. Seeing the young Duke of Gloucester silent and unhappy once, she sharply asked him the cause of his silence. "I am thinking," said the poor child. "Thinking, sir! and of what?" "I am thinking if ever I have a son I will not make him so unhappy as you make me." The other sons were all wild, except George. Dutifully every evening George and Charlotte paid their visit to the King's mother at Carlton House. She had a throat complaint, of which she died; but to the last persisted in driving about the streets to show she was alive. The night before her death the resolute woman talked with her son and daughter-in-law as usual, went to bed, and was found dead there in the morning. "George, be a king!" were the words which she was forever croaking in the ears of her son: and a king the simple, stubborn, affectionate, bigoted man tried to be.

He did his best; he worked according to his lights; what

virtue he knew, he tried to practise; what knowledge he could master, he strove to acquire. He was forever drawing maps, for example, and learned geography with no small care and industry. He knew all about the family histories and genealogies of his gentry, and pretty histories he must have known. He knew the whole " Army List; " and all the facings, and the exact number of the buttons, and all the tags and laces, and the cut of all the cocked hats, pigtails, and gaiters in his army. He knew the personnel of the Universities; what doctors were inclined to Socinianism, and who were sound Churchmen; he knew the etiquettes of his own and his grandfather's courts to a nicety, and the smallest particulars regarding the routine of ministers, secretaries, embassies, audiences; the humblest page in the ante-room, or the meanest helper in the stables or kitchen. These parts of the royal business he was capable of learning, and he learned. But, as one thinks of an office, almost divine, performed by any mortal man,— of any single being pretending to control the thoughts, to direct the faith, to order the implicit obedience of brother millions, to compel them into war at his offence or quarrel; to command, " In this way you shall trade, in this way you shall think; these neighbors shall be your allies whom you shall help, these others your enemies whom you shall slay at my orders; in this way you shall worship God,"—who can wonder that, when such a man as George took such an office on himself, punishment and humiliation should fall upon people and chief?

Yet there is something grand about his courage. The battle of the King with his aristocracy remains yet to be told by the historian who shall view the reign of George more justly than the trumpery panegyrists who wrote immediately after his decease. It was he, with the people to back him, who made the war with America; it was he and the people who refused justice to the Roman Catholics; and on both questions he beat the patricians. He bribed: he bullied: he darkly dissembled on occasion: he exercised a slippery perseverance, and a vindictive resolution, which one almost admires as one thinks his character over. His courage was never to be beat. It trampled North under foot: it beat the stiff neck of the younger Pitt: even his illness never conquered that indomitable spirit. As soon as his brain was clear, it resumed the scheme, only laid aside when his reason left him: as soon as his hands were out of the strait-waistcoat, they took up the pen and the plan which had engaged him up to the moment of his malady. I believe it is by persons believing themselves in the right that nine tenths of the tyranny of this world has been perpetrated. Arguing on that convenient premiss, the Dey of Algiers would cut off twenty heads of a morning; Father Dominic would burn a score of Jews in the presence of the Most Catholic King, and the Archbishops of Toledo and Salamanca sing Amen. Protestants were roasted, Jesuits hung and quartered at Smithfield, and witches burned at Salem, and all by worthy people, who believed they had the best authority for their actions.

And so, with respect to old George, even Americans, whom he hated, and who conquered him, may give him credit for having quite honest reasons for oppressing them. Appended to Lord Brougham's biographical sketch of Lord North, are some autograph notes of the King, which let us most curiously into the state of his mind. "The times certainly require," says he, "the concurrence of all who wish to prevent anarchy. I have no wish but the prosperity of my own dominions; therefore, I must look upon all who would not heartily assist me as bad men, as well as bad subjects." That is the way he reasoned. "I wish nothing but good, therefore, every man who does not agree with me is a traitor and a scoundrel." Remember that he believed himself anointed by a Divine commission; remember that he was a man of slow parts and imperfect education; that the same awful will of heaven which placed a crown upon his head, which made him tender to his family, pure in his life, courageous and honest, made him dull of comprehension, obstinate of will, and at many times deprived him of reason. He was the father of his people; his rebellious children must be flogged into obedience. He was the defender of the Protestant faith; he would rather lay that stout head upon the block than that Catholics should have a share in the government of England. And you do not suppose that there are not honest bigots enough in all countries to back kings in this kind of statesmanship? Without doubt the American war was popular in England. In 1775 the address in favor of coercing the colonies was carried by 304 to 105 in the Commons, by 104 to 29 in the House of Lords. Popular? — so was the Revocation of the Edict of Nantes popular in France: so was the massacre of St. Bartholomew: so was the Inquisition exceedingly popular in Spain.

Wars and revolutions are, however, the politician's province. The great events of this long reign, the statesmen and orators who illustrated it, I do not pretend to make the subjects of an hour's light talk. Let us return to our humbler duty of court gossip. Yonder sits our little Queen, surrounded by many stout sons and fair daughters whom she bore to her faithful George. The history of the daughters, as little Miss Burney has painted them to us, is delightful. They were handsome — she calls them beautiful; they were most kind, loving, and lady-like; they were gracious to every person, high and low, who served them. They had many little accomplishments of their own. This one drew: that one played the piano: they all worked most prodigiously, and fitted up whole suites of rooms — pretty, smiling Penelopes — with their busy little needles. As we picture to ourselves the society of eighty years ago, we must imagine hundreds of thousands of groups of women in great high caps, tight bodies, and full skirts, needling away, whilst one of the number, or, perhaps, a favored gentleman in a pigtail, reads out a novel to the company. Peep into the cottage at Olney, for example, and see there Mrs. Unwin and Lady Hesketh, those high-bred ladies, those sweet, pious women, and William Cowper, that delicate wit, that trembling pietist, that refined gentleman, absolutely reading out "Jonathan Wild" to the ladies! What a change in our manners, in our amusements, since then!

King George's household was a model of an English gentleman's household. It was early; it was kindly; it was charitable; it was frugal; it was orderly; it must have been stupid to a degree which I shudder now to contemplate. No wonder all the princes ran away from the lap of that dreary domestic virtue. It always rose, rode, dined at stated intervals. Day after day was the same. At the same hour at night the King kissed his daughters' jolly cheeks; the Princesses kissed their mother's hand; and Madame Thielke brought the royal nightcap. At the same hour the equerries and women in waiting had their little dinner and cackled over their tea. The King had his backgammon or his evening concert; the equerries yawned themselves to death in the anteroom; or the King and his family walked on Windsor slopes, the King holding his darling little Princess Amelia by the hand; and the people crowded round quite good-naturedly; and the Eton boys thrust their chubby cheeks under the crowd's elbows; and, the concert over, the King never failed to take his enormous cocked hat off, and salute his band, and say, " Thank you, gentlemen."

A quieter household, a more prosaic life than this of Kew or Windsor cannot be imagined. Rain or shine, the King rode every day for hours, poked his red face into hundreds of cottages round about, and showed that shovel-hat and Windsor uniform to farmers, to pig-boys, to old women making apple dumplings; to all sorts of people, gentle and simple, about whom countless stories are told. Nothing can be more undignified than these stories. When Haroun Alraschid visits a subject incog., the latter is sure to be very much the better for the caliph's magnificence. Old George showed no such royal splendor. He used to give a guinea sometimes: sometimes feel in his pockets and find he had no money: often ask a man a hundred questions: about the number of his family, about his oats and beans, about the rent he paid for his house, and ride on. On one occasion he played the part of King Alfred and turned a piece of meat with a string at a cottager's house. When the old woman came home, she found a paper with an enclosure of money, and a note written by the royal pencil: " Five guineas to buy a jack." It was not splendid, but it was kind and worthy of Farmer George. One day, when the King and Queen were walking together, they met a little boy — they were always fond of children, the good folks — and patted the little white head. " Whose little boy are you?" asks the Windsor uniform. " I am the King's beef-eater's little boy," replied the child. On which the King said, " Then kneel down and kiss the Queen's hand." But

the innocent offspring of the beefeater declined this treat.
" No," said he, " I won't kneel, for if I do I shall spoil my
new breeches." The thrifty King ought to have hugged
him and knighted him on the spot. George's admirers wrote
pages and pages of such stories about him. One morning
before anybody else was up, the King walked about Gloucester town; pushed over Molly the housemaid with her
pail, who was scrubbing the doorsteps; ran upstairs and
woke all the equerries in their bedrooms; and then trotted
down to the bridge, where, by this time, a dozen of louts were
assembled. " What! is this Gloucester New Bridge?"
asked our gracious monarch; and the people answered him,
" Yes, your Majesty." " Why, then, my boys," said he,
" let us have a huzzay! " After giving them which intellectual gratification he went home to breakfast. Our fathers
read these simple tales with fond pleasure; laughed at these
very small jokes; liked the old man who poked his nose into
every cottage; who lived on plain wholesome roast and
boiled; who despised your French kickshaws; who was a true
hearty old English gentleman. You may have seen Gilray's
famous print of him — in the old wig, in the stout old hideous Windsor uniform — as the King of Brobdingnag,
peering at a little Gulliver, whom he holds up in his hand,
whilst in the other he has an opera-glass, through which he
surveys the pigmy? Our fathers chose to set up George
as the type of a great king; and the little Gulliver was the
great Napoleon. We prided ourselves on our prejudices
we blustered and bragged with absurd vainglory; we dealt
to our enemy a monstrous injustice of contempt and scorn;
we fought him with all weapons, mean as well as heroic.
There was no lie we would not believe; no charge of crime
which our furious prejudice would not credit. I thought at

one time of making a collection of the lies which the French had written against us, and we had published against them during the war; it would be a strange memorial of popular falsehood.

Their Majesties were very sociable potentates: and the Court Chronicler tells of numerous visits which they paid to their subjects, gentle and simple: with whom they dined; at whose great country houses they stopped; or at whose poorer lodgings they affably partook of tea and bread-and-butter. Some of the great folks spent enormous sums in entertaining their sovereigns. As marks of special favor, the King and Queen sometimes stood as sponsors for the children of the nobility. We find Lady Salisbury was so honored in the year 1786; and in the year 1802, Lady Chesterfield. The "Court News" relates how her ladyship received their Majesties on a state bed "dressed with white satin and a profusion of lace: the counterpane of white satin embroidered with gold, and the bed of crimson satin lined with white." The child was first brought by the nurse to the Marchioness of Bath, who presided as chief nurse. Then the Marchioness handed baby to the Queen. Then the Queen handed the little darling to the Bishop of Norwich, the officiating clergyman; and, the ceremony over, a cup of caudle was presented by the Earl to his Majesty on one knee, on a large gold waiter, placed on a crimson velvet cushion. Misfortunes would occur in these interesting genuflectory ceremonies of royal worship. Bubb Doddington, Lord Melcombe, a very fat, puffy man, in a most gorgeous court suit, had to kneel, Cumberland says, and was so fat and so tight that he could not get up again. "Kneel, sir, kneel!" cried my lord-in-waiting to a country mayor who had to read an address, but who went on with his compliment standing.

7 " Kneel, sir, kneel ! " cries my lord, in dreadful alarm.
" I can't ! " says the mayor, turning round; " don't you see
I have got a wooden leg ? " In the capital Burney Diary
and Letters, the home and court life of good old King George
and good old Queen Charlotte are presented at portentous
length. The King rose every morning at six: and had two
hours to himself. He thought it effeminate to have a carpet
in his bedroom. Shortly before eight, the Queen and the
royal family were always ready for him, and they proceeded
to the King's chapel in the castle. There were no fires in the
passages: the chapel was scarcely alight; princesses, govern-
esses, equerries, grumbled and caught cold: but cold or hot,
it was their duty to go: and, wet or dry, light or dark, the
stout old George was always in his place to say amen to
the chaplain.

The Queen's character is represented in Burney at full
length. She was a sensible, most decorous woman; a very
grand lady on state occasions, simple enough in ordinary
life; well read as times went, and giving shrewd opinions
about books; stingy, but not unjust; not generally unkind
to her dependents, but invincible in her notions of etiquette,
and quite angry if her people suffered ill-health in her service. She gave Miss Burney a shabby pittance, and led the
poor young woman a life which well-nigh killed her. She
never thought but that she was doing Burney the greatest
favor, in taking her from freedom, fame, and competence,
and killing her off with languor in that dreary court. It was
not dreary to her. Had she been servant instead of mistress,
her spirit would never have broken down; she never would
have put a pin out of place, or been a moment from her
duty. She was not weak, and she could not pardon those
who were. She was perfectly correct in life, and she hated

poor sinners with a rancor such as virtue sometimes has.
She must have had awful private trials of her own: not
merely with her children, but with her husband in those
long days about which nobody will ever know anything
now; when he was not quite insane; when his incessant
tongue was babbling folly, rage, persecution; and she had
to smile and be respectful and attentive under this intoler-
able *ennui*. The Queen bore all her duties stoutly, as she
expected others to bear them. At a State christening, the
lady who held the infant was tired and looked unwell, and
the Princess of Wales asked permission for her to sit down.
" Let her stand," said the Queen, flicking the snuff off her
sleeve. She would have stood, the resolute old woman, if
she had had to hold the child till his beard was grown. " I
am seventy years of age," the Queen said, facing a mob of
ruffians who stopped her sedan: " I have been fifty years
Queen of England, and I never was insulted before."
Fearless, rigid, unforgiving little Queen! I don't wonder
that her sons revolted from her.

Of all the figures in that large family group which surrounds George and his Queen, the prettiest, I think, is the
father's darling, the Princess Amelia, pathetic for her beauty,
her sweetness, her early death, and for the extreme passionate tenderness with which her father loved her. This
was his favorite amongst all the children: of his sons, he
loved the Duke of York best. Burney tells a sad story of
the poor old man at Weymouth, and how eager he was to
have this darling son with him. The King's house was not
big enough to hold the Prince; and his father had a portable
house erected close to his own, and at huge pains, so that his
dear Frederick should be near him. He clung on his arm
all the time of his visit: talked to no one else; had talked of

no one else for some time before. The Prince, so long
expected, stayed but a single night. He had business in
London the next day, he said. The dulness of the old King's
court stupefied York and the other big sons of George III.
They scared equerries and ladies, frightened the modest
little circle with their coarse spirits and loud talk. Of little
comfort, indeed, were the King's sons to the King.

But the pretty Amelia was his darling; and the little
maiden, prattling and smiling in the fond arms of that old
father, is a sweet image to look on. There is a family
picture in Burney, which a man must be very hard-hearted
not to like. She describes an after-dinner walk of the royal
family at Windsor:—" It was really a mighty pretty procession," she says. " The little Princess, just turned of
three years old, in a robe-coat covered with fine muslin, a
dressed close cap, white gloves, and fan, walked on alone and
first, highly delighted with the parade, and turning from
side to side to see everybody as she passed; for all the ter-
racers stand up against the walls, to make a clear passage for
the royal family the moment they come in sight. Then
followed the King and Queen, no less delighted with the joy
of their little darling. The Princess Royal leaning on Lady
Elizabeth Waldegrave, the Princess Augusta holding by the
Duchess of Ancaster, the Princess Elizabeth led by Lady
Charlotte Bertie, followed. Office here takes place of rank,"
says Burney — to explain how it was that Lady E. Waldegrave, as lady of the bedchamber, walked before a
duchess,—" General Bude, and the Duke of Montague,
and Major Price as equerry, brought up the rear of the procession." One sees it; the band playing its old music, the
sun shining on the happy, loyal crowd; and lighting the
ancient battlements, the rich elms, and purple landscape,

and bright greensward: the royal standard drooping from the great tower yonder; as old George passes, followed by his race, preceded by the charming infant, who caresses the crowd with her innocent smiles.

" On sight of Mrs. Delany the King instantly stopped to speak to her; the Queen, of course, and the little Princess, and all the rest, stood still. They talked a good while with the sweet old lady, during which time the King once or twice addressed himself to me. I caught the Queen's eye, and saw in it a little surprise, but by no means any displeasure, to see me of the party. The little Princess went up to Mrs. Delany, of whom she is very fond, and behaved like a little angel to her. She then, with a look of inquiry and recollection, came behind Mrs. Delany to look at me. ' I am afraid,' said I, in a whisper, and stooping down, ' your Royal Highness does not remember me ? ' Her answer was an arch little smile, and a nearer approach, with her lips pouted out to kiss me."

The Princess wrote verses herself, and there are some pretty plaintive lines attributed to her, which are more touching than better poetry : —

> " Unthinking, idle, wild, and young
> I laughed, and danced, and talked, and sung:
> And, proud of health, of freedom vain,
> Dreamed not of sorrow, care, or pain;
> Concluding, in those hours of glee,
> That all the world was made for me.
>
> " But when the hour of trial came,
> When sickness shook this trembling frame,
> When folly's gay pursuits were o'er,
> And I could sing and dance no more,
> It then occurred, how sad 'twould be,
> Were this world only made for me."

The poor soul quitted it — and ere yet she was dead the agonized father was in such a state that the officers round about him were obliged to set watchers over him, and from November, 1810, George III ceased to reign. All the world knows the story of his malady: all history presents no sadder figure than that of the old man, blind and deprived of reason, wandering through the rooms of his palace, addressing imaginary Parliaments, reviewing fancied troops, holding ghostly courts. I have seen his picture as it was taken at this time, hanging in the apartment of his daughter, the Landgravine of Hesse Hombourg — amidst books and Windsor furniture, and a hundred fond reminiscences of her English home. The poor old father is represented in a purple gown, his snowy beard falling over his breast — the star of his famous Order still idly shining on it. He was not only sightless: he became utterly deaf. All light, all reason, all sound of human voices, all the pleasures of this world of God, were taken from him. Some slight lucid moments he had; in one of which, the Queen, desiring to see him, entered the room, and found him singing a hymn, and accompanying himself at the harpsichord. When he had finished, he knelt down and prayed aloud for her, and then for his family, and then for the nation, concluding with a prayer for himself, that it might please God to avert his heavy calamity from him, but if not, to give him resignation to submit. He then burst into tears and his reason again fled.

What preacher need moralize on this story; what words save the simplest are requisite to tell it? It is too terrible for tears. The thought of such a misery smites me down in submission before the Ruler of kings and men, the Monarch Supreme over empires and republics, the inscrutable Dispenser of life, death, happiness, victory. " O brothers," I said to those who heard me first in America —" O brothers! speaking the same dear mother tongue — O comrades!

enemies no more, let us take a mournful hand together as we stand by this royal corpse, and call a truce to battle! Low he lies to whom the proudest used to kneel once, and who was cast lower than the poorest: dead, whom millions prayed for in vain. Driven off his throne; buffeted by rude hands; with his children in revolt; the darling of his old age killed before him untimely; our Lear hangs over her breathless lips and cries, ' Cordelia, Cordelia, stay a little!'

> " Vex not his ghost—oh! let him pass—he hates him
> That would upon the rack of this tough world
> Stretch him out longer!"

Hush! Strife and Quarrel, over the solemn grave! Sound, trumpets, a mournful march. Fall, dark curtain, upon his pageant, his pride, his grief, his awful tragedy."

SIMPSON

MATTHEW SIMPSON, a famous American pulpit orator, was born in Cadiz, Ohio, June 20, 1811, and was educated at Madison (now Alleghany) College, in Meadville, Pennsylvania. After leaving college he studied and practised medicine for a short time, but in 1834 entered the Methodist ministry. From 1839 to 1848 he was president of Asbury (now De Pauw) University, and in 1852 was elected bishop. He went to Europe in 1878 as delegate to the World's Evangelical Alliance in Berlin, and the sermons and addresses which he delivered on this tour gave him a wide reputation as an orator, particularly his sermon before the Alliance. Before returning to America he made an extended tour in the Orient. In 1859 he removed to Evanston, Illinois, where he was connected with the Garrett Biblical Institute, and subsequently to Philadelphia. His fame as a preacher was continually increasing, and during the Civil War he delivered many patriotic addresses. He officiated at the funeral of Abraham Lincoln at Springfield, Illinois, and while in England in 1881 delivered an address at Exeter Hall upon the death of President Garfield. He was asked to deliver a series of addresses at Yale University on preaching, which were published as "Lectures on Preaching" (1879). His other works include: "A Hundred Years of Methodism" (1879); "Cyclopædia of Methodism" (1878); "Sermons" (1885). His death took place in Philadelphia, June 18, 1884.

SERMON ON THE RESURRECTION OF OUR LORD

DELIVERED EASTER SUNDAY, 1866

"But now is Christ risen from the dead, and become the firstfruits of them that slept."—1 Cor. xv, 20.

A LITTLE more than eighteen hundred years ago, as the light of the morning was breaking around the walls of Jerusalem, there was a guard placed about a sepulchre in a small garden near the walls of the city. They were guarding a grave. Some strange scenes had occurred on the Friday before. While a man whom they had taken from the hills of Galilee and around the little lake of Capernaum had been hanging on the cross crucified as a malefactor, strange signs appeared in the heavens, and on the earth, and in the temple.

It was rumored that he had said he would rise the third

morning. The third morning was coming, and as the light began to break in the East, there came two women silently and sadly wending their way among the tents that were pitched all around the city of Jerusalem; they had sojourned all night in the tents, for as yet the gates of the city had not been opened. They came to see the sepulchre and were bringing spices in their hands. They loved the man who had been crucified as a malefactor, because of his goodness, his purity, and his compassion. They seemed to be almost the only hearts on earth that did love him deeply, save the small circle of friends who had gathered around him. There had been curses upon his head as he hung on the cross—curses from the bystanders, curses from the soldiers, curses from the people. They cried: "Away with him; his blood be on us and on our children!" and on that morning there were none but a few feeble, obscure, heart-broken friends that dared to come near his grave.

A little more than eighteen hundred years have passed and on the anniversary of that day, the morning of the first day of the week, the first Sabbath after the full moon and the vernal equinox, at the same season, the whole world comes to visit that grave. The eyes of princes and of statesmen, the eyes of the poor and the humble in all parts of the earth are turned toward that sepulchre.

All through Europe men and women are thinking of that grave and of him who lay in it. All over western lands, from ocean to ocean, on mountain top and in valley, over broad prairies and deep ravines, the eyes and hearts of people are gathered round that grave. In the darkness of Africa, here and there, we see them stretching out their hands toward it. Along from the coasts of India and the heights of the Himalayas they have heard of that grave and are bending toward it. The Chinese, laying aside their prejudices, have turned their eyes westward and are looking toward that sepulchre. Along the shores of the seas, over the mountain tops and in the valleys, the hearts of the people have not only been gathering around the grave, but they have caught a glimpse of the rising inmate who ascended in his glory toward heaven.

The song of jubilee has gone forth, and the old men are saying, " The Lord is risen from the dead." The young men and matrons catch up the glowing theme, and the little children around our festive boards, scarcely comprehending the source of their joy, with glad hearts are now joyful, because Jesus has risen from the dead. All over the earth tidings of joy have gone forth, and as the valleys have been ringing out their praises on this bright Sabbath morning how many hearts have been singing—

" Our Jesus is gone up on high! "

Why this change? What hath produced such a wonderful difference in public feeling? The malefactor once cursed, now honored; the obscure and despised, now sought for; the rising Redeemer, not then regarded by men, now universally worshipped. What is the cause of this great change?—how brought about? The subject of this morning, taken from the associations of this day, call us to consider as briefly as we may the fact of the resurrection of Christ from the dead and some of the consequences which flow to us from that resurrection.

It is important for us to fix clearly in our mind the fact that this is one reason why such days are remembered in the annals of the church as well as in the annals of nations; for our faith rests on facts, and the mind should clearly embrace the facts that we may feel that we are standing on firm ground. This fact of the resurrection of Christ is the foundation of the Christian system; for the Apostle says: "And if Christ be not raised, your faith is vain, ye are yet in your sins; then they also which are fallen asleep in Christ will perish." If Christ be not risen, we shall never see the fathers and the mothers who have fallen asleep in Jesus; we shall never see the little ones which have gone up to be, as we believe, angels before the throne of God. If Christ be not raised, we are of all men the most miserable, because we are fancying future enjoyment which never can be realized; but if Christ be raised, then shall we also rise, and them that sleep in Jesus will God bring with him. And that our minds may rest as to the fact of Christ's resurrection, let us notice how God hath arranged the evidences to secure the knowledge of this fact clearly to man.

The first point to which our attention is invited is the fact of Christ's death. Were not this fact clearly established it would be in vain to try to prove his resurrection from the dead. Christ might have suffered for man in some obscure place; he might have laid down his life as a ransom, and yet there would have been no legal evidence of it. God allowed the wrath of man to become the instrument of praising him, in that he suffered Christ to be taken under what was then the legal process—arrested first by the great council of the Jews, and then by the authority of the Roman governor, so that the matter became a matter of public record—a legal transaction. The highest power, both of the Jewish and Roman governments, united in this fact of his arrest, his trial, and his condemnation to death.

Not only was this permitted, but the time of the occurrence was wisely arranged. It was at the feast of the Jews, the Passover, when all the Jews came up to keep the Passover.

They came not only from Egypt but from all the country through which they were scattered. Jerusalem could not hold the people that came together; they pitched their tents all around the city, on the hills and in the valleys. It was the time of full moon, when there was brightness all night, and they came together with safety and security. The multitude, then, was there to witness the scene, so that it might be attested by people from all parts of Judea and from all countries round about Judea.

Then, again, the form of the death was such as to be not a sudden one, but one of torture, passing through many hours. Had the execution been a very sudden one, as it might have been, the death would have been equally efficacious, yet it would not have been witnessed by so many; but as he hung those dreadful hours, from nine until three, the sun being darkened, what an opportunity was given to the people passing by to be impressed with the scene! The crucifixion was near the city; the crowd was there; the temple worship was in process; the strangers were there; and as one great stream passes on some festive day through the great thoroughfare of your city, so passed the stream of men, women, and children by that cross on which the Saviour hung. They wagged their heads and reviled as they passed by. The very ones whom Jesus had healed, whose fathers had been cured of leprosy or fever, whose mothers' eyes had been opened; the ones who had been raised up from beds of sickness by the touch of that Saviour, passed by and reviled, and said: "He saved others, himself he cannot save." The multitude saw him as he hung suffering on the cross.

Then, again, the circumstances attending his death were such as to invite universal attention. It was not designed that the death should be a private one; not merely a legal

transaction, a matter soon over, but a protracted and agoniz-
ing spectacle—one to be seen and known by the multitude;
but, in addition, that man's attention should be drawn to something to be connected with that wonderful scene; hence God
called upon the heavens and the earth, the air and the graves,
and the temple itself for testimony. It is said that before
the coronation of a prince in olden time in Europe—and in
some kingdoms the custom is still observed—there is sent
forth a herald, sometimes three days in advance, at different
periods according to the custom, to issue a challenge to any
one that dares to claim the kingdom to come and prove his
right, and to announce that the coronation of his prince is to
take place.

Methinks it was such a challenge God gave to all the powers
of humanity and to all the powers of darkness. There hung
suffering on the cross he who died for human woe, and as he
hung God was about to crown him King of kings and Lord of
lords on the morning of the third day. He sends forth his
voice of challenge, and as he speaks the earth rocks to its
centre; that ground, shaking and convulsing, was a call to
man to witness what was about to occur.

Not only is there a voice of earth. Yonder the sun clothed
himself in sackcloth for three hours, as much as to say:
" There may be gloom for three days; the great source of
light hath veiled himself, as in a mantle of night, for three
days. As for three hours this darkness hangs, but as out of
the darkness the light shines forth, so at the end of the three
days shall the Sun of Righteousness shine out again, the great
centre of glory, with that glory which he had with the
Father from the foundation of the world." It was the
herald's voice that passed through the heavens, and that spoke
through all the orbs of light, " Give attention, ye created

beings, to what is to happen!" But it was not alone in the earth, which is the great centre, nor in the heavens, which is the great source of light, that the tidings were proclaimed.

Look in yonder valley. The tombs are there; the prophets have been buried there. Yon hillside is full of the resting-places of the dead; generations on generations have been buried there; friends are walking in it, and they are saying, "Yonder is a mighty judge in Israel; there is the tomb of a prophet." They were passing to and fro through that valley of death when the earthquake's tread was heard, and behold! the tombs were opened, the graves displayed the dead within, and there was a voice that seemed to call from the very depths of the graves, "Hear, O sons of men!"

What feelings must have thrilled through the hearts of those who stood by those monuments and bended over those graves, when, thrown wide open, the doors bursting, and the rocks giving way, they saw the forms of death come forth and recognized friends that once they had known. What was to occur? What could all this mean? Then the great sacrifice was offered. It was at three o'clock in the afternoon when Christ was to give up the ghost. Yonder the multitude of pious people were gathered toward the temple. The outer court was full; the doors and gates which led into the sanctuary were crowded; the lamb was before the altar; the priest in his vestments had taken the sacrificial knife; the blood was to be shed at the hour of three; the multitude were looking.

Yonder hangs a veil; it hides that inner sanctuary; there are cherubim in yonder with their wings spread over the mercy-seat; the shekinah once dwelt there; God himself in his glory was there and the people are bending to look in. No one enters into that veil save the high priest, and he, with

blood and in the midst of incense, but once a year; but it was
the mercy-seat and the eye of every pious Jew was directed
toward that veil, thinking of the greater glory which lay beyond it.

As the hour of three came and as the priest was taking the
sacrificial knife from the altar and was about to slay the
lamb, behold! an unseen hand takes hold of that veil and
tears it apart from top to bottom, and has thrown open the
mercy-seat, not before seen by men.   The cherubim are
there; the altar with its covering of blood is there; the resting-place of the ark is there; it is the holiest of holies.
Methinks the priest drops the knife, the lamb goes free, for
the lamb that was slain from the foundation of the world is
suffering for man.   The way to the holy of holies is open,—
a new and a living way, which man may not close, which
priest alone cannot enter; but a way is open whereby humanity, oppressed and downtrodden, from all parts of the earth,
may find its way to the mercy-seat of God.   There was a
call to the pious worshipper by voices which seemed to say:
"An end to all the sacrifices, an end to all the suffering
victims, an end to all the sprinkled hyssop that is used in
purification, for one has come to do the will of God on whom
the burden of man had been laid."

Now here were all these calls to humanity from all parts,
as if to announce the great transaction.   While all this was
occurring Christ was on the cross, suffering the agony of
crucifixion.   How deep that agony we need not attempt to
tell you; it was fearful; and yet no complaint escaped his lips,
no murmuring was there.   He bore the sins of many in his
own flesh on the tree.   He heard the multitudes revile him;
he saw them wag their heads; he remembered that the disciples had fled from him—one followed afar off, but the

rest had gone; and yet he complained not. Friends and kindred had all left him and he trod the wine-press alone. He drank the cup in all its bitterness and no complaint escaped from him. One left him that had never forsaken him before. "The world is gone, the disciples I have fed and taught have all fled and passed away,—all have forsaken me."

But there was no time until that moment of fearful darkness came, when all the load of guilt was upon him and for our sins he was smitten, that his spirit was crushed, and he called out, "My God, my God, why hast thou forsaken me?" All else might go—it were little; "Why hast *thou* forsaken me?" But it is over; the darkness is past; the load is borne; and I hear him say, "It is finished;" he bows his head and dies.

Now there is publicity for the transaction. It demanded public investigation, it received it. There was not only the mental agony united with the agony of crucifixion, but there was the voluntary giving up of his life; yet, lest there might be some suspicion, to all this was added the proof of the fact of his death. When the limbs of the others were broken and he was perceived to be dead, the soldier thrust the spear into his side and there came out of that side both water and blood.

There is a peculiarity in the sacred writings. A little incident that seems to be mentioned without care becomes the strongest possible proof, not only of the fact of Christ's death, but of the nature of his death. When that sentence was written the human frame was not understood, the circulation of the blood was not understood. Anatomists had not then, as they have now, unveiled the human system; the great science of pathology had not yet been clearly taught to man; and yet in that sentence we have almost a world of meaning. For it is well attested now that where persons die from violent mental emotion, by what is termed a broken heart, a crushed spirit, there is always formed a watery secretion around the heart. It was not known then to the soldier who lifted up that spear and pierced the body; but so much of that water had secreted around the heart that he saw it issuing forth from the pierced side, unstained by blood, which showed that that great heart had been crushed by agony within.

When taken from the cross he was put in the sepulchre. His friends had given him up, his disciples had forsaken him; some of them saw him die; they knew that he was crucified and they abandoned him. They were returning to their former employments; but his enemies remembered he had said he would rise the third day, and they put a guard around him. The Roman soldiers were there; the king's seal was on the stone rolled over the mouth of the sepulchre; they made everything secure. Here again God ordered that we should have abundant proof of Christ's crucifixion.

He was crucified on Friday, which was to them the last day of the week, resting in the grave on our Saturday, which is their Sabbath, and then comes the first day of the week, our Sabbath morning, made our Sabbath because of Christ's resurrection from the dead. There came an humble visitant to the tomb, Mary Magdalene; she had been healed of much, forgiven much and she loved much. Mary, the mother of James, came also and beheld the scenes that occurred; but there had been strange commotions elsewhere.

Heaven had been gathering around that grave. Angels had been watching there; they had seen the Roman guard; they had seen the shining spear and the polished shield; they had seen that Christ was held as a prisoner by the greatest powers on earth. Methinks I see the angelic host as they gathered around the throne of God and looked up into the face of Omnipotence, and if ever there was a time when there was silence in heaven for half an hour it was before the morning light of the third day dawned. I hear them say, " How long shall man triumph? How long shall human power exalt itself? How long shall the powers of darkness hold jubilee? Let us away and roll away the stone; let us away and frighten yonder Roman guard and drive them from the sepulchre."

They waited until permission was given. I see the angel coming down from the opening doors of glory; he hastens outside the walls of Jerusalem and down to the sepulchre; when they saw him coming the keepers shook, they became like dead men; he rolls away the stone and sets himself by the mouth of the sepulchre. Christ, girding himself with all the power of his divinity, rises from the grave. He leads captivity captive, tears the crown from the head of death, and makes light the darkness of the grave. Behold him as he rises just preparatory to his rising up to glory. Oh, what a moment was that! Hell was preparing for its jubilee; the powers of earth were preparing for a triumph; but as the grave yields its prey, Christ, charged with being an impostor, is proved to be the Son of God with power; it is the power of his resurrection from the dead.

There was Christ's resurrection from the dead. He became the first fruits of them that slept. But to give the amplest proofs of his resurrection he lingered on earth to be seen of men, and to be seen in such a manner as to show that he was still the Saviour Christ. In my younger days I used often to wonder why was it that Mary Magdalene came

very morning. On this glad day blessings are dropping from
the throne of God upon us from this risen Saviour. He hath
ascended up on high, the gates have opened for him, and he
hath gone to his throne in glory.

Let us look at a few of the results that flow to us from
these facts thus sustained of his death and resurrection from
the dead!

In the first place it establishes all Bible declarations. It
had been predicted that he should not stay in the grave, and
when he arose it put the seal to the Old Testament as the
Word of God. The prophecy in him fulfilled gave glorious
proof that the other parts of it should be also fulfilled as the
word of an unchanging God.

Again in his resurrection we see a proof of his divine
power. No man hath been raised from the dead by his own
power. All died, from Adam to Moses, with the exception
of Enoch and Elijah, who, because of their devotion and
acknowledgment of the divine head, themselves became prophets of a coming Saviour. He rose by his own power. He
conquered death itself, the grave, and the whole powers of
humanity.

Jupiter is represented by an old classic writer as saying to
the lesser gods that if all of them combined together and
should endeavor to throw down his throne—if all power was
arrayed against him—he, by his own might, would be able to
overcome them all. What was fiction with the ancients becomes gloriously realized in Christ. Take all the powers of
humanity—the Jewish power, the Roman power; the power
of learning, of art, of public opinion; take all the powers of
earth and hell, death and the grave, and combine them all
against the Saviour and, without one effort, without one single
apparent movement—the sleeper lies in death, his eyes are

sealed, and, as if all unconscious, for the warning had not been given before—in an instant those eyes were opened, that frame rises, the grave yields up its prey, death retires conquered, and Christ demonstrates himself to be the ruler of the whole universe. He made the earth to tremble, the sun to put on sackcloth, the very air to grow dark, the graves to open, the dead to come forth, and proclaimed himself to be the conqueror of death and hell. So we have proof of his being the Son of God with power.

In that resurrection from the dead we have a pledge of our own resurrection. Christ has become the first-fruits of them that slept. You know the figure of the first-fruits as understood by the Jews. Their religion was connected with the seasons of the year—with the harvest crops; one of their feasts was called the feast of the first-fruits, and was on this wise: When the first heads of grain began to ripen in the field and there was thus a pledge of harvest, they cut off those first ripened heads and went up to Jerusalem.

Before that the grain was not crushed, no bread was baked out of it, and nothing was done to appropriate that crop to man's use until first those ripened heads of grain were brought up to Jerusalem and presented to the Lord as a thank-offering. He was acknowledged as Lord of the harvest and they were laid up as a kind of thank-offering before God. They were the first-fruits. Then they went away to the fields and all through Judea the sickle was thrust in, the grain was reaped and gathered into sheaves, and when the harvest was secured they baked the bread for their children out of this first grain. They came up to the temple, where the first-fruits had been laid, and they held a feast of thanksgiving and shouted harvest home. The old harvest feast seems to be descended from this ancient custom.

Christ rose as the first-fruits, and there is to be a glorious resurrection. Christ came, the first man to rise in this respect, by his own power, from the grave, having snatched the crown from death, having thrown light into the grave, having himself ascended up toward glory. He goes up in the midst of the shouts of angels; the heavens open before him; yonder is the altar; there is the throne and around it stand the seraphim and the cherubim; and Christ enters the victor and sits down upon the throne, from henceforth expecting until his enemies be made his footstool. He is the first-fruits of the harvest, but the angels are to be sent out like the reapers, and by and by humanity is coming.

As Christ, the first-fruits, passed through the grave and went up to glory, so there shall come from their sleeping dust in Asia, in Africa, in Europe, and in America, from every mountain top, from the depths of the sea, from deep ravines, and from plains outspread—oh, there shall come in the time of the glorious harvest—the uprising of humanity, when all the nations, waking from their long sleep, shall rise and shall shout the harvest home! Thank God! at that time none shall be wanting.

Oh, they come, they come, from the nations of the past and from the generations yet unborn! I see the crowd gathering there. Behold the angels are waiting, and as the hosts rise from the dead they gather round the throne. Christ invites his followers to overcome and sit down with him on his throne, as he overcame and sat down with the Father on his throne. In that is the pledge of our resurrection from the dead. Can I not suffer, since Christ suffered? Can I not die, since Christ died? Let the grave be my resting-place, for Christ rested there. Is it cold? The warmth of his animation is in it. Is it lonely? He shall be beside me in all his

spirit's power.   Does the load of earth above me and beneath which I am placed press upon me?   Christ hath power
to burst the tomb; he shall burst the tomb, though deep it be,
and I shall rise through his almighty power.

Yes, let the malice of men be directed against me; let me
be taken, if it must be, as a martyr and be bound to the stake;
let the fagots be kindled, let the flame ascend, let my body
be burned; gather my ashes, grind my bones to powder, scat-
ter them on the ocean's surface; or carry those ashes to the
top of yonder volcano and throw them within its consuming
fire—let them be given to the dust—and yet I can sing:

> " God, my Redeemer, lives,
> And ever from the skies
> Looks down and watches all my dust,
> Till he shall bid it rise."

Thank God! it may be scattered on the wings of the wind—
Christ is everywhere present; he has marked every particle
and it shall rise again by his own almighty power.   And what
is it to sleep awhile if I am Christ's?   To die, if I am like
Christ in dying? and be buried, if I am like Christ in being
buried?   I trust I shall be like him when he comes forth in
his glory.   I shall be like him, for the Apostle says, We shall
be like him, for we shall see him as he is; we shall be changed
from glory into glory, into the same image as by the Spirit of
God.

It would be a great change to be changed from glory to
glory, from saints to angels, from angels to cherubim, from
cherubim to seraphim, from glory to glory; but, thank God!
we shall not stop being changed; for the change shall go on
from glory to glory until we shall be transformed into the
likeness of the Son of God, brighter than angels ever shone,
more glorious than were ever cherubim.

We shall be near the throne; we shall sit beside him, for he hath made room for us there. Then, if we can calmly look at death and face him, because his strength has been overcome, it reconciles us to parting a little while with friends. A father or a mother may be taken from us, but we shall see them again; they shall not sleep forever. The little ones that drop from our arms, we can almost see them this morning; some of us can almost feel them in our arms—can see the glance of that beautiful eye and hear the sound of that little prattling lip; they seem to be with us now, as a little while ago they dropped from out of our arms. We followed them to the grave and we left them there, where the winter's storm has been howling around them.

Sometimes loneliness like that terrible storm has swept over our hearts and left them almost in despair; but through Christ's resurrection we see our children yonder in glory, safe in the Saviour's arms. Their little forms shall rise all-glorious from the tomb in the morning of the resurrection; we shall find them, for Jesus is the resurrection and the life.

All this comes to us from the resurrection of Christ from the dead. He died once; he dies no more; the condemnation of death is forever gone; he sits on the throne of everlasting dominion; his kingdom is an eternal kingdom; and as he died once and has risen to die no more, so when we have died once and gone to the grave and entered the dark valley and shadow of death and we come up safely on the other side, thank God! death is passed forever; we shall then put our feet on the neck of the monster and shall be able to say:

> "Oh death, where is thy sting?
> Oh grave, where is thy victory?"

Looking at the resurrection of Christ we exclaim, Thanks be unto God who hath given us the victory! Such is the eternity of glory and blessedness that awaits us. Thank God for a spiritual body! Here some of us long to triumph over nature. We would grasp, if we could, angelic wisdom; but our brows will ache with pain, our frames decay, our eyes grow dim, our hearing fail. This flesh of ours will not stand hours of painful study and seasons of protracted labor; but, thank God! when the body that now oppresses us is laid in the grave a spiritual body will be given to us, pure, ethereal, and holy. Oh, what an extent of knowledge shall flash upon us! what light and glory! what spirituality and power! Then we shall not need to ask an angel anything. We shall know as we are known. Jesus will be our teacher; the Everlasting God, the Man whose name is Wonderful, the Counsellor, the Prince of Peace. He himself shall be our Leader. We shall know then as also we are known.

Then rejoice in God. Dry up those tears. Cast away that downcast look. Child of the dust, you are an heir of glory. There is a crown all burnished for you; there is a mansion all ready for you; there is a white robe prepared for you; there is eternal glory for you; angels are to be your servants and you are to reign with the King of kings forever. But while you wait on earth, be witnesses for God; attest the glory of your Master; rise in the greatness of his strength; bind sin captive to your chariot wheels; go onward in your heavenly career, and be as pure as your ascended Head is pure. Be active in works of mercy; be angels of light; be flames of fire; go on your mission of mercy and convert the world unto God before you go up higher. When you go, not only go forward to present yourself, but may every one of you be able to say: " Here am I, and those which thou hast given me."

STEPHENS

ALEXANDER HAMILTON STEPHENS, a distinguished American statesman, was born near Crawfordsville, Georgia, February 11, 1812, and was educated at the University of Georgia. He studied law and was admitted to the bar in 1834. Two years later he began political life with his entrance into the lower house of the State legislature, where he continued until 1840. In 1841 he became State senator, and from 1843 to 1859 was a representative in Congress from his State. He was an ardent advocate of the annexation of Texas, but opposed the Mexican war policy and was a supporter of the compromise of 1850. He was greatly opposed to the dissolution of the Union, and delivered a strong Union speech in 1860. He supported the nomination of Stephen A. Douglas, and early the next year, in the Georgia State convention, he eloquently opposed secession. When, however, the ordinance of secession was passed, he acquiesced in the result, for although he doubted the wisdom of the policy he still maintained the right of secession. He was chosen Vice-President of the provisional government of the Confederacy and was elected to the office in the following autumn, but it was soon evident that he and President Davis differed widely on several important matters. After the fall of the Confederacy Stephens was imprisoned for five months in Fort Warren in Boston Harbor, but was released on parole in the October following. In February, 1866, he delivered a strong speech in favor of reconstruction, and in the same month was elected to Congress as senator, but was not allowed to take his seat, as Congress ignored the return of Georgia to the Union under President Johnson's proclamation. In 1874 he was permitted to re-enter Congress and served there until he became governor of Georgia in 1882. He died in office at Atlanta, March 4, 1883. His political course often seemed extremely contradictory, but he always acted upon some principle quite clear to himself, but not always at first sight apparent to others with entire distinctness. A lifelong believer in State rights and local self-government, he claimed for every citizen the largest liberty consonant with protection to property and preservation of order.

ON THE EVILS OF SECESSION

DELIVERED IN THE SECESSION CONVENTION OF GEORGIA,
JANUARY, 1861

THIS step [the secession of Georgia], once taken, can never be recalled; and all the baleful and withering consequences that must follow (as you will see) will rest on the Convention for all coming time. When we and our posterity shall see our lovely South desolated by the demon of war, which this act of yours will inevitably invite and call forth; when our green fields of waving harvests shall be trodden down by the murderous soldiery and fiery car of war sweeping over our land; our temples of justice laid in ashes; all the horrors and desolations of war upon us,—who but this Convention will be held responsible for it? and who but him who shall have given his vote for this unwise and ill-timed measure (as I honestly think and believe) shall be held to strict account for this suicidal act by the present generation, and probably cursed and execrated by posterity for all coming time, for the wide and desolating ruin that will inevitably follow this act you now propose to perpetrate?

Pause, I entreat you, and consider for a moment what reasons you can give that will even satisfy yourselves in calmer moments,—what reasons you can give to your fellow sufferers in the calamity that it will bring upon us? What reason can you give to the nations of the earth to justify it? They will be the calm and deliberate judges in the case; and to what cause or one overt act can you name or point on which to rest the plea of justification? What right has the North assailed? What interest of the South has been invaded? What justice has been denied, and what claim founded in justice and right has been withheld?

Can either of you to-day name one governmental act of wrong, deliberately and purposely done by the government of Washington, of which the South has a right to complain? I challenge the answer! While, on the other hand, let me show the facts (and believe me, gentlemen, I am not here the advocate of the North; but I am here the friend, the firm friend and lover of the South and her institutions, and for this reason I speak thus plainly and faithfully, for yours, mine, and every other man's interest, the words of truth and sober-ness) of which I wish you to judge, and I will only state facts which are clear and undeniable and which now stand as records authentic in the history of our country.

When we of the South demanded the slave-trade or the importation of Africans for the cultivation of our lands, did they not yield the right for twenty years? When we asked a three-fifths representation in Congress for our slaves, was it not granted? When we asked and demanded the return of any fugitive from justice or the recovery of those persons owing labor or allegiance, was it not incorporated in the con-stitution and again ratified and strengthened in the fugitive-slave law of 1850?

But do you reply that in many instances they have violated this compact and have not been faithful to their engage-ments? As individuals and local communities they may have done so, but not by the sanction of government; for that has always been true to Southern interests. Again, gentle-men, look at another fact. When we have asked that more territory should be added, that we might spread the institution of slavery, have they not yielded to our demands in giving us Louisiana, Florida, and Texas, out of which four States have been carved, and ample territory for four more to be added in due time if you by this unwise and impolitic act do not destroy this hope and perhaps by it lose all and have your last slave wrenched from you by stern military rule, as South America and Mexico were, or by the vindictive decree of a universal emancipation, which may reasonably be expected to follow.

But again, gentlemen, what have we to gain by this proposed change of our relation to the general government? We have always had the control of it, and can yet if we remain in it and are as united as we have been. We have had a majority of the Presidents chosen from the South as well as the control and management of most of those chosen from the North. We have had sixty years of Southern Presidents to their twenty-four, thus controlling the executive department.

So of the judges of the supreme court, we have had eighteen from the South and but eleven from the North; although nearly four fifths of the judicial business has arisen in the free States, yet a majority of the court has always been from the South. This we have required so as to guard against any interpretation of the constitution unfavorable to us.

In like manner we have been equally watchful to guard our interests in the legislative branch of government. In choosing the presiding Presidents (*pro tem.*) of the Senate we have had twenty-four to their eleven. Speakers of the House we have had twenty-three and they twelve. While the majority of the representatives, from their greater population, have always been from the North, yet we have so generally secured the Speaker, because he to a great extent shapes and controls the legislation of the country. Nor have we had less control in every other department of the general government. Attorney-generals we have had fourteen while the North have had but five.

Foreign ministers we have had eighty-six, and they but fifty-four. While three fourths of the business which demands diplomatic agents abroad is clearly from the free States, from their greater commercial interests, yet we have had the principal embassies, so as to secure the world markets for our cotton, tobacco, and sugar, on the best possible terms.

We have had a vast majority of the higher offices of both army and navy, while a larger proportion of the soldiers and sailors were drawn from the North. Equally so of clerks, auditors, and comptrollers filling the executive department; the records show for the last fifty years that of the three thousand thus employed we have had more than two thirds of the same, while we have but one third of the whole population of the republic.

Again, look at another item, and one, be assured, in which we have a great and vital interest; it is that of revenue, or means of supporting government. From official documents we learn that a fraction over three fourths of the revenue collected for the support of government has uniformly been raised from the North.

Pause, now, while you can, gentlemen, and contemplate carefully and candidly these important items. Look at another necessary branch of government and learn from stern statistical facts how matters stand in that department. I mean the mail and post-office privileges that we now enjoy under the general government as it has been for years past. The expense for the transportation of the mail in the free States was by the report of the Postmaster-General for the year 1860 a little over $13,000,000, while the income was $19,000,000. But in the slave States the transportation of the mail was $14,716,000, while the revenue from the same was $8,001,026, leaving a deficit of $6,115,735 to be supplied by the North for our accommodation, and without it we must have been entirely cut off from this most essential branch of government.

Leaving out of view for the present the countless millions of dollars you must expend in a war with the North, with tens of thousands of your sons and brothers slain in battle and offered up as sacrifices upon the altar of your ambition,— and for what, we ask again? Is it for the overthrow of the American government, established by our common ancestry, cemented and built up by their sweat and blood, and founded on the broad principles of right, justice, and humanity? And as such I must declare here, as I have often done before, and which has been repeated by the greatest and wisest of statesmen and patriots in this and other lands, that it is the best and freest government, the most equal in its rights, the most just in its decisions, the most lenient in its measures, and the most inspiring in its principles to elevate the race of men, that the sun of heaven ever shone upon.

Now, for you to attempt to overthrow such a government as this, under which we have lived for more than three quarters of a century,—in which we have gained our wealth, our standing as a nation, our domestic safety,—while the elements of peril are around us, with peace and tranquillity accompanied with unbounded prosperity and rights unassailed, is the height of madness, folly, and wickedness, to which I can lend neither my sanction nor my vote.

GREAT CORNERSTONE SPEECH

DELIVERED AT SAVANNAH, MARCH 22, 1861

THE new constitution has put at rest forever all agitating questions relating to our peculiar institution, African slavery as it exists among us,—the proper status of the negro in our form of civilization. This was the immediate cause of the late rupture and present revolution. Jefferson, in his forecast, had anticipated this as the "rock upon which the old Union would split." He was right. What was conjecture with him is now a realized fact. But whether he fully comprehended the great truth upon which that rock stood and stands may be doubted. The prevailing ideas entertained by him and most of the leading statesmen at the time of the formation of the old constitution were that the enslavement of the African was in violation of the laws of nature; that it was wrong in principle, socially, morally, and politically.

It was an evil they knew not well how to deal with, but the general opinion of the men of that day was that somehow or other, in the order of Providence, the institution would be evanescent and pass away. This idea, though not incorporated in the constitution, was the prevailing idea at the time.

The constitution, it is true, secured every essential guaranty to the institution while it should last, and hence no argument can be justly used against the constitutional guaranties thus secured, because of the common sentiment of the day. Those ideas, however, were fundamentally wrong. They rested upon the assumption of the equality of races. This was an error. It was a sandy foundation, and the idea of the government built upon it; when the storm came and the wind blew, it fell.

Our new government is founded upon exactly the opposite idea; its foundations are laid, its corner-stone rests, upon the great truth that the negro is not equal to the white man; that slavery—subordination to the superior race—is his natural and moral condition.

This, our new government, is the first in the history of the world based upon this great physical, philosophical, and moral truth. This truth has been slow in the process of its development, like all other truths in the various departments of science. It has been so even among us. Many who hear me perhaps can recollect well that this truth was not generally admitted even within their day. The errors of the past generation still clung to many as late as twenty years ago. Those

8　at the North who still cling to these errors with a zeal above
knowledge we justly denominate fanatics.

All fanaticism springs from an aberration of the mind, from
a defect in reasoning. It is a species of insanity. One of the
most striking characteristics of insanity, in many instances, is
forming correct conclusions from fancied or erroneous premises. So with the anti-slavery fanatics; their conclusions are
right, if their premises are. They assume that the negro is
equal, and hence conclude that he is entitled to equal privileges and rights with the white man. If their premise were
correct, their conclusions would be logical and just; but, their
premise being wrong, their whole argument fails. I recollect
once having heard a gentleman from one of the northern
States, of great power and ability, announce in the House of
Representatives, with imposing effect, that we of the South
would be compelled, ultimately, to yield upon this subject of
slavery; that it was as impossible to war successfully against a
principle in politics as it was in physics or mechanics; that the
principle would ultimately prevail; that we, in maintaining
slavery as it exists with us, were warring against a principle,
a principle founded in nature, the principle of the equality of
man. The reply I made to him was that upon his own
grounds we should succeed, and that he and his associates in
their crusades against our institutions would ultimately fail.
The truth announced, that it was as impossible to war successfully against a principle in politics as in physics and mechanics, I admitted, but told him that it was he and those acting
with him who were warring against a principle. They were
attempting to make things equal which the Creator had made
unequal.

In the conflict thus far success has been on our side, complete throughout the length and breadth of the Confederate

we can get on very well without them, even if they should not. . . .

Will everything commenced so well continue as it has begun? In reply to this anxious inquiry I can only say it all depends upon ourselves. A young man starting out in life on his majority, with health, talent, and ability, under a favoring Providence, may be said to be the architect of his own fortunes. His destinies are in his own hands. He may make for himself a name of honor or dishonor, according to his own acts. If he plants himself upon truth, integrity, honor, and uprightness, with industry, patience, and energy, he cannot fail of success. So it is with us; we are a young republic just entering upon the arena of nations; we will be the architect of our own fortunes. Our destiny, under providence, is in our own hands. With wisdom, prudence, and statesmanship on the part of our public men, and intelligence, virtue, and patriotism on the part of the people, success, to the full measures of our most sanguine hopes, may be looked for.

But if we become divided; if schisms arise; if dissensions spring up; if factions are engendered; if party spirit, nourished by unholy personal ambition, shall rear its hydra head,—I have no good to prophesy for you. Without intelligence, virtue, integrity, and patriotism on the part of the people, no republic or representative government can be durable or stable.

We have intelligence, and virtue, and patriotism. All that is required is to cultivate and perpetuate these. Intelligence will not do without virtue. France was a nation of philosophers. These philosophers became Jacobins. They lacked that virtue, that devotion to moral principle, and that patriotism which is essential to good government. Organized upon principles of perfect justice and right, seeking amity and friendship with all other Powers, I see no obstacle in the way of our upward and onward progress.

Our growth by accessions from other States will depend greatly upon whether we present to the world, as I trust we shall, a better government than that to which they belong. If we do this, North Carolina, Tennessee, and Arkansas cannot hesitate long; neither can Virginia, Kentucky, and Missouri. They will necessarily gravitate to us by an imperious law. We made ample provision in our constitution for the admission of other States; it is more guarded—and wisely so, I think—than the old constitution on the same subject, but not too guarded to receive them as fast as it may be proper.

Looking to the distant future, and perhaps not very distant either, it is not beyond the range of possibility and even probability that all the great States of the Northwest shall gravitate this way as well as Tennessee, Kentucky, Missouri, Arkansas, etc. Should they do so our doors are wide enough to receive them, but not until they are ready to assimilate with us in principle.

The process of disintegration in the old Union may be expected to go on with almost absolute certainty. We are now the nucleus of a growing power which, if we are true to ourselves, our destiny, and high mission, will become the controlling power on this continent. To what extent accession will go on in the process of time, or where it will end, the future will determine. So far as it concerns States of the old Union, they will be upon no such principle of reconstruction as now spoken of, but upon reorganization and new assimilation. Such are some of the glimpses of the future as I catch them.

But at first we must necessarily meet with the inconveni-

WILSON

HENRY WILSON, an American statesman of note, was born in Farmington, New Hampshire, February 16, 1812. He was the son of a farm laborer, and at the age of ten was apprenticed to a farmer for eleven years, during which period he had very little schooling, but read over a thousand books. Till his majority his name had been Jeremiah Jones Colbath, but he now assumed the name of Henry Wilson. After leaving the farm at twenty-one he learned the shoemaker's trade in Natick, Massachusetts, and presently came into notice as a speaker at political meetings and an outspoken opponent of slavery. In 1840 he entered the State legislature and from 1844 to 1846 was State senator. He was actively opposed to the admission of Texas as a slave State, and, with the poet Whittier, presented a petition to Congress against it, signed by thousands. He was a delegate to the Whig convention at Philadelphia in 1848, but withdrew because of its rejection of anti-slavery resolutions. He was again in the State senate, 1850-53, and, succeeding Everett in the senate of the United States in 1855, remained there as member continuously for eighteen years. He took part in all debates of importance, and although his speeches are not distinguished by especial grace of style they are statesmanlike and effective. Wilson was a man of very positive convictions, but his statements of fact were uttered with the greatest care and were seldom successfully challenged. He was elected vice-president on the ticket with General Grant in November, 1872, and accordingly resigned from the senate on the 3d of March following. Wilson died in office at Washington November 22, 1875. His published writings comprise, besides single speeches: " History of the Anti-Slavery Measures of the Thirty-seventh and Thirty-eighth Congresses " (1865); " Military Measures of the United States Congress " (1866); " History of the Reconstruction Measures of the Thirty-ninth and Fortieth Congresses " (1868); " History of the Rise and Fall of the Slave Power in America " (1872-77).

SPEECH ON BILL TO CONFISCATE THE PROPERTY AND FREE THE SLAVES OF REBELS

DELIVERED IN THE SENATE, MAY 1, 1862

MR. PRESIDENT,—The senator from Vermont [Mr. Collamer], in submitting this amendment to the original bill proposes to authorize the President of the United States, if in his judgment it shall be necessary for the more speedy suppression of this insurrection, to appoint a day when all persons held to service or labor in any State whose inhabitants he has declared by proclamation to be in a state of insurrection shall be declared free. That honorable senator, in the course of his speech, said that it seemed to be the chief object of some of the supporters of the original bill to carry that provision of the bill emancipating the slaves of rebels; and yesterday the senator from Virginia [Mr. Carlisle] alluded to and indorsed that declaration.

Now, sir, I am free to confess here that it is with me the chief object of solicitude. I care something for the confiscation of the property of the leading rebels; but I do not wish to touch the property of the masses of the people. I think the distinction is a just one,—that the leaders should be punished, and that the masses of the people should feel that they will be forgiven and protected if they return to their loyalty.

I do not expect that we shall realize any large amount of property by any confiscation bill that we shall pass. After the conflict, when the din of battle has ceased, the humane and kindly and charitable feelings of the country and of the world will require us to deal gently with the masses of the people who are engaged in this rebellion. It will be pleaded that wives and children will suffer for the crimes of husbands and fathers; and such appeals will have more or less effect upon the future policy of the government.

. But, sir, take from rebel masters their bondmen, and from the hour you do so until the end of the world, to "the last syllable of recorded time," the judgment of the country and the judgment of the world will sanction the act and it will be stronger every day while the world lasts. Therefore, sir, I am in favor of emancipating the slaves of all the rebels who are engaged in this rebellion.

Sir, with the lights of to-day I do not see how any man

can be for slavery and at the same time be a loyal man. Slavery and treason this day and this hour in this country are one and the same. Slavery and treason are synonymous words. I can conceive how a man of intelligence and character can recognize the existence of slavery, look upon it as it is as an evil, and yet not see how it is to be abolished or when it is to be got rid of. I can appreciate the position of such a man, and I think I do appreciate it.

But, sir, how can any man looking over this broad land to-day and seeing flashing from every quarter of the heavens the crimes of human slavery against this country, labor to uphold, strengthen, and support human slavery in America? It is the cause and the whole cause of this rebellion. We talk about " Jeff " Davis, Slidell, Mason, and Toombs, and their treasonable confederates; but they are not the cause of this rebellion; they are simply the hands, the tools: the heart, the brain, the soul is slavery; the motive power is slavery. Slavery is the great rebel; Davis and his compeers are but its humble tools and instruments.

Slavery for thirty years has been hostile to and aggressive upon the free institutions of America. There is not a principle embodied in our free institutions, there is not an element of our government that elevates or blesses mankind, there is not anything in our government or our institutions worth preserving, that slavery for a generation has not warred against and upon.

It smote down thirty years ago the great right of petition in these halls. It destroyed in large sections of the country the constitutional freedom of the press. It suppressed freedom of speech. It corrupted presses, churches, and political organizations. It plunged the nation into a war for the acquisition of slave-holding territory. It enacted a fugitive-slave law, inhuman, unchristian, disgraceful to the country and to the age. It repealed the prohibition of slavery over half a million square miles in the central regions of the continent. It seized the ballot-boxes in Kansas; it usurped the government of the Territory; it enacted inhuman and unchristian laws; it made a slave constitution and attempted to force it upon a free people; it bathed the virgin sods of that magnificent Territory with the blood of civil war. It mobbed, flogged, expelled, and sometimes murdered Christian men and women in the slave-holding States for no offence against law, humanity, or religion. It turned the hearts of large masses of men against their brethren, against the institutions of their country, against the glorious old flag, and the constitution of their fathers. It has now plunged this nation into this unholy rebellion, into this gigantic civil war that rends the country, and stains our waters and reddens our fields with fraternal blood.

Sir, I never see a loyal soldier upon a cot of sickness, sorrow, or death, without feeling that slavery has laid him there. I never gaze upon the wounds of a loyal soldier fallen in support of the flag of the republic without feeling that slavery inflicted those wounds upon him. I never see a loyal soldier wounded and maimed hobbling through your streets without feeling that he was wounded and maimed by slavery. I never gaze upon the lowly grave of a loyal soldier dying for the cause of his country without feeling that he was murdered by slavery. I never see a mourning wife or sorrowing children without realizing that slavery has made that mourning wife a widow and those sorrowing children orphans.

Sir, all these sacrifices of property, of health, of life, all this sorrow, agony, and death, now upon us, are born of slavery. Slavery is the prolific mother of all these woes that blight our land and fill the heart of our people with sorrows.

Slavery pronounced long ago against the free elements of our popular institutions; it scoffed at the Declaration of Independence; it pronounced free society a failure; it jeered and sneered at the laboring masses as mudsills and white slaves. Scoffing at everything which tended to secure the rights and enlarge the privileges of mankind, it has pronounced against the existence of democratic institutions in America. Proud, domineering, defiant, it has pronounced against the supremacy of the government, the unity and life of the nation.

Sir, slavery is the enemy, the clearly pronounced enemy of the country. Slavery is the only clearly pronounced enemy our country has on God's earth. There it stands. Hate is in its heart, scorn in its eye, defiance in its mien. It hates our cherished institutions, despises our people, defies our government. Slavery is the great rebel, the giant criminal, the murderer striving with bloody hands to throttle our government and destroy our country.

Senators may talk round it if they please, they may scold at its agents and denounce its tools. I care little about its agents or its tools. I think not of Davis and his compeers in crime; I look at the thing itself, to the great rebel with hands dripping with the blood of my murdered countrymen. I give the criminal no quarter. If I with the lights I have could utter a word or give a vote to continue for one moment the life of the great rebel that is now striking at the vitals of my country I should feel that I was a traitor to my native land and deserved a traitor's doom. Sir, I believe that every word spoken in Congress or out of Congress, every act that continues, strengthens, or keeps the breath of life in human slavery in America, is against the existence and perpetuity of democratic institutions; against the dignity of the toiling millions of my country; against the peace, the honor, the glory, and the life of the nation.

Sir, slavery being the criminal, slavery being the rebel, it should be stricken down through the agents it employs. It has its hundreds of thousands of rebels in arms against the country. To punish its instruments I will strike at it and destroy it if I can. I believe that we have a constitutional right to free the slaves of rebel masters, and I think it would be a crime against my country if I did not give a vote to free the slaves of every rebel on this continent. If this Congress adjourns without putting upon the statute-book of the country an act to free the slaves of every rebel in the United States I believe it will be false and recreant to the cause of the country.

I believe it is policy to emancipate the slaves of rebels. Gentlemen tell us that they do not see success in this direction. I do not see success in any other direction. I expect the armies to win brilliant victories. I have no doubt of success either on the Mississippi or at Yorktown, under Halleck or McClellan. I have no doubt but that the brave men whose hearts are burning with love of liberty and of country and hatred of this criminal that is striving to destroy the republic will, with arms in their hands, smite down its agents on land or wave. Victory I am sure will flash upon the banners of the republic.

I believe that we are to win victories, but how are we to change the hearts of the masses of men that have plunged into this rebellion? What made them hate the people of this country? What made them jeer at the toiling millions of the free States as mudsills of society? What made them scoff at the Declaration of Independence and at the free institutions that do not pull down the highest to elevate the lowly up? What made them hate the old flag of our country? What made them raise their hands for the overthrow of our institutions, the destruction of this government and this nation?

Slavery made them do it. It was slavery, nothing more, nothing less, that perverted their hearts, clouded their reason, blinded their consciences, and made them traitors. Just in proportion to the strength of slavery in any locality in the country is the hate of the people against our institutions, our government, and our people; and so long as slavery shall live, so long as it shall have vitality, so long as it shall be an institution to be nurtured and strengthened, upheld and sustained, so long as it shall be an element of power on this continent, just so long will the people now in rebellion against the government hate our people and hate our country.

An intelligent man who believes in slavery, who would strengthen and spread it, who would nurture it, who would make it an element of political power, cannot love the democratic institutions of this country; he cannot love the country itself. It is an impossibility—a moral impossibility.

You have all cast your eyes over the country in rebellion. Where live the loyal men? In western Virginia, in eastern Tennessee, in western North Carolina, in Missouri, in the mountain regions where there are few slaves. There you have men who are not seduced or conquered by slavery; men who yet love our institutions, love our government, love our people, love our old flag. But wherever slavery is strong it has seduced, subdued, or conquered the hearts of the people, made them disloyal against the country; and they will hate us so long as slavery is a power on earth.

Sir, casting aside all regard for the bondman, looking at

this question simply in the light of action for the suppression of the rebellion and the restoration of the future harmony and repose of the country, I believe it is our duty to destroy the cause that has changed the hearts of millions of our people. Destroy slavery and you take from the heart of that people the sole motive for hating us and hating our country. When they shall see that the cause of all their hate and disloyalty lies low in the dust they will rise again and support your institutions and your government, and be proud again to recognize the flag of their country. Slavery has intoxicated and maddened the people of the slave-holding States. Take the cup from the trembling hand of the drunkard, who is ready, in his delirium, to smite down wife and child, and the drunkard will be a man again and love and protect that wife and child. Strike the chains from the limbs of the slaves of rebel masters and those masters will become loyal again, ready to pour out their blood for the institutions they now hate and the government they so madly assail.

Every hour of thought and reflection brings me to the conclusion that death to slavery is life to the republic. Believing this, I think it is our duty to walk up to the extreme verge of our constitutional power, and I would go no farther, but I would walk up to the extreme verge of constitutional power to destroy slavery. If there is a doubt I would not give that doubt to slavery, but I would give that doubt to my country. If I have any doubts on these points I give the doubts in favor of my country against slavery, and not for slavery against my country. But, sir, I have no doubt. We have a right to take the life, take the property, and free the slaves of every rebel on this continent. While I would not take the lives of many, if any; while I would not take the property of more than the leaders, I would take the bondmen from every rebel on the continent, and in doing it I should have the sanction of my own judgment, the sanction of the enlightened world, the sanction of the coming ages, and the blessings of Almighty God. Every day, while the world stands, that act would be approved and applauded by the human heart all over the globe.

Sir, it seems to me our duty is as clear as the track of the sun across the heavens, and that duty is, before the adjournment of this Congress, to lay low in the dust under our feet, so that iron heels will rest upon it, this great rebel, this giant criminal, this guilty murderer, that is warring upon the existence of the country. It is in our power to do it, and we ought to meet it; and I must confess I have no sort of respect for any of those doubts that have been thrown out during this session of Congress in regard to this policy of freeing the slaves of rebel masters.

Why, sir, I remember, from the time the flag of rebellion was raised, that every act of the government to uphold its authority has been denounced in Congress and out of Congress as offensive to the rebels. We could not propose anything to sustain the authority of the government without being told, " Oh, you will offend the loyal men of the border States, and you will exasperate the rebels." We disregarded it in many cases, and this country has lost many lives and millions of dollars because we did not disregard it in the commencement and boldly act up to our constitutional obligations.

Last summer when it was proposed to free the slaves who had been actually employed by their masters, with arms in their hands, to smite down our brethren, we were told: " It will not do; you offend these rebels; you will unite the hearts of the people of the slave States against you; you will offend the loyal border-State men." Well, sir, we passed the act in spite of these doubts, and it is the law of the land to-day. I only regret that it is not more faithfully executed by the government and by the military men in the service of the government. When we proposed to abolish slavery in this District the other day we were told it would not do; we would unite the hearts of traitors against the country and strengthen their hands, and it would be a rock of offence before our border-State men. We passed the bill, and this day and this hour thirteen thousand black men in this District in their churches are offering up prayers to Almighty God for blessings on us for that beneficent act. Sir, every movement we make, every proposition we make, we are met with this same talk about giving offence to rebels. I do not fear these rebels. Our bayonets will be as bright and as sharp after we act upon this subject as they are now.

Sir, every day that slavery stands, every moment that it breathes the breath of life in all its power, there stands an enemy that can never love our people, our institutions, or our government. It is a moral impossibility. Then destroy it, and when it is gone will come back the old sentiments of the Washingtons and the Jeffersons and the great men of the revolutionary era in the slave-holding States. Then will come back the love for the Declaration of Independence, for the constitution of the United States, for the free institutions that adorn, bless, and elevate the masses of mankind. Then will come back the reverence for the glorious memories of the past. Then will come back the love for the Stars and Stripes of our country. Then will come back a feeling of amazement and of shame that men were so perverted by the monster slavery as to imbrue their hands in the blood of their countrymen. Rebels will come back with a feeling of repentance for these crimes against their country. Then, when slavery is stricken down, they will come back again and offer their hands, red though they be with the blood of our brethren, and we shall forgive the past, take them to our bosoms, and be again one people. But, senators, keep slavery; let it stand; shrink from duty; let men whose hands are stained with the blood of our countrymen, whose hearts are disloyal to our country, hold fast to the chains that bind three millions of men in bondage, and we shall have an enemy to hate us, ready to seize on all fit opportunities to smite down all that we love, and again to raise their disloyal hands against the perpetuity of the republic. Sir, I believe this to be as true as the Holy Evangelist of Almighty God, and nothing but the prejudices of association on the one side, or timidity on the other, can hold us back from doing the duty we owe to our country in this crisis.

The senator from Vermont has proposed in his amendment to authorize the President of the United States, whenever he shall believe it necessary for the suppression of this rebellion, to issue his proclamation declaring the slaves of rebels free. This proposition gives up the whole question. If I understand it, it is a full concession. It concedes the right of this Congress to authorize the President of the United States to emancipate the slaves of rebels in all the States where he has made proclamation that the people are in insurrection.

I accept it, sir, and if Congress has the right to authorize the President to issue a proclamation emancipating these slaves, if in his judgment he believes it necessary, then Congress has the right to authorize and require the President to do it if Congress believes it necessary, for the suppression of the rebellion, that such a proclamation shall be issued. The senator from Vermont has laid down a doctrine upon which we can stand; and therefore I propose to amend his proposition and not allow any discretion anywhere but in the law, and let the law say that, for the more speedy and efficient suppression of this rebellion, the President shall be authorized and required to issue his proclamation. We decide that question for ourselves. With the lights that are flashing upon us this day, how can we doubt for a moment? If the Senate will sustain the amendment I have proposed, we shall require the President, thirty days after the passage of this act, for the speedy and more effectual suppression of this rebellion, to issue a proclamation declaring the slaves of rebels, in these States and parts of States, free. I hope the Senate will thus amend this proposition so that we shall leave nothing to accident, nothing to contingencies. With the lights of to-day let us meet the responsibilities of to-day and do our whole duty.

I feel, sir, that if we adjourn, if we go hence without putting upon the statute-book of our country a law declaring the slaves of rebels free men, we shall be guilty of the blood of the brave men who are to uphold the flag of our country the hot and sickly climes of the South. Many of them lie to-day in humble graves in the land of strangers. Many of them are now marching to the far South. They are to die by thousands with the disease and sickness of the climate. They are to perish by thousands on battle-fields.

Shall we permit this power to stand in front of them, ready to overwhelm them? Shall we permit this power to stand unbroken, because we are afraid of offending timid or doubting men? Sir, I care for the blood of the brave men from my State, from the loyal part of the country, who are fighting this battle for freedom and for national life. Their lives are dearer to me than the doubtful constitutional rights of criminals. We are very tender of the constitutional rights of

crime. Hardly a day passes that the constitutional rights
of crime are not illustrated in this chamber or in the other
House. Sir, I joyfully give my vote and my voice for the
cause of my countrymen and my country, against the great
criminal that stands to-day with bloody hands ready to pull
down the institutions and destroy the existence of my country.
In thus acting I am cheered and sustained by the proud consciousness that I am actuated by a patriotism that embraces
our whole country and the present and future welfare of the
republic.

MARTIN

JOHN MARTIN, an eminent Irish revolutionist, was born at Loughorne, County Down, September 8, 1812. His father was a well-to-do farmer and linen-merchant. He was educated at Dr. Henderson's school at Newry and at Trinity College, Dublin. In 1832 he took his degree and began the study of medicine, which he relinquished in 1836 when he inherited the estates of his uncle at Loughorne. In 1839 he visited America and travelled widely over the United States and Canada. On his return he became a member of the Association of the Confederates, but was expelled because he demanded the publication of the accounts. He became a contributor to the "United Irishman," and when that was suppressed, he issued the "Irish Felon" from the same publishing rooms. Before his sixth number was out he was arrested for treason-felony. He was sentenced to be transported for ten years. He remained in Van Diemen's Land until 1854, when he was conditionally pardoned and returned to Paris, where he expected to live in exile, but the death of a relative in Ireland called him home in 1858. In January, 1864, he established in Dublin a Repeal association called the "National League." When the famous public funeral procession was organized in Dublin in December, 1867, in memory of the three Irishmen executed in Manchester on the twenty-third of November, John Martin delivered the address at the cemetery, and, having been again arrested, was tried for sedition; but this time the jury disagreed and the prisoner was discharged.

THE NATIONAL INDEPENDENCE OF IRELAND

SPEECH DELIVERED FROM THE DOCK AT DUBLIN, AUGUST 18, 1849

MY LORDS,—I have no imputation to cast upon the bench, neither have I anything to charge the jury with, of unfairness toward me. I think the judges desired to do their duty honestly, as upright judges and men, and that the twelve men who were put into the box, as I believe, not to try, but to convict me, voted honestly, according to their prejudices. I have no personal enmity against the sheriff, sub-sheriff, or any of the gentlemen connected with the arrangement of the jury-panel, nor against the attorney-general or any other person engaged in the proceedings called

my trial; but, my lords, I consider that I have not been yet
tried.   There have been certain formalities carried on here
for three days regarding me, ending in a verdict of guilty;
but I have not been put upon my country, as the constitution
said to exist in Ireland requires.   Twelve of my countrymen,
" indifferently chosen," have not been put into that jury-box
to try me, but twelve men who, I believe, have been selected
by the parties who represent the Crown, for the purpose of
convicting and not of trying me.

I believe they were put into that box because the parties
conducting the prosecution knew their political sentiments
were hostile to mine, and because the matter at issue here is
a political question,—a matter of opinion, and not a matter of
fact.   I have nothing more to say as to the trial, except to
repeat that, having watched the conduct of the judges, I consider them upright and honest men.   I have this to add, that
as to the charge I make with respect to the constitution of the
panel and the selection of the jury I have no legal evidence
of the truth of my statement, but there is no one who has a
moral doubt of it.   Every person knows that what I have
stated is the fact; and I would represent to the judges, most
respectfully, that they, as upright and honorable men, and
judges, and as citizens, ought to see that the administration
of justice in this country is above suspicion.   I have nothing
more to say with regard to the trial; but I would be thankful
to the court for permission to say a few words in vindication
of my character and motives after sentence is passed.

[Baron Pennefather,—" No; we will not hear anything
from you after sentence."
Chief Baron,—" We cannot hear anything from you after
sentence has been pronounced."]

Then, my lords, permit me to say that, admitting the narrow and confined constitutional doctrines which I have heard preached in this court to be right, I am not guilty of the charge, according to this act. I did not intend to devise or levy war against the Queen, or to depose the Queen. In the article of mine on which the jury framed their verdict of guilty, which was written in prison and published in the last number of my paper, what I desired to do was this,—to advise and encourage my countrymen to keep their arms, because that is their inalienable right, which no act of Parliament, no proclamation, can take away from them. It is, I repeat, their inalienable right. I advised them to keep their arms; and further, I advised them to use their arms in their own defence against all assailants,—even assailants that might come to attack them unconstitutionally and improperly using the Queen's name as their sanction.

My object in all my proceedings has been simply to assist in establishing the national independence of Ireland, for the benefit of all the people of Ireland,—noblemen, clergymen, judges, professional men,—in fact, all Irishmen. I have sought that object, first, because I thought it was our right,— because I think national independence is the right of the people of this country; and, secondly, I admit that, being a man who loves retirement, I never would have engaged in politics did I not think it was necessary to do all in my power to make an end of the horrible scenes that this country presents—the pauperism, starvation, and crime, and vice, and hatred of all classes against each other. I thought there should be an end to that horrible system, which, while it lasted, gave me no peace of mind; for I could not enjoy anything in my native country so long as I saw my countrymen forced to be vicious, forced to hate each other, and degraded to the level of paupers and brutes. That is the reason I engaged in politics. I ac-

knowledge, as the solicitor-general has said, that I was but a
weak assailant of the English power. I am not a good writer,
and I am no orator. I had only two weeks' experience in conducting a newspaper until I was put into jail; but I am satisfied to direct the intention of my countrymen to everything I
have written and said, and to rest my character on a fair and
candid examination of what I have put forward as my
opinions. I shall say nothing in vindication of my motives
but this,—that every fair and honest man, no matter how
prejudiced he may be, if he calmly considers what I have
written and said, will be satisfied that my motives were pure
and honorable. I have nothing more to say.

THE IRISH MARTYRS

ADDRESS AT THE CEMETERY IN DUBLIN, DECEMBER 8, 1867

FELLOW COUNTRYMEN,—This is a strange kind of
funeral procession in which we are engaged to-day.
We are here, a vast multitude of men, women, and
children, in a very inclement season of the year, under rain
and through mud. We are here escorting three empty hearses
to the consecrated last resting-place of those who die in the
Lord. The three bodies that we would tenderly bear to the
churchyard and would bury in consecrated ground with all
the solemn rites of religion are not here. They are away in
a foreign and hostile land, where they have been thrown into
unconsecrated ground, branded by the triumphant hatred of
our enemies as the vile remains of murderers. Those three
men whose memories we are here to-day to honor—Allen,
O'Brien, and Larkin—they were not murderers. These men
were pious men, virtuous men, they were men who feared

God and loved their country. They sorrowed for the sorrows of the dear old native land of their love. They wished, if possible, to save her, and for that love and for that wish they were doomed to an ignominious death at the hands of the British hangman. It was as Irish patriots that these men were doomed to death, and it was as Irish patriots that they met their death.

For these reasons, my countrymen, we here to-day have joined in this solemn procession to honor their memories. For that reason we say from our hearts, "May their souls rest in peace." For that reason, my countrymen, we join in their last prayer, "God save Ireland."

The death of these men was an act of English policy, a legal murder, and that legal murder was an act of English policy, of the policy of that nation which, through jealousy and hatred of our nation, destroyed by fraud and force our just government sixty-seven years ago.

They have been sixty-seven sad years of insult and robbery —of impoverishment—of extermination—of suffering beyond what any other subject-people but ours have ever endured from the malignity of foreign masters. Nearly through all these years the Irish people continued to pray for the restoration of their Irish national rule. They offered their forgiveness to England. They offered even their friendship to England, if she would only give up her usurped power to tyrannize over us, and leave us to live in peace and as honorable neighbors. But in vain. England felt herself strong enough to continue to insult and rob us, and she was too greedy and too insolent to cease from robbing and insulting us.

Now it has come to pass, as a consequence of that malignant policy pursued for so many years,—it has come to pass that the great body of the Irish people despair of obtaining peaceful restitution of our national rights. And it has also come to pass that vast numbers of Irishmen whom the oppression of English rule forbade to live by honest industry in their own country have in America learned to become soldiers, and those Irish soldiers seem resolved to make war against England.

And England is in a panic of rage and fear in consequence of this, and being in a panic about Fenianism, she hopes to strike terror into her Irish malcontents by a legal murder.

England wanted to show that she was not afraid of Fenianism, but she has only shown that she is not afraid to do injustice in the face of Heaven and of man. Many a wicked statute she has framed—many a jury she has packed, in order to dispose of her Irish political offenders—but in the case of Allen, O'Brien, and Larkin, she has committed such an outrage on justice and decency as to make even many Englishmen stand aghast.

I shall not detain you with entering into details with which you are all well acquainted, as to the shameful scenes of the handcuffing of the untried prisoners—as to the shameful scenes of the trials up to the last moment, when the three men—our dearly beloved Irish brethren—were forced to give up their innocent lives as a sacrifice for the cause of Ireland; and fellow countrymen, these three humble Irishmen who represented Ireland on that sad occasion demeaned themselves as Christians, as patriots, modestly, courageously, piously, nobly.

We need not blush for them. They bore themselves all through with a courage worthy of the greatest heroes that ever obtained glory upon eartth. They behaved through all the trying scenes I referred to with Christian patience, with resignation to the will of God, with modest, yet proud and firm adherence to principle. They showed their love to Ireland and their fear of God from the first to the last.

It is vain for me to attempt to detain you with many words upon this matter. I will say this, that all who are here do not approve of the schemes for the relief of Ireland that these men were supposed to have contemplated; but all who love Ireland, all generous, Christian men, and women, and children of Ireland—all the children growing up to be men and women of Ireland—all those feel an intense sympathy, an intense love for the memories of these three men whom England has murdered in form of law by way of striking terror into her Irish subjects.

Fellow countrymen, it is almost idle for me to persist in addressing weak words of mine to you; for your presence here to-day, you demeanor all through, the solemn conduct of the vast multitude assembled directly under the terrorism of a hostile government, say more than the words of the greatest orator,—more than the words of a Meagher could say for you. You have behaved yourselves all through this day with most admirable spirit as good Irish men and women—as good boys and girls of holy Ireland ought to do—and I am sure you will behave so to the end.

This demonstration is mainly one of mourning for the fate of these three good Irishmen; but, fellow countrymen, and women, and boys, and girls, it is also one of protest and indignation against the conduct of our rulers. Your attendance here to-day is a sufficient protest. Your orderly behavior—your good temper all through this wretched weather—your attendance here in such vast numbers for such a purpose—avowedly and in the face of the terrorism of the government, which falls most directly upon the metropolis—that is enough for protest. You, in your multitudes, men, women, and

children, have to-day made that protest. Your conduct has
been admirable for patience, for good nature, for fine spirit,
for solemn sense of that great duty you were resolved to do.
You will return home with the same good order and inoffen-
siveness. You will join with me now, in repeating the prayer
of the three martyrs whom we mourn—" God save Ireland!"
And all of you, men, women, and boys and girls that are to
be men and women of holy Ireland, will ever keep the sentiment of that prayer in your heart of hearts.

THE INDICTMENT OF MILLIONS

SPEECH DELIVERED FROM THE DOCK AT DUBLIN, FEBRUARY 21, 1868

MY LORDS, AND GENTLEMEN OF THE JURY,—
I am going to trouble this court with some reply to
the charge made against me in this indictment. But
I am sorry that I must begin by protesting that I do not
consider myself as being now put upon my country to be
tried as the constitution requires—and therefore I do not
address you for my legal defence, but for my vindication
before the tribunal of conscience—a far more awful tribunal,
to my mind, than this.

Gentlemen, I regard you as twelve of my fellow countrymen, known or believed by my prosecutors to be my political
opponents, and selected for this reason for the purpose of
obtaining a conviction against me in form of law.

Gentlemen, I have not the smallest purpose of casting an
imputation against your honesty, or the honesty of my prosecutors who have selected you. This is a political trial, and
in this country political trials are always conducted in this
way. It is considered by the Crown prosecutor to be their

duty to exclude from the jury-box every juror known or suspected to hold or agree with the accused in political sentiment.

Now, gentlemen, I have not the least objection to see men of the most opposite political sentiments to mine placed in the jury-box to try me, provided they be placed there as the constitution commands—provided they are twelve of my neighbors indifferently chosen. As a loyal citizen I am willing and desirous to be put upon my country and fairly tried before any twelve of my countrymen, no matter what may happen to be the political sentiments of any of them. But I am sorry and indignant that this is not such a trial. This system by which, over and over again, loyal subjects of the Queen in Ireland are condemned in form of law for seeking, by such means as the constitution warrants, to restore her Majesty's kingdom of Ireland to the enjoyment of its national rights,—this system of selecting anti-Repealers, and excluding Repealers from the jury-box, when a Repealer like me is to be tried, is calculated to bring the administration of justice into disesteem, disrepute, and hatred. I here protest against it.

My lords, and gentlemen of the jury, before I offer any reply to the charges in this indictment, and the further development of those charges made yesterday by the learned gentleman whose official duty it was to argue the government's case against me, I wish to apologize to the court for declining to avail myself of the professional assistance of the bar upon this occasion. It is not through any want of respect for the noble profession of the bar that I decline that assistance. I regard the duties of a lawyer as among the most respectable that a citizen can undertake. His education has taught him to investigate the origin and to understand the principles of law and the true nature of loyalty. He has had to consider how the interests of individual citizens may harmonize with the interests of the community, how justice and liberty may be united, how the state may have both order and contentment. The application of the knowledge which he has gained from the study of law to the daily facts of human society sharpens and strengthens all his faculties, clears his judgment, helps him to distinguish true from false, and right from wrong.

It is no wonder, gentlemen, that an accomplished and virtuous lawyer holds a high place in the aristocracy of merit in every free country. Like all things human, the legal profession has its dark as well as its bright side, has in it germs of decay and rotten foulness as well as of health and beauty; but yet it is a noble profession and one which I admire and respect. But, above all, I would desire to respect the bar of my own country, and the Irish bar,—the bar made illustrious by such memories as those of Grattan and Flood, and the Emmets, and Curran, and Plunket, and Sourin, and Holmes, and Sheil, and O'Connell. I may add, too, of Burke, and of Sheridan, for they were Irish in all that made them great. The bar of Ireland wants this day only the ennobling inspirations of national freedom to raise it to a level with the world. Under the Union very few lawyers have been produced whose names can rank in history with any of the great names I have mentioned. . . .

But to this attack upon my character as a good citizen, and upon my liberty, my lords, and gentlemen, the only defence I could permit to be offered would be a full justification of my political conduct, morally, constitutionally, legally,— a complete vindication of my acts and words alleged to be seditious and disloyal,—and to retort against my accusers the

charge of sedition and disloyalty. Not, indeed, that I would
desire to prosecute these gentlemen upon that charge, if I
could count upon convicting them and sending them to the
dungeon instead of myself. I don't desire to silence them,
or to hurt a hair of their wigs, because their political opinions
differed from mine. Gentlemen, this prosecution against
me, like the prosecution just accomplished against two national newspapers, is part of a scheme of the ministers of
the Crown for suppressing all voice of protest against the
Union, for suppressing all public complaint against the deadly
results of the Union, and all advocacy by act, speech, or
writing for Repeal of the Union.

Now, I am a Repealer so long as I have been a politician
at all—that is for at least twenty-four years past. Until
the national self-government of my country be first restored,
there appears to me to be no place, no *locus standi* (as lawyers
say), for any other Irish political question, and I consider it
to be my duty as a patriotic and loyal citizen to endeavor by
all honorable and prudent means to procure the repeal of
the Act of Union and the restoration of the independent Irish
government of which my country was (as I have said in my
prosecuted speech), " by fraud and force," and against the
will of the vast majority of its people of every race, creed,
and class, though under false forms of law, deprived sixty-
seven years ago. . . .

Now, gentlemen, such being my convictions, were I to
entrust my defence in this court to a lawyer, he must speak
as a Repealer, not only for me, but for himself, not only as
a professional advocate, but as a man and from the heart. I
cannot doubt but that there are very many Irish lawyers
who privately share my convictions about Repeal. Believing
as I do in my heart and conscience, and with all the force of

the mind that God has given me, that Repeal is the right and the only right policy for Ireland—for healing all the wounds of our community, all our sectarian feuds, all our national shame, suffering, and peril—for making our country peaceful, industrious, prosperous, respectable, and happy —I cannot doubt but that in the enlightened profession of the bar there must be very many Irishmen who, like me, consider Repeal to be right, and best, and necessary for the public good.

But, gentlemen, ever since the Union, by fraud and force, and against the will of the Irish people, was enacted—ever since that act of usurpation by the English Parliament of the sovereign rights of the Queen, lords, and commons of Ireland—ever since this country was thereby rendered the subject instead of the sister of England—ever since the Union, but especially for about twenty years past, it has been the policy of those who have got possession of the sovereign rights of the Irish Crown to appoint to all places of public trust, emolument, or honor in Ireland only such men as would submit, whether by parol or by tacit understanding, to suppress all public utterance of their desire for the repeal of the Union.

Such has been the persistent policy toward this country of those who command all the patronage of the Irish offices, paid and unpaid—the policy of all English ministers, whether Whig or Tory. Combined with the disposal of the public forces, such a policy is naturally very effective in not really reconciling, but in keeping Ireland quietly subject to the Union. It is a hard trial of men's patriotism to be debarred from all career of profitable and honorable distinction in the public service of their own country. . . .

I shall trouble you for a short time longer, while I en-

9 deavor to show that I have not acted in a way unbecoming a good citizen. The charge against me in this indictment is that I took a part in the illegal procession and violated the statute entitled the " Party Processions Act." His lordship enumerated seven conditions, the violation of some one of which is necessary to render an assembly illegal at common law. These seven conditions are:

1. That the persons forming the assembly met to carry out an unlawful purpose.

2. That the numbers in which the persons met endangered the public peace.

3. That the assembly caused alarm to the peaceful subjects of the Queen.

4. That the assembly created disaffection.

5. That the assembly incited her Majesty's Irish subjects to hate her Majesty's English subjects—his lordship did not say anything to the case of an assembly inciting the Queen's English subjects to hate the Queen's Irish subjects, but no such case is likely to be tried here.

6. That the assembly intended to asperse the right and constitutional administration of justice.

7. That the assembly intended to impair the functions of justice and to bring the administration of justice into disrepute.

I say that the procession of the 8th of December did not violate any one of these conditions.

1. In the first place, the persons forming that procession did not meet to carry out any unlawful purpose—their purpose was peaceably to express their opinion upon a public act of the public servants of the Crown.

2. In the second place, the numbers in which those persons met did not endanger the public peace. None of those per-

sons carried arms. Thousands of those persons were women and children. There was no injury or offence attempted to be committed against anybody, and no disturbance of the peace took place.

3. In the third place, the assembly caused no alarm to the peaceable subjects of the Queen—there is not a tittle of evidence to that effect.

4. In the fourth place, the assembly did not create disaffection, neither was it intended or calculated to create disaffection. On the contrary, the assembly served to give peaceful expression to the opinion entertained by vast numbers of her Majesty's peaceful subjects upon a public act of the servants of the Crown, an act which vast numbers of the Queen's subjects regretted and condemned. And thus the assembly was calculated to prevent or remove disaffection. For such open and peaceful manifestations of the real opinions of the Queen's subjects upon public affairs is the proper, safe, and constitutional way in which they may aid to prevent disaffection.

5. In the fifth place, the assembly did not incite the Irish subjects of the Queen to hate her Majesty's English subjects. On the contrary, it was a proper constitutional way of bringing about a right understanding upon a transaction which, if not fairly and fully explained and set right, must produce hatred between the two peoples. That transaction was calculated to produce hatred. But those who protest peaceably against such a transaction are not the party to be blamed, but those responsible for the transaction.

6. In the sixth place, the assembly had no purpose of aspersing the right and constitutional administration of justice. Its tendency was peaceably to point out faults in the conduct of the servants of the Crown, charged with the

administration of justice, whose faults were calculated to bring the administration of justice into disrepute.

7. Nor, in the seventh place, did the assembly impair the functions of justice, or intend or tend to do so. Even my prosecutors do not allege that judicial tribunals are infallible. It would be too absurd to make such an allegation in plain words. It is admitted on all hands that judges have sometimes given wrong directions, that juries have given wrong verdicts, that courts of justice have wrongfully appreciated the whole matter for trial.

When millions of the Queen's subjects think that such wrong has been done, is it sedition for them to say so peaceably and publicly? On the contrary, the constitutional way for good citizens to act in striving to keep the administration of justice pure and above suspicion of unfairness is by such open and peaceable protests. Thus, and thus only, may the functions of justice be saved from being impaired. In this case wrong had been done. Five men had been tried together upon the same evidence, and convicted together upon that evidence, and while one of the five was acknowledged by the Crown to be innocent, and the whole conviction was thus acknowledged to be wrong and invalid, three of the five men were hanged upon that conviction.

My friend, Mr. Sullivan, in his eloquent and unanswerable speech of yesterday, has so clearly demonstrated the facts of that unhappy and disgraceful affair of Manchester that I shall merely say of it that I adopt every word he spoke upon the subject for mine, and to justify the sentiment and purpose with which I engaged in the procession of the 8th of December. I say persons responsible for that transaction are fairly liable to the charge of acting so as to bring the administration of justice into contempt, unless, gentlemen, you hold those persons to be infallible, and hold that they can do no wrong. But, gentlemen, the constitution does not say that the servants of the Crown can do no wrong. According to the constitution the sovereign can do no wrong, but her servants may. In this case they have done wrong. . . .

By indicting me for the expression of that opinion the public prosecutors virtually indict some millions of the Queen's peaceable Irish subjects. It is only the convenience of this court—which could not hold the millions in one batch of traversers, and which would require daily sittings for several successive years to go through the proper formalities for duly trying all those millions; it is only the convenience of this court that can be pretended to relieve the Crown prosecutors from the duty of trying and convicting all those millions, if it is their duty to try and convict me. . . .

And to select one man, or six men for trial, condemnation, and punishment, out of, say, four millions who have really participated in the same alleged wicked, malicious, seditious, evil-disposed, and unlawful proceedings, is unfair to the six men, and unfair to the other 3,999,994 men, is a dereliction of duty on the part of the officers of the law, and is calculated to bring the administration of justice into disrepute.

Equal justice is what the constitution demands. Under military authority an army may be decimated, and a few offenders may properly be punished, while the rest are left unpunished. But under a free constitution it is not so. Whoever breaks the law must be made amenable to punishment, or equal justice is not rendered to the subjects of the Queen. It is not pertinent, therefore, gentlemen, for me to say to you, this is an unwise proceeding which my prosecutors bid you to sanction by a verdict. I have heard it asked by a lawyer addressing the court, as a question that must be answered in the negative — Can you indict a whole nation?

If such a proceeding as this prosecution against the peaceable procession of the 8th of December receives the sanction of your verdict, that question must be answered in the affirmative. It will need only a Crown prosecutor, an·attorney-general, and a solicitor-general, two judges, and twelve jurors, all of the one mind, while all the other subjects of the Queen in Ireland are of a different mind, and the five millions and a half of the Queen's subjects of Ireland outside that circle of seventeen of her Majesty's subjects may be indicted, convicted, and consigned to penal imprisonment in due form of law—as law is understood in political trials in Ireland. . . .

The learned judge in his charge told the grand jury that under this act all processions are illegal which carry weapons of offence, or which carry symbols calculated to promote the animosity of some other class of her Majesty's subjects. Applying the law to this case, his lordship remarked that the procession of the 8th of December had something of military array—that is, they went in regular order, with a regular step. But, gentleman, there were no arms in that procession, there were no symbols in that procession intended or calculated to provoke animosity in any other class of the Queen's subjects, or in any human creature. There was neither symbol, deed, or word intended to provoke animosity. And as to the military array—is it not absurd to attribute warlike character to an unarmed and perfectly peaceful assemblage in which there were some thousands of women and children? No offence was given or offered any human being. . . .

The speech delivered on that occasion is an important element in forming a judgment upon the character and object of the procession. The speech declared the procession to be a peaceable expression of the opinion of those who composed it upon an important public transaction, an expression of sorrow and indignation at an act of the ministers of the government.

It was a protest against that act—a protest which those who disapproved of it were entitled by the constitution to make, and which they made, peaceably and legitimately. Has not every individual of the millions of the Queen's subjects the right to say openly whether he approves or disapproves of any public act of the Queen's ministers? Have not all the Queen's subjects the right to say so together, if they can without disturbance of the Queen's peace? The procession enabled many thousands to do that without the least inconvenience or danger to themselves, and with no injury or offense to their neighbors. To prohibit or punish peaceful, inoffensive, orderly, and perfectly innocent processions upon pretence that they are constructively unlawful, is unconstitutional tyranny. . . .

I would not have held the procession had I not understood that it was permitted. But understanding that it was permitted, and so believing that it might serve the people for a safe and useful expression of their sentiments, I held the procession. I did not hold the procession because I believed it to be illegal, but because I believed it to be legal, and understood it to be permitted. . . .

Gentlemen of the jury, I have said enough to convince any twelve reasonable men that there was nothing in my conduct in the matter of that procession which you can declare on your oaths to be "malicious, seditious, ill-disposed, and intended to disturb the peace and tranquillity of the realm."

I shall trouble you no further except by asking you to listen to the summing up of the indictment, and, while you listen, to judge between me and the attorney-general. I shall read you my words and his comment. Judge, Irish jurors, which of us two is guilty: " Let us, therefore, conclude this proceeding by joining heartily, with hats off, in the prayer of those three men—' God save Ireland.' " " Thereby," says the attorney-general in his indictment, " meaning, and intending to excite hatred, dislike, and animosity against her Majesty and the government, and bring into contempt the administration of justice and the laws of this realm, and cause strife and hatred between her Majesty's subjects in Ireland and in England, and to excite discontent and disaffection against her Majesty's government." Gentlemen, I have now done.

BEECHER

HENRY WARD BEECHER was born at Litchfield, Connecticut, in 1813, and graduated from Amherst College in 1834. After studying theology at Lane's Seminary he settled in 1837 as a Presbyterian minister in Lawrenceberg, Indiana, whence he shortly removed to Indianapolis, and preached there until 1847, when he received a call to Plymouth Church, Brooklyn. Here he acquired and maintained throughout his life a reputation as a pulpit orator of the first rank. He became deeply interested in politics, discussed frequently from the platform the great political questions of the day, and in 1856 and 1860 took an active part in the campaigns. The oration here reproduced was one of a series of addresses delivered by Mr. Beecher in England during the autumn of 1863. By supporting Mr. Cleveland for the Presidency in 1884, Beecher alienated many of his former political admirers. He died in Brooklyn on March 8, 1887.

ADDRESS AT LIVERPOOL, OCTOBER 16, 1863

FOR more than twenty-five years I have been made perfectly familiar with popular assemblies in all parts of my country except the extreme South. There has not for the whole of that time been a single day of my life when it would have been safe for me to go south of Mason and Dixon's line in my own country, and all for one reason: my solemn, earnest, persistent testimony against that which I consider to be the most atrocious thing under the sun— the system of American slavery in a great free republic. (Cheers.) I have passed through that early period when right of free speech was denied to me. Again and again I have attempted to address audiences that, for no other crime than that of free speech, visited me with all manner

(7254)

of contumelious epithets; and now since I have been in England, although I have met with greater kindness and courtesy on the part of most than I deserved, yet, on the other hand, I perceive that the Southern influence prevails to some extent in England. (Applause and uproar.) It is my old acquaintance; I understand it perfectly—(laughter) —and I have always held it to be an unfailing truth that where a man had a cause that would bear examination he was perfectly willing to have it spoken about. (Applause.) And when in Manchester I saw those huge placards: "Who is Henry Ward Beecher?"—(laughter, cries of "Quite right," and applause)—and when in Liverpool I was told that there were those blood-red placards, purporting to say what Henry Ward Beecher had said, and calling upon Englishmen to suppress free speech—I tell you what I thought. I thought simply this: "I am glad of it." (Laughter.) Why? Because if they had felt perfectly secure that *you* are the minions of the South and the slaves of slavery, they would have been perfectly still. (Applause and uproar.) And, therefore, when I saw so much nervous apprehension that, if I were permitted to speak—(hisses and applause)—when I found they were afraid to have me speak—(hisses, laughter, and "No, no!")—when I found that they considered my speaking damaging to their cause—(applause)—when I found that they appealed from facts and reasonings to mob law —(applause and uproar)—I said, no man need tell me what the heart and secret counsel of these men are. They tremble and are afraid. (Applause, laughter, hisses, "No, no!" and a voice: "New York mob.") Now, personally, it is a matter of very little consequence to me whether I speak here to-night or not. (Laughter and cheers.) But, one thing is very certain, if you do permit me to speak here to-night you will hear very plain talking. (Applause and hisses.) You will not find a man—(interruption)—you will not find me to be a man that dared to speak about Great Britain 3,000 miles off, and then is afraid to speak to Great Britain when he stands on her shores. (Immense applause and hisses.) And if I do not mistake the tone and temper of Englishmen, they had rather have a man who opposes them in a manly way—(applause from all parts of the hall)—than a sneak that agrees with them in an unmanly way. (Applause and "Bravo!") Now, if I can carry you with me by sound convictions, I shall be immensely glad (applause); but if I cannot carry you with me by facts and sound arguments, I do not wish you to go with me at all; and all that I ask is simply *fair play*. (Applause, and a voice: "You shall have it, too.")

Those of you who are kind enough to wish to favor my speaking—and you will observe that my voice is slightly husky, from having spoken almost every night in succession for some time past—those who wish to hear me will do me the kindness simply to sit still, and to keep still; and I and my friends the Secessionists will make all the noise. (Laughter.)

There are two dominant races in modern history—the Germanic and the Romanic races. The Germanic races tend to personal liberty, to a sturdy individualism, to civil and to political liberty. The Romanic race tends to absolutism in government; it is clannish; it loves chieftains; it develops a people that crave strong and showy governments to support and plan for them. The Anglo-Saxon race belongs to the great German family, and is a fair exponent of its peculiarities. The Anglo-Saxon carries self-government and self-development with him wherever he goes.

He has popular *government* and popular *industry;* for the effects of a generous civil liberty are not seen a whit more plain in the good order, in the intelligence, and in the virtue of a self-governing people, than in their amazing enterprise and the scope and power of their creative industry. The power to create riches is just as much a part of the Anglo-Saxon virtues as the power to create good order and social safety. The things required for prosperous labor, prosperous manufactures, and prosperous commerce are three. First, liberty; second, liberty; third, liberty. (Hear, hear!) Though these are not merely the same liberty, as I shall show you. First, there must be liberty to follow those laws of business which experience has developed, without imposts or restrictions or governmental intrusions. Business simply wants to be let alone. (Hear, hear!) Then, secondly, there must be liberty to distribute and exchange products of industry in any market without burdensome tariffs, without imposts, and without vexatious regulations. There must be these two liberties—liberty to create wealth, as the makers of it think best, according to the light and experience which business has given them; and then liberty to distribute what they have created without unnecessary vexatious burdens. The comprehensive law of the ideal industrial condition of the world is free manufacture and free trade. (Hear, hear! A voice: "The Morrill tariff." Another voice: "Monroe.") I have said there were three elements of liberty. The third is the necessity of an intelligent and free race of customers. There must be freedom among producers; there must be freedom among the distributors; there must be freedom among the customers. It may not have occurred to you that it makes any difference what one's customers are, but it does in all regular and prolonged business. The condition of the customer determines how much he will buy, determines of what sort he will buy. Poor and ignorant people buy little and that of the poorest kind. The richest and the intelligent, having the more means to buy, buy the most, and always buy the best. Here, then, are the three liberties: liberty of the producer, liberty of the distributor, and liberty of the consumer. The first two need no discussion; they have been long thoroughly and brilliantly illustrated by the political economists of Great Britain and by her eminent statesmen; but it seems to me that enough attention has not been directed to the third; and, with your patience, I will dwell upon that for a moment, before proceeding to other topics.

It is a necessity of every manufacturing and commercial people that their customers should be very wealthy and intelligent. Let us put the subject before you in the familiar light of your own local experience. To whom do the tradesmen of Liverpool sell the most goods at the highest profit? To the ignorant and poor, or to the educated and prosperous? (A voice: "To the Southerners." Laughter.) The poor man buys simply for his body; he buys food, he buys clothing, he buys fuel, he buys lodging. His rule is to buy the least and the cheapest that he can. He goes to the store as seldom as he can; he brings away as little as he can; and he buys for the least he can. (Much laughter.) Poverty is not a misfortune to the poor only who suffer it, but it is more or less a misfortune to all with whom he deals. On the other hand, a man well off—how is it with him? He buys in far greater quantity. He can afford to do it; he has the money to pay for it. He buys in far greater variety, because he seeks to gratify not merely physical wants, but also mental wants. He buys for the satisfaction of sentiment and taste, as well as of sense. He buys silk, wool, flax, cotton; he buys all metals—iron, silver, gold, platinum; in short, he buys for all necessities and all substances. But that is not all. He buys a better quality of goods. He buys richer silks, finer cottons, higher grained wools. Now a rich silk means so much skill and care of somebody's that has been expended upon it to make it finer and richer; and so of cotton and so of wool. That is, the price of the finer goods runs back to the very beginning, and remunerates the workman as well as the merchant. Now, the whole laboring community is as much interested and profited as the mere merchant, in this buying and selling of the higher grades in the greater varieties and quantities. The law of price is the skill; and the amount of skill expended in the work is as much for the market as are the goods. A man comes to market and says: "I have a pair of hands," and he obtains the lowest wages. Another man comes and says: "I have something more than a pair of hands; I have truth and fidelity." He gets a higher price. Another man comes and says: "I have something more; I have hands, and strength, and fidelity, and skill." He gets more than either of the others. The next man comes and says: "I have got hands, and strength, and skill, and fidelity; but my hands work more than that. They know how to create things for the fancy, for the affections, for the moral sentiments"; and he gets more than any of the others. The last man comes and says: "I have all these qualities, and have them so highly that it is a peculiar genius"; and genius carries the whole market and gets the highest price. (Loud applause.) So that both the work-man and the merchant are profited by having purchasers that demand quality, variety, and quantity. Now, if this be so in the town or the city, it can only be so because it is a law. This is the specific development of a general or universal law, and therefore we should expect to find it as true of a nation as of a city like Liverpool. I know that it is so, and you know that it is true of all the world; and it is just as important to have customers educated, intelligent, moral, and rich out of Liverpool as it is in Liverpool. (Applause.) They are able to buy; they want variety, they want the very best; and those are the customers you want. That nation is the best customer that is freest, because freedom works prosperity, industry, and wealth. Great Britain, then, aside from moral considerations, has a direct commercial and pecuniary interest in the liberty, civilization, and wealth of every nation on the globe. (Loud applause.) You also have an interest in this, because you are a moral and religious people. ("Oh, oh!" laughter and applause.) You desire it from the highest motives; and godliness is profitable in all things, having the promise of the life that now is, as well as of that which is to come; but if there were no hereafter, and if man had no progress in this life, and if there were no question of civilization at all, it would be worth your while to protect civilization and liberty, merely as a commercial speculation. To evangelize has more than a moral and religious import—it comes back to temporal relations. Wherever a nation that is crushed, cramped, degraded under despotism is struggling to be free, you, Leeds, Sheffield, Manchester, Paisley, all have an interest that that nation should be free. When depressed and backward people demand that they may have a chance to rise—Hungary, Italy, Poland—it is a duty for humanity's sake, it is a duty for the highest moral motives, to sympathize with them;

but besides all these there is a material and an interested reason why you should sympathize with them. Pounds and pence join with conscience and with honor in this design. Now, Great Britain's chief want is—what?

They have said that your chief want is cotton. I deny it. Your chief want is consumers. (Applause and hisses.) You have got skill, you have got capital, and you have got machinery enough to manufacture goods for the whole population of the globe. You could turn out fourfold as much as you do, if you only had the market to sell in. It is not so much the want, therefore, of fabric, though there may be a temporary obstruction of it; but the principal and increasing want—increasing from year to year—is, where shall we find men to buy what we can manufacture so fast? (Interruption, and a voice, "The Morrill tariff," and applause.) Before the American war broke out, your warehouses were loaded with goods that you could not sell. (Applause and hisses.) You had over-manufactured; what is the meaning of over-manufacturing but this: that you had skill, capital, machinery, to create faster than you had customers to take goods off your hands? And you know that rich as Great Britain is, vast as are her manufactures, if she could have fourfold the present demand, she could make fourfold riches to-morrow; and every political economist will tell you that your want is not cotton primarily, but customers. Therefore, the doctrine, how to make customers, is a great deal more important to Great Britain than the doctrine how to raise cotton. It is to that doctrine I ask from you, business men, practical men, men of fact, sagacious Englishmen—to that point I ask a moment's attention. (Shouts of "Oh, oh!" hisses, and applause.) There are no more continents to be discovered. (Hear, hear!) The market of the future must be found—how? There is very little hope of any more demand being created by new fields. If you are to have a better market there must be some kind of process invented to make the old fields better. (A voice, "Tell us something new," shouts of order, and interruption.) Let us look at it, then. You must civilize the world in order to make a better class of purchasers. (Interruption.)

If you were to press Italy down again under the feet of despotism, Italy, discouraged, could draw but very few supplies from you. But give her liberty, kindle schools throughout her valleys, spur her industry, make treaties with her by which she can exchange her wine, and her oil, and her silk for your manufactured goods; and for every effort that you make in that direction there will come back profit to you by increased traffic with her. (Loud applause.) If Hungary asks to be an unshackled nation— if by freedom she will rise in virtue and intelligence, then by freedom she will acquire a more multifarious industry, which she will be willing to exchange for your manufactures. Her liberty is to be found—where? You will find it in the Word of God, you will find it in the code of history; but you will also find it in the Price Current (Hear, hear!); and every free nation, every civilized people—every people that rises from barbarism to industry and intelligence, becomes a better customer.

A savage is a man of one story, and that one story a cellar. When a man begins to be civilized, he raises another story. When you Christianize and civilize the man, you put story upon story, for you develop faculty after faculty; and you have to supply every story with your productions. The savage is a man one story deep; the civilized man is thirty stories deep. (Applause.) Now, if you go to a lodging house, where there are three or four men, your sales to them may, no doubt, be worth something; but if you go to a lodging house like some of those which I saw in Edinburgh, which seemed to contain about twenty stories ("Oh, oh!" and interruption), every story of which is full, and all who occupy buy of you—which is the better customer, the man who is drawn out, or the man who is pinched up? (Laughter.) Now, there is in this a great and sound principle of economy. ("Yah, yah!" from the passage outside the hall, and loud laughter.) If the South should be rendered independent—(at this juncture mingled cheering and hissing became immense; half the audience rose to their feet, waving hats and handkerchiefs, and in every part of the hall there was the greatest commotion and uproar.) You have had your turn now; now let me have mine again. (Loud applause and laughter.) It is a little inconvenient to talk against the wind; but after all, if you will just keep good-natured—I am not going to lose my temper; will you watch yours? (Applause.) Besides all that, it rests me, and gives me a chance, you know, to get my breath. (Applause and hisses.) And I think that the bark of those men is worse than their bite. They do not mean any harm—they don't know any better. (Loud laughter, applause, hisses, and continued uproar.) I was saying, when these responses broke in, that it was worth our while to consider both alternatives. What will be the result if this present struggle shall eventuate in the separation of America, and making the South—(loud applause, hisses, hooting and cries of "Bravo!")—a slave Territory exclusively—(cries of "No, no!" and laughter)—and the

North a free territory—what will be the final result? You
will lay the foundation for carrying the slave population
clear through to the Pacific Ocean. This is the first step.
There is not a man that has been a leader of the South
any time within these twenty years that has not had this
for a plan. It was for this that Texas was invaded, first
by colonists, next by marauders, until it was wrested from
Mexico. It was for this that they engaged in the Mexican
War itself, by which the vast territory reaching to the Pacific was added to the Union. Never for a moment have
they given up the plan of spreading the American institutions, as they call them, straight through toward the
West, until the slave, who has washed his feet in the Atlantic, shall be carried to wash them in the Pacific. (Cries
of "Question," and uproar.) There! I have got that state
ment out, and you cannot put it back. (Laughter and applause.) Now, let us consider the prospect. If the South
becomes a slave empire, what relation will it have to you
as a customer? (A voice: "Or any other man." Laughter.) It would be an empire of 12,000,000 of people. Now,
of these, 8,000,000 are white, and 4,000,000 are black.
(A voice: "How many have you got?" Applause and
laughter. Another voice: "Free your own slaves.") Consider that one-third of the whole are the miserably poor,
unbuying blacks. (Cries of "No, no!" "Yes, yes!" and
interruption.) You do not manufacture much for them.
(Hisses, "Oh!" "No.") You have not got machinery
coarse enough. (Laughter, and "No.") Your labor is
too skilled by far to manufacture bagging and linsey-
woolsey. (A Southerner: "We are going to free them,
every one.") Then you and I agree exactly. (Laughter.)
One other third consists of a poor, unskilled, degraded

white population; and the remaining one-third, which is a large allowance, we will say, intelligent and rich.

Now here are twelve million of people, and only one-third of them are customers that can afford to buy the kind of goods that you bring to market. (Interruption and uproar.) My friends, I saw a man once, who was a little late at a railway station, chase an express train. He did not catch it. (Laughter.) If you are going to stop this meeting, you have got to stop it before I speak; for after I have got the things out, you may chase as long as you please—you would not catch them. (Laughter and interruption.) But there is luck in leisure; I'm going to take it easy. (Laughter.) Two-thirds of the population of the Southern States to-day are non-purchasers of English goods. (A voice: "No, they are not"; "No, no!" and uproar.) Now you must recollect another fact—namely, that this is going on clear through to the Pacific Ocean; and if by sympathy or help you establish a slave empire, you sagacious Britons—("Oh, oh!" and hooting)—if you like it better, then, I will leave the adjective out—(Laughter, Hear! and applause)—are busy in favoring the establishment of an empire from ocean to ocean that should have fewest customers and the largest non-buying population. (Applause, "No, no!" A voice: "I thought it was the happy people that populated fastest.")

Now, what can England make for the poor white population of such a future empire, and for her slave population? What carpets, what linens, what cottons can you sell them? What machines, what looking-glasses, what combs, what leather, what books, what pictures, what engravings? (A voice: "We'll sell them ships.") You may sell ships to a few, but what ships can you sell to two-thirds of the population of poor whites and blacks? (Applause.) A little bagging and a little linsey-woolsey, a few whips and manacles, are all that you can sell for the slave. (Great applause and uproar.) This very day, in the slave States of America there are eight millions out of twelye millions that are not and cannot be your customers from the very laws of trade. (A voice: "Then how are they clothed?" and interruption.) . . .

But I know that you say, you cannot help sympathizing with a gallant people. (Hear, hear!) They are the weaker people, the minority; and you cannot help going with the minority who are struggling for their rights against the majority. Nothing could be more generous, when a weak party stands for its own legitimate right against imperious pride and power, than to sympathize with the weak. But who ever sympathized with a weak thief, because three constables had got hold of him? (Hear, hear!) And yet the one thief in three policemen's hands is the weaker party. I suppose you would sympathize with him. (Hear, hear! laughter and applause.) Why, when that infamous king of Naples, Bomba, was driven into Gaeta by Garibaldi with his immortal band of patriots, and Cavour sent against him the army of Northern Italy, who was the weaker party then? The tyrant and his minions; and the majority was with the noble Italian patriots, struggling for liberty. I never heard that Old England sent deputations to King Bomba, and yet his troops resisted bravely there. (Laughter and interruption.) To-day the majority of the people of Rome is with Italy. Nothing but French bayonets keep her from going back to the kingdom of Italy, to which she belongs. Do you sympathize with the minority in Rome or the majority in Italy? (A voice: "With Italy.") To-day the South is the minority in America, and they are fighting for *independence!* For what? (Uproar. A voice: "Three cheers for independence!" and hisses.) I could wish so much bravery had a better cause, and that so much self-denial had been less deluded; that the poisonous and venomous doctrine of State rights might have been kept aloof; that so many gallant spirits, such as Jackson, might still have lived. (Great applause and loud cheers, again and again renewed.) The force of these facts, historical and incontrovertible, cannot be broken, except by diverting attention by an attack upon the North. It is said that the North is fighting for Union, and not for emancipation. The North is fighting for Union, for that insures emancipation. (Loud cheers, "Oh, oh!" "No, no!" and cheers.) A great many men say to ministers of the Gospel: "You pretend to be preaching and working for the love of the people. Why, you are all the time preaching for the sake of the Church." What does the minister say? "It is by means of the Church that we help the people," and when men say that we are fighting for the Union, I too say we are fighting for the Union. (Hear, hear! and a voice: "That's right.") But the motive determines the value; and why are we fighting for the Union? Because we never shall forget the testimony of our enemies. They have gone off declaring that the Union in the hands of the North was fatal to slavery. (Loud applause.) There is testimony in court for you. (A voice: "See that," and laughter.) . . .

In the first place I am ashamed to confess that such was the thoughtlessness—(interruption)—such was the stupor of the North—(renewed interruption)—you will get a word at a time; to-morrow will let folks see what it is you don't want to hear—that for a period of twenty-five years she went to sleep, and permitted herself to be drugged and poisoned with the Southern prejudice against black men. (Applause and uproar.) The evil was made worse, because, when any object whatever has caused anger between political parties, a political animosity arises against that object, no matter how innocent in itself; no matter what were the original influences which excited the quarrel. Thus the colored man has been the football between the two parties in the North, and has suffered accordingly. I confess it to my shame. But I am speaking now on my own ground, for I began twenty-five years ago, with a small party, to combat the unjust dislike of the colored man. (Loud applause, dissension, and uproar. The interruption at this point became so violent that the friends of Mr. Beecher throughout the hall rose to their feet, waving hats and handkerchiefs, and renewing their shouts of applause. The interruption lasted some minutes.) Well, I have lived to see a total revolution in the Northern feeling—I stand here to bear solemn witness of that. It is not my opinion; it is my knowledge. (Great uproar.) Those men who undertook to stand up for the rights of all men—black as well as white—have increased in number; and now what party in the North represents those men that resist the evil prejudices of past years? The Republicans are that party. (Loud applause.) And who are those men in the North that have oppressed the negro? They are the Peace Democrats; and the prejudice for which in England you are attempting to punish me, is a prejudice raised by the men who have opposed me all my life. These pro-slavery Democrats abused the negro. I defended him, and they mobbed me for doing it. Oh, justice! (Loud laughter, applause, and hisses.) This is as if a man should commit an assault, maim and wound a neighbor, and a surgeon being called in should begin to dress his wounds, and by and by a policeman should come and collar the surgeon and haul him off to prison on account of the wounds which he was healing. Now, I told you I would not flinch from anything. I am going to read you some questions that were sent after me from Glasgow, purporting to be from a workingman. (Great interruption.) If those pro-slavery interrupters think they will tire me out, they will do more than eight millions in America could. (Applause and renewed interruption.) I was reading a question on your side too. "Is it not a fact that in most of the Northern States laws exist precluding negroes from equal civil and political rights with the whites? That in the State of New York the negro has to be the possessor of at least two hundred and fifty dollars' worth of property to entitle him to the privileges of a white citizen? That in some of the Northern States the colored man, whether bond or free, is by law excluded altogether, and not suffered to enter the State limits, under severe penalties? and is not Mr. Lincoln's own State one of them? and in view of the fact that the $20,000,000 compensation which was promised to Missouri in aid of emancipation was defeated in the last Congress (the strongest Republican Congress that ever assembled), what has the North done toward emancipation?" Now, then, there's a dose for you. (A voice: "Answer it.") And I will address myself to the answering of it. And first, the bill for emancipation in Missouri, to which this money was denied, was a bill which was drawn by what we call "log-rollers," who inserted in it an enormously disproportioned price for the slaves. The Republicans offered to give them $10,000,000 for the slaves in Missouri, and they outvoted it because they could not get $12,000,000.

Already half the slave population had been "run" down South, and yet they came up to Congress to get $12,000,000 for what was not worth ten millions, nor even eight millions. Now as to those States that had passed "black" laws, as we call them; they are filled with Southern emigrants. The southern parts of Ohio, the southern part of Indiana, where I myself lived for years, and which I knew like a book, the southern part of Illinois, where Mr. Lincoln lives—(great uproar)—these parts are largely settled by emigrants from Kentucky, Tennessee, Georgia, Virginia, and North Carolina, and it was their vote, or the Northern votes pandering for political reasons to theirs, that passed in those States the infamous "black" laws; and the Republicans in these States have a record, clean and white, as having opposed these laws in every instance as "infamous." Now as to the State of New York; it is asked whether a negro is not obliged to have a certain freehold property, or a certain amount of property, before he can vote. It is so still in North Carolina and Rhode Island for *white* folks-- it is so in New York State. (Mr. Beecher's voice slight.y failed him here, and he was interrupted by a person who tried to imitate him. Cries of "Shame!" and "Turn him out!") I am not undertaking to say that these faults of the North, which were brought upon them by the bad example and influence of the South, are all cured; but I do say that they are in *prócess* of cure which promises, if unimpeded by foreign influence, to make all such odious distinctions vanish.

There is another fact that I wish to allude to—not for the sake of reproach or blame, but by way of claiming your more lenient consideration—and that is, that slavery was entailed upon us by your action. (Hear, hear!) Against the earnest protests of the colonists the then government of Great Britain—I will concede not knowing what were the mischiefs—ignorantly, but in point of fact, forced slave traffic on the unwilling colonists. (Great uproar, in the midst of which one individual was lifted up and carried out of the room amid cheers and hisses.)

The Chairman—If you would only sit down no disturbance would take place.

The disturbance having subsided, Mr. Beecher said:

I was going to ask you, suppose a child is born with hereditary disease; suppose this disease was entailed upon him by parents who had contracted it by their own misconduct, would it be fair that those parents that had brought into the world the diseased child, should rail at that child because it was diseased.   ("No, no!")   Would not the child have a right to turn round and say: "Father, it was your fault that I had it, and you ought to be pleased to be patient with my deficiencies."   (Applause and hisses, and cries of "Order!"   Great interruption and great disturbance here took place on the right of the platform; and the chairman said that if the persons around the unfortunate individual who had caused the disturbance would allow him to speak alone, but not assist him in making the disturbance, it might soon be put an end to.   The interruption continued until another person was carried out of the hall.)   Mr. Beecher continued: I do not ask that you should justify slavery in us, because it was wrong in you two hundred years ago; but having ignorantly been the means of fixing it upon us, now that we are struggling with mortal struggles to free ourselves from it, we have a right to your tolerance, your patience, and charitable constructions.

No man can unveil the future; no man can tell what

revolutions are about to break upon the world; no man
can tell what destiny belongs to France, nor to any of the
European powers; but one thing is certain, that in the exigencies of the future there will be combinations and recom-
binations, and that those nations that are of the same faith,
the same blood, and the same substantial interests, ought
not to be alienated from each other, but ought to stand
together. (Immense cheering and hisses.) I do not say
that you ought not to be in the most friendly alliance with
France or with Germany; but I do say that your own children, the offspring of England, ought to be nearer to you
than any people of strange tongue. (A voice: "Degenerate
sons," applause and hisses; another voice: "What about
the 'Trent'?") If there had been any feelings of bitterness
in America, let me tell you that they had been excited,
rightly or wrongly, under the impression that Great Britain
was going to intervence between us and our own lawful
struggle. (A voice—"No!" and applause.) With the evidence that there is no such intention all bitter feelings will
pass away. (Applause.) We do not agree with the recent
doctrine of neutrality as a question of law. But it is past,
and we are not disposed to raise that question. We accept
it now as a fact, and we say that the utterance of Lord
Russell at Blairgowrie—(Applause, hisses, and a voice:
"What about Lord Brougham?")—together with the declaration of the government in stopping war-steamers here—
(great uproar, and applause)—has gone far toward quieting
every fear and removing every apprehension from our
minds. (Uproar and shouts of applause.) And now in
the future it is the work of every good man and patriot
not to create divisions, but to do the things that will make
for peace. ("Oh, oh!" and laughter.) On our part it shall

be done. (Applause and hisses, and "No, no!") On your part it ought to be done; and when in any of the convulsions that come upon the world, Great Britain finds herself struggling single-handed against the gigantic powers that spread oppression and darkness—(applause, hisses, and uproar)—there ought to be such cordiality that she can turn and say to her first-born and most illustrious child, "Come!" (Hear, hear! applause, tremendous cheers and uproar.) I will not say that England cannot again, as hitherto, single-handed manage any power—(applause and uproar)—but I will say that England and America together for religion and liberty—(A voice: "Soap, soap," uproar, and great applause)—are a match for the world. (Applause; a voice: "They don't want any more soft soap.") Now, gentlemen and ladies—(A voice: "Sam Slick"; and another voice: "Ladies and gentlemen, if you please")—when I came I was asked whether I would answer questions, and I very readily consented to do so, as I had in other places; but I will tell you it was because I expected to have the opportunity of speaking with some sort of ease and quiet. (A voice: "So you have.") I have for an hour and a half spoken against a storm—(Hear, hear!)—and you yourselves are witnesses that, by the interruption, I have been obliged to strive with my voice, so that I no longer have the power to control this assembly. (Applause.) And although I am in spirit perfectly willing to answer any question, and more than glad of the chance, yet I am by this very unnecessary opposition to-night incapacitated physically from doing it. Ladies and gentlemen, I bid you good-evening.

EFFECT OF THE DEATH OF LINCOLN

DELIVERED IN BROOKLYN, APRIL 16, 1865

AGAIN a great leader of the people has passed through toil, sorrow, battle, and war, and come near to the promised land of peace, into which he might not pass over. Who shall recount our martyr's sufferings for this people? Since the November of 1860, his horizon has been black with storms. By day and by night, he trod a way of danger and darkness. On his shoulders rested a government dearer to him than his own life. At its integrity millions of men were striking at home. Upon this government foreign eyes lowered. It stood like a lone island in a sea full of storms, and every tide and wave seemed eager to devour it. Upon thousands of hearts great sorrows and anxieties have rested, but not on one such, and in such measure, as upon that simple, truthful, noble soul, our faithful and sainted Lincoln. Never rising to the enthusiasm of more impassioned natures in hours of hope, and never sinking with the mercurial in hours of defeat to the depths of despondency, he held on with unmovable patience and fortitude, putting caution against hope, that it might not be premature, and hope against caution, that it might not yield to dread and danger. He wrestled ceaselessly, through four black and dreadful purgatorial years, wherein God was cleansing the sin of his people as by fire.

At last, the watcher beheld the gray dawn for the country. The mountains began to give forth their forms from out the darkness, and the East came rushing toward us with arms full of joy for all our sorrows. Then it was for him to be glad exceedingly that had sorrowed immeasurably. Peace could bring to no other heart such joy, such rest, such honor, such trust, such gratitude. But he looked upon it as Moses looked upon the promised land. Then the wail of a nation proclaimed that he had gone from among us. Not thine the sorrow, but ours, sainted soul. Thou hast, indeed, entered the promised land, while we are yet on the march. To us remains the rocking of the deep, the storm upon the land, days of duty and nights of watching; but thou art sphered high above all darkness and fear, beyond all sorrow and weariness. Rest, O weary heart! Rejoice exceedingly, thou that hast enough suffered! Thou hast beheld him who invisibly led thee in this great wilderness. Thou standest among the elect. Around thee are the royal men that have ennobled human life in every age. Kingly art thou, with glory on thy brow as a diadem. And joy is upon thee for evermore. Over all this land, over all the little cloud of years that now from thine infinite horizon moves back as a speck, thou art lifted up as high as the star is above the clouds that hide us, but never reach it. In the goodly company of Mount Zion thou shalt find that rest which thou hast sorrowing sought in vain; and thy name, an everlasting name in heaven, shall flourish in fragrance and beauty as long as men shall last upon the earth, or hearts remain, to revere truth, fidelity, and goodness.

Never did two such orbs of experience meet in one hemisphere, as the joy and the sorrow of the same week in this land. The joy was as sudden as if no man had expected it, and as entrancing as if it had fallen a sphere from heaven. It rose up over sobriety, and swept business from its moorings, and ran down through the land in irresistible course. Men embraced each other in brotherhood that were strangers in the flesh. They sang, or prayed, or, deeper yet, many could only think thanksgiving and weep gladness. That peace was sure; that government was firmer than ever; that the land was cleansed of plague; that the ages were opening to our footsteps, and we were to begin a march of blessings; that blood was stanched, and scowling enmities were sinking like storms beneath the horizon; that the dear fatherland, nothing lost, much gained, was to rise up in unexampled honor among the nations of the earth—these thoughts, and that indistinguishable throng of fancies, and hopes, and desires, and yearnings, that filled the soul with tremblings like the heated air of midsummer days—all these kindled up such a surge of joy as no words may describe.

In one hour joy lay without a pulse, without a gleam or breath. A sorrow came that swept through the land as huge storms sweep through the forest and field, rolling thunder along the sky, dishevelling the flowers, daunting every singer in thicket or forest, and pouring blackness and darkness across the land and up the mountains. Did ever so many hearts, in so brief a time, touch two such boundless feelings? It was the uttermost of joy; it was the uttermost of sorrow—noon and midnight, without a space between.

The blow brought not a sharp pang. It was so terrible that at first it stunned sensibility. Citizens were like men awakened at midnight by an earthquake and bewildered to find everything that they were accustomed to trust wavering and falling. The very earth was no longer solid. The first feeling was the least. Men waited to get straight to feel. They wandered in the streets as if groping after some impending dread, or undeveloped sorrow, or some one to tell them what ailed them. They met each other as if each would ask the other, "Am I awake, or do I dream?" There was a piteous helplessness. Strong men bowed down and wept. Other and common griefs belonged to some one in chief; this belonged to all. It was each and every man's. Every virtuous household in the land felt as if its first-born were gone. Men were bereaved and walked for days as if a corpse lay unburied in their dwellings. There was nothing else to think of. They could speak of nothing but that; and yet of that they could speak only falteringly. All business was laid aside. Pleasure forgot to smile. The city for nearly a week ceased to roar. The great Leviathan lay down, and was still. Even avarice stood still, and greed was strangely moved to generous sympathy and universal sorrow. Rear to his name monuments, found charitable institutions, and write his name above their lintels; but no monument will ever equal the universal, spontaneous, and sublime sorrow that in a moment swept down lines and parties, and covered up animosities, and in an hour brought a divided people into unity of grief and indivisible fellowship of anguish. . . .

This nation has dissolved—but in tears only. It stands four-square, more solid to-day than any pyramid in Egypt. This people are neither wasted, nor daunted, nor disordered. Men hate slavery and love liberty with stronger hate and love to-day than ever before. The government is not weakened, it is made stronger. How naturally and easily were the ranks closed! Another steps forward, in the hour that the one fell, to take his place and his mantle; and I avow my belief that he will be found a man true to every instinct of liberty; true to the whole trust that is reposed in him; vigilant of the Constitution; careful of the laws; wise for liberty, in that he himself, through his life, has known what it was to suffer from the stings of slavery, and to prize liberty from bitter personal experiences.

Where could the head of government in any monarchy be smitten down by the hand of an assassin, and the funds not quiver or fall one-half of one per cent? After a long period of national disturbance, after four years of drastic war, after tremendous drafts on the resources of the country, in the height and top of our burdens, the heart of this people is such that now, when the head of government is stricken down, the public funds do not waver, but stand as the granite ribs in our mountains.

Republican institutions have been vindicated in this experience as they never were before; and the whole history of the last four years, rounded up by this cruel stroke, seems, in the providence of God, to have been clothed, now, with an illustration, with a sympathy, with an aptness, and with a significance, such as we never could have expected nor imagined. God, I think, has said, by the voice of this event, to all nations of the earth, "Republican liberty, based upon true Christianity, is firm as the foundation of the globe."

Even he who now sleeps has, by this event, been clothed with new influence. Dead, he speaks to men who now willingly hear what before they refused to listen to. Now his simple and weighty words will be gathered like those of Washington, and your children and your children's children shall be taught to ponder the simplicity and deep wisdom of utterances which, in their time, passed, in party heat, as idle words. Men will receive a new impulse of patriotism for his sake and will guard with zeal the whole country which he loved so well. I swear you, on the altar

10 of his memory, to be more faithful to the country for which he has perished. They will, as they follow his hearse, swear a new hatred to that slavery against which he warred, and which, in vanquishing him, has made him a martyr and a conqueror. I swear you, by the memory of this martyr, to hate slavery with an unappeasable hatred. They will admire and imitate the firmness of this man, his inflexible conscience for the right, and yet his gentleness, as tender as a woman's, his moderation of spirit, which not all the heat of party could inflame, nor all the jars and disturbances of his country shake out of place. I swear you to an emulation of his justice, his moderation, and his mercy.

You I can comfort; but how can I speak to that twilight million to whom his name was as the name of an angel of God? There will be wailing in places which no minister shall be able to reach. When in hovel and in cot, in wood and in wilderness, in the field throughout the South, the dusky children, who looked upon him as that Moses whom God sent before them to lead them out of the land of bondage, learn that he has fallen, who shall comfort them? O, thou Shepherd of Israel, that didst comfort thy people of old, to thy care we commit the helpless, the long-wronged, and grieved.

And now the martyr is moving in triumphal march, mightier than when alive. The nation rises up at every stage of his coming. Cities and States are his pallbearers, and the cannon beats the hours with solemn progression. Dead, dead, dead, he yet speaketh. Is Washington dead? Is Hampden dead? Is David dead? Is any man that ever was fit to live dead? Disenthralled of flesh, and risen in the unobstructed sphere where passion never comes, he begins his illimitable work. His life now is grafted upon the infinite, and will be fruitful as no earthly life can be. Pass on, thou that hast overcome. Your sorrows, O people, are his peace. Your bells and bands and muffled drums sound triumph in his ear. Wail and weep here; God made it echo joy and triumph there. Pass on.

Four years ago, O Illinois, we took from your midst an untried man and from among the people. We return him to you a mighty conqueror. Not thine any more, but the nation's; not ours, but the world's. Give him place, O ye prairies. In the midst of this great continent his dust shall rest, a sacred treasure to myriads who shall pilgrim to that shrine to kindle anew their zeal and patriotism. Ye winds that move over the mighty places of the West, chant his requiem. Ye people, behold a martyr whose blood, as so many articulate words, pleads for fidelity, for law, for liberty.

ON MAN AND HIS INSTITUTIONS

DELIVERED IN BOSTON, MAY 28, 1856

MAN is born, by God's ordaining power, with a separate nature, with special personal powers, which he cannot alienate and which none can take from him. His reason is his own; his affections are his own; his moral nature is his own. Into that individuality he is born, upon it he lives, on account of it God holds him accountable. He dies in his own personality, and goes alone, by himself, to the judgment. God respects and maintains the individuality of man and will not let society rub it out. He cannot, like a chemical agent, go out of one nature, by combination, into another. Like a thread, he may go to the composition of a fabric, but comes out of the loom of society a single, continuous, perfect thread, retaining its own nature and color through all the figures of the pattern.

Man combines in himself harmoniously two apparently incompatible elements, perfect independence and perfect cohesion with others. He is at the same time sharply individual and thoroughly composite. He is at once solitary and social, a perfect single being, and yet organized as an element into a community of beings.

It is the individuality of man that is the source of his power; and the strength and power of the individual is the secret of the strength of society itself. A state of society which finds it necessary to repress the individual, to prevent his development, to curtail and absorb him, so that society is greater than its citizens, the state more important than the men that live in it, is at variance with the designs of God and the nature of man. And that society is the strongest, the most normal and healthy, which leaves its individual citizens their utmost liberty, their utmost growth, and their fullest strength.

Nothing else on earth is so various in endowment, so far-reaching in capacity, so wonderful in development, so complex in relations, as man. All the stores of art; all the fruits of human endeavor; all temples and sculpture; all pictures and embellishments; all treasures of skill and books; all cities and inventions; all laws, philosophies, and ordinances,— are not to be compared for value with any one single man that uses them and is yet superior to them. They are but servants. He alone is master.

The tree is yet more than the apple which drops from it. Man is of more worth than all the effects which he produces. Next to God, man is God! And it should be so. He is the son of God.

But this original power of individual man needs means of exercising itself. God works by thinking. Effects follow volitions. But between human volitions and effects there must be some intermediate instrument. Men pour forth their power through material instrumentalities. Society is the aggregate of all those instruments by which individuals exert their separate personalities.

A man without institutions is a fountain without an egress; like a soul without bodily members to work with; like a body without a hand, or a hand without fingers.

Man is the elementary power and the supreme value. But for his own greatest good he requires institutions; they are the means by which man acts and without which he never could develop himself or make use of his power were it developed.

While the first of all civic truths is the liberty, power, and individuality of man, the second truth must be the necessity of the civil state, of laws, of wise institutions.

And it must never be forgotten that, indispensable as they are, institutions and society can give nothing to man. They only afford him the means of using that which belongs to him by the right of creation. Man is the master of himself — society his indispensable servant; this is the one truth in its two elements.

Where society interferes with individual rights and limits the action of citizens, it is not ever because society requires something which is inconsistent with the liberty of the individual, but because the individual requires for his full development and growth, often, that one part of his nature should be held in that the other parts may grow. Men's passions must be kept back to let their affections grow. Man's secular nature must not be absorbing and tyrannical, refusing to give scope and growth-room to his moral nature. All penal restrictions in society are, in the root philosophy, not aimed at the repression of power in the individual, but rather toward his augmentation, his greater power. They are, in their large effects, toward liberty and not away from it. No law, no institution, no society that diminishes the individual for the sake of making the whole strong, is sound.

The strength of society lies in the power and wide freedom of its citizens. The wisdom of an institution is not in what it gets from men, but in what it can do to express their powers, and serve them.

This distinction in favor of the liberty of men as against their own laws and institutions is fundamental. It is in this philosophy that governments are separated and characterized.

All monarchic governments claim that society is greater than man — the whole, than the individuals; that man's laws and institutions are greater and more sacred than he is.

All governments of true liberty must recognize in man the source of power and sacredness. Man is greater than law. Man is holier than government. Man is the master of law. Institutions are the servants of men. One doctrine leads to tyranny; the other leads to liberty.

With these guards and explanations I proceed to develop the nature of institutions.

1. When, for the sake of greater force, several or many men come together to pursue a common end, they are styled an "association;" but if they bring together their means or instruments of working, and organize them in some material form, by investment or buildings, they grow to be an institution. An institution is, then, a principle organized into a material shape. It is an incarnated moral principle. It is a truth born into a body.

The name "institution," however, is select, being applied chiefly to organizations of intellectual or moral power.

If a man gather together his neighbors, that by speech he may exert a moral influence upon them, it is but a casual gathering; but if he erect a building; if provision is made for continual assemblies; if it is ordained that speakers shall be successively employed, that when one dies, his place shall be supplied by another,— then there is an "institution" of instruction.

If a kind heart, in teaching his own children, gather up also a few from among the ignorant, it is but a casual work. If, now, he add to this the element of continuance and the physical means of continuing, it becomes an institution of learning. A school is an everlasting schoolmaster. It is a device by which, when the first schoolmaster dies, he shall leave an artificial body which is to receive in succession the separate souls of unnumbered schoolmasters; and thus, by the metempsychosis of institutions, the children shall never be left without rule and ferule.

A mother, in caring for her own babes, is tenderly touched that in her neighborhood are babes that have no mother. She brings them to her nursery and is for the time a mother to them. But she must die, while orphans are always living somewhere. If maternal love can be embodied and made both constant and perpetual, then that incarnation of a mother's love is an institution. An orphan's institution is a body to which God gives the permission of never dying, by supplying new mothers' hearts to throb in it. The element of beauty makes art institutions. Mathematical truths make scientific institutions of various kinds.

An "institution," therefore, may be defined to be an artificial body animated by some principle for the sake of prolonging its influence through the successive lives of different individuals who administer it. It splices men's lives together and makes a bridge over the space between generations over which a truth may pass and travel on forever. It is artificial immortality.

It is this element of enduring that distinguishes "institution" from "association." By association and organization men gain power and scope; they grow widthwise. By institutions they gain continuance; they grow lengthwise. And thus we return to our first expression, that men increase their power, incarnating and organizing moral influences, so that there may be both latitude and longitude to their power.

Institutions are of two classes: those whose office it is to develop man's power; and those whose office it is to furnish to that developed power the machinery for activity.

The first are educational institutions; the others range from the bottom of society to the top, representing each grade of faculty in the human soul. They are industrial, commercial, social, and civil. They concentrate the scattered forces of individual men, apply them continuously, and perpetuate their existence through long periods.

Although our theme more especially regards educational institutions, yet we shall speak of all those which apply, as well as those which develop, individual force, in those respects in which they have a common nature.

The first want of society is the fulness, the liberty, the vivacity and freshness of its individual citizens. No state is permanently strong which absorbs the liberty of the individual into the body politic. If the state is the great value; if men are only bricks, separately worthless, and good only when laid in orderly rows and held by the cement of laws, then it will come to pass that in a little time men will begin to shrink, to dry up, to wither away. A state whose citizens are but the pabulum of the state will soon have nothing to feed on and will be no better than a pyramid enormously built for the pitiful purpose of holding dead men's dust through worthless ages. Men are the roots and leaves; society is the tree which they make. The trunk and branches are but the frame; the life lies in the extremities.

But individualism needs help. Men are stronger to conceive than to execute, and one man may devise what only a hundred can achieve. Common good requires association. This is the first step toward institution. Association is simply combination. It does not yet incarnate a principle so that it shall work by physical instruments and continue by its own enduring nature. Men are short-lived; they drop the thread before the pattern is half done. The shuttle moves slower and slower after sixty, and the loom stops often at half that number of years. How shall the threads be taken up again? What shall unite men to carry forward common enterprises? How shall the variableness of the individual, crippled by sickness sometimes, and sometimes swayed by casual attractions — wearied often, and sometimes quite cast down, daunted, or cajoled — pushed too hard, or held back too far by all the influences which throng life,— how shall we give continuity to the force of the individual, concentrate it, and carry it forward over long periods of time, except by supplementing one man by another, and, as the unequal expansion of metals works steadiness for the pendulum, so, by the inequality of dispositions, work a symmetrical whole for the individual? Setting a fresh man over against one man's weariness, a strong man over against his weakness, a wise man where he is unskilled, thus using one man to fill up another with, and by succession, as a kind of splicing, draw out the life of a design, through many men's natural lives, giving immortality to our purposes.

If, then, societies become dry and mechanical, falling into routine and losing new growths, when men are swallowed up in institutions; so, on the other hand, without the converging and perpetuating power of institutions, men are variable, scattering, discordant, lying along the shore of time like sand, rather than lifting up society, like a mountain promontory, the brow of whose cliff defies the wave and looks far out over the ocean, not afraid of its storms.

That institutions furnish coverts for power, that they may be turned against men and with subtile suction draw out his life-blood, that they may be made serviceable to the malignant passions as much as to the normal sentiments, cannot be doubted. Institutions are to be watched. We are to keep the most zealous guard over them. They are not only to be more trusted than men, but they are to be more vigorously suspected. They tend to deteriorate. They are easily and often turned against the very things for which they were created. The principle of which the institution was an incarnation dies within it and leaves but a husk or shell.

Thus institutions for benevolence become sinecures of selfishness; institutions to enable men safely to despise the world become hospitable mansions in which men entertain the world; institutions of religion become secular forces; institutions for the truth become the strongholds of error; institutions for exemption from temptation, for devout meditation, for purity, become the hot-beds of impurity, the very webs of indolence on which vices hang innumerable. This only teaches us that this world requires vigilance. The best things must be kept good.

Even if we would, we could not change the nature of

things. The malignant passions are instituted; they maintain their power by this wisdom. Selfishness is instituted in the world. Power is instituted; pride is instituted. All the evils of the soul are incarnated, organized, and connected, working into each other and perpetuating the reign of sin and crime on earth.

We cannot meet the drilled and disciplined battalions of evil with a scattering guerilla warfare. We must institute justice, truth, love, peace, purity.

Men are showers; associations are streams and reservoirs. Institutions are hydraulic and hydrostatic instruments by which to apply the liquid force. Men cannot live without institutions, and institutions cannot live vigorously without great, free men. They are not antagonistic; they are co-operative. They are like father and son. The parent protects the weakness of infancy and leads the son up to his manhood. That manhood, in turn, takes the weakness of age into its arms, and the old man is strong in the cradle of his son's bosom.

Without institutions men stand still. The wanderers of the desert, nomadic, and without institutions, stand now where Abraham stood four thousand years ago. Nothing is collected and transmitted from generation to generation. Each generation consumes all that it raises. There is no overplus — no transmission — nothing to transmit. Under such circumstances men are not ligneous, growing upon old growths, but herbaceous, planted every spring and dying every winter.

By their institutions men are a race; by institutions they outlive time. By these institutions they become ubiquitous; they redeem their souls from death, leaving them on earth to work after their forms decay. For men, living as isolated individuals, die; institutions catch their genius and live on, and are like trees whose leaves do fall every season, but trunk and bough carry forward the life of the tree through a hundred winters.

The first and universal danger of institutions is materialization. Men form institutions by giving to a principle a body, that it may walk or work among men. Once incarnated, the soul of the principle is apt to be neglected, and its body supremely cared for.

Churches are institutions designed to bring the spirit of religion to bear upon human life. Once created, they are perverted when the safety of the organization is more thought of than the power of its central principle. Christ may be imprisoned in Christian churches. There is death when the soul dies and the form only is left.

Denominations are tending perpetually to this mistake, maintaining ecclesiastical institutions by the repression of moral power. To keep the form of the institution they sacrifice the principle for which it was created. They quarrel about the candlestick till the candle falls and is extinguished. In this way an institution is transformed and resists the influences which it was erected to express. Laws may be employed to destroy that justice which they were intended to guard. Constitutions may come to protect the very evils they were made to exclude, and to destroy the very principle they were formed to cherish.

The transformation of institutions, by which they continue to express the life of the age, is like that of plants,—some plants, dying every year, replant themselves by new seed. Some continue by overlaying the past with a new growth, and give to every summer new branches and fresh leaves.

Those institutions that are nearest to human life, that feel its transforming power most, will quietly change as it changes, like skull to brain, and live on without revolution; while those that are fortified against change, and meant by donors to be forever the same, will in the end not only be changed, but undergo changes by the worst revolutionary processes.

The peculiar training of the East has been by institutions and toward them. Nowhere else have they been wiser, more in consonance with man's nature and true liberty. Nowhere else have men had so wisely blended the power of institutions with the everlasting variety and freshness of individuality. Nowhere else have institutions sprung so directly from the people, and in their whole influence served to augment and improve the people. We are what we are by reason of our institutions. Our civilization is characterized by them. Like all strong growths, it is infested with over-growths and water-sprouts. There is some danger that we shall institute too minutely and shall cease to act individually, spontaneously. Our people seek to organize everything. We organize for inquiry. We organize to answer. We organize to give advice. We organize for pleasure. We distribute tracts by system. We institute our charity until we are in danger of seeking to do nothing with the generous glow of personality, and everything in corporate character.

A pound of tea is to be sent to the poor. One way is for the heart that pitied to put a hand into the pocket, procure the tea, carry it with a hearty good will, shake hands with all the children, comfort the parents with hopeful words and sympathy, and go home a happier and a better man.

But our people tend to institute everything. A meeting is called and regularly formed. The constitution is adopted, officers with specified duties elected, a committee appointed, and the pound of tea is borne forth upon official hands and constitutionally delivered. Nobody is to be thanked; a committee gave it; a society sent it; but the human heart never thanks anything but men.

And yet this excess is the indication of the nature of our people, who are the most individually free on earth, but whose unbounded freedom is saved from license by this innate or inbred disposition to institute action. It is our mission to create institutions which shall express, but never control, the power of free citizens.

God has prepared a field. The West broods upon her nest for young States and leads them forth as an eagle its eaglets.

The special want of the new States is that which is the special abundance of the East. The want and the supply are happily proportioned. Civil institutions will spring forth without help. Industrial institutions will come forth under the strong suggestions of interest. Religious and educational institutions are those which are in need of fostering care. Colleges and theological institutions, with their wealth of library, cabinets, and apparatus, are a gift which includes all gifts. You never can convey to a people the details and fruits of civilization, but only the awakening, creative force of civilization. Civilization must go as yeast, not as bread. The only proper supply of a people's wants is to teach them how to supply themselves.

That which the West needs is not so much the educated men of the East, as the institutions by which to educate her own men. These are the suns that spread the East with harvests and fill the hands with bounty that were held out for supply.

Colleges stimulate society through every nerve. They give power to the liberal professions. They foster industry by giving intelligence to the citizen. Colleges civilize the hand and put brains into its palm. The hand of an intelligent freeman thinks more than the head of a slave. Give colleges, and you give necessarily everything which manhood can perform. You give that which arouses manhood within men — which inspires them to become inspirers. Institutions which develop men are the bosoms of God from which society draws its life.

There is an impression with many that our colleges and universities do but favor the children of the rich, and the wants of those who are to be scholars by profession, of literary men, and of those who are by the prescriptive right of certain callings, to walk above the level of common occupations, while the children of laborers, of artisans, of the mass of citizens, cannot experience their benefits.

Even if this were so, we know not why colleges should be discouraged. A man is a man, if his father was rich. The exclusion is not arbitrary and forceful, but arises simply from the inability or indisposition of men to meet the expenses of advantages which are equally proffered to all. Are not the apples that hang in the top of the tree the largest and ripest, because the children that look wistfully up are too small to reach and too weak to club them?

But it is not so. Our colleges do serve the necessities of society, from the top to the bottom, in a way which will require for its exposition some insight into the law by which influences in society work.

Society reaches up as a plant does, with successive joints from root to blossom. The mind itself affords the scale on which society deploys. The physical forms and passions are the mind's lowest faculties; and that part of society which in the main represents these forces is the lowest. The executive and selfish powers are next above, and that part of society which represents physical executive life stands next.

The domestic affections are yet higher in the mind; and those whose force in life is through these hold a corresponding rank. Then the moral sentiments are highest; and they that represent these hold the highest rank in a truly developed society.

Although this classification will not be found to be developed with such even edges in real life, it is because society is yet like an abused tree in a poor soil, unevenly grown, and cramped and dwarfed. But as a tree, however treated, is always seeking to follow out and express the image which God wrapped up in it, so society is forever swaying to the influence of an inward form and seeking to develop an expression of it, and the relative gradations and value of society are found in the scale of man's mind.

Thus society is not a level expanse of men without depth. It is a thing of vast depth and thickness. It is made up of innumerable little circles touching each other on every side, and ascending and descending from a middle point by successive layers and strata.

It is to be remarked, too, that the enlightenment and civilization of society increases the number of circles and increases the distance between the top and bottom. Growth in civilization is never toward simplicity, but toward complexity. Growth in the individual is never toward fewer wants, but toward more. There are as many appetites in the full man as there are parts and faculties in his being. Every power needs its own food. The same is true of society. And in its expansion there are formed new gradations, new circles, new strata, one above the other. The bottom of society may be steadily rising, and it may reach by-and-by where the top once stood, but the top will have gone up yet more rapidly, and the distance will be greater than ever between top and bottom. There will always be somebody found to be at the top. Nor is there a present likelihood that we shall not find enough to represent the bottom. And there will be as many intermediate circles as can be made up, not only by the number of human faculties in the soul, but by all their infinite combinations. These successive spheroids of society will be indistinguishable to the most subtile analysis, as drops of water are, while in the sea, inseparable one from another, as cells and cellules are in the living plant, which we know to be there, though the eye cannot detect nor the unaided hand separate.

It is more than a question of curiosity — What is the law of the circulation of influence between these parts and tissues of organized society? The answer must furnish the philosophy of education.

We shall mention only the working of influence in one direction, namely, from the top downward. To all superior influences there is a double way of working: first, by a general and diffused power over the whole of society, as the sun shines over the whole continent at once; and second, by a permeating and leaching way, as the rain which falls first upon the surface works down from particle to particle, from stratum to stratum.

The highest minds most powerfully affect the minds only second to them, and enter into and form a part of those which, in their turn, do not so much reflect the influence as exert an influence of their own upon those minds next below, derived from the working upon them of those above; and these, again, being educated by that which they receive, turn and insensibly work upon those below them. While in one way superior influences work upon men, as individuals, at once and upon all alike, in the second way influence works upon society by setting one circle to exert itself upon that which is next to it.

The power of each circle downward will be in proportion to the power which it has received from above. Now, it is to be observed that influence is not transmitted through these successive portions of society as through lenses, so that the truth, the influence, the power, at the end of its journey, is just what it was at the start; but influence is digested at each stage, and that which the last circle does is not the repetition of what the first did, but is a new and separate influence of its own, wrought in it by a stimulative power above; and that stimula tion is an effect wrought again within it, so that a power may begin at the top, as the merest speculation, as the most airy and subtile moral conception, which, if falling directly upon the bottom of society, would be utterly unfelt and wasted. But it falls upon a class of appreciative minds just beneath it and educates them. They, in turn, do not attempt to transmit that which educated them, but something that shall produce the same effect in those next below. Thus there arises a series of creative forces. The highest creates life. That life creates a lower life. That, again, works another, to the end.

The astronomical observatory on Mount Adams, near Cincinnati, was built by the voluntary contributions of merchants, artisans, and laborers. It would at first be thought that nothing could have been done which would repay so little good to the donors. Is it so?

We believe that in time the masses of laboring men will stand many degrees higher than they would have done.

Its influence in the beginning will be upon a few. But it will make them capable of breeding power upon yet more, and these will be aroused and will in turn arouse others. And that which at the beginning was abstract science, or science applied to things utterly removed from human necessities, will in the end work forth in fruits appropriate to all the levels of society, to the very lowest.   To measure and weigh the sun; to find out hidden sparks of stars; to drive up nebula and compress them to a shape; to watch the coquettings and conjunctions and flirting transits of planets,— what will be the end of all these things?   Better roads, lighter wheelbarrows, finer kerchiefs, lighter fingers to make them, neater carpenters and snugger homes, fewer needs and more supplies; in short, civilization among the masses.

It is doubtful whether in Bacon's lifetime one hundred men felt the direct influence of his philosophical thoughts.   It is doubtful yet whether two hundred men lived who have studied his apothegms, maxims, and propositions.   But they have been digested and have passed into the arteries of science as blood, and they beat all over the world with vital throbs and propulsions of knowledge.   There is not a peasant to whom science has given more and better food; there is not a mechanic in the world to whom knowledge has given more luxuries than crowned heads had three hundred years ago, who does not owe it to the mind of Bacon.   It is what men's deeds do that measures mental longevity.   It seems to us as if the light which falls upon our path to-day, and glorifies grass, moss, flowers, and leaves, had just fallen from the sun.   We seem to think that it leaped forth from the fountain but a moment ago and ran to greet us with but a moment's life within it.   But the light that falls upon your land to-day has been a solitary traveller for centuries through the long distance.   When this light which now flames about your dwelling sprang forth, Rome was yet imperial.   The Parthenon stood, and Phidian Jupiter sat in colossal glory, the wonder of the world.

The common comforts of life which to-day solace our way were a century ago the rare and marvelous wonder of a few. The maxims of the nursery were, five hundred years ago, the abstract speculations of cloistered men. The airy and subtile principles which a thousand years ago were as high above men's heads as the top of Himalaya above its base are now familiar truths. For truths are first clouds, then rain, and then harvests and food. Thus the philosophy of one age is the common sense of the next. Men are called imbecile for not understanding what they were called crazy for pretending to know some hundreds of years ago. The influences at the top of society affect society to the bottom. They may work circuitously; they may work slowly; but it is because they work with such enormous fruitfulness. We may not recognize what of our advantages we owe to our higher institutions. We must not expect to find the learning, but only the effect of the learning. When men go into the orchard to see what the sun is good for, they must not expect little identical suns, balls of light, hanging on the trees. They that search for sunlight find apples.

We must not look for mathematicians, for lawyers, for physicians, for deep-read and philosophical men, as the only fruits of colleges. We must accept fruit of other kinds, better workmen, more intelligent artisans, more sagacious mechanics, more skilful inventors, more enterprising commercialists, more common people who read, think, and grow stout by reading and thinking. If colleges give learning to the few, they give intelligence to the many.

There is no antagonism between the highest forms of institutions and the lowest, any more than there is between the higher and lower boughs of a common tree. Common schools are the fruits which drop from the boughs of colleges.

Colleges are not aristocratic. If they stand upon a higher plane, it is as stationary engines, to draw society up the long inclination. Where the higher circles, institutions, and classes of society are kept open, so that entrance and exit depends upon the capacity of those who will, they are never invidious or undemocratic. For democracy does not mean a dead level. It means the liberty of being just what God made man to be, forbidding any to be propped up above their own worth, and any to be kept below their own capacity. In short, democracy is a theory of government which declares that every man shall find his own level. And men at the top of society are as democratic as men at the bottom, if they have their right level.

Since the world began I know of nothing so remarkable as the formation of society along our western border. Old nations have abandoned their former seats and overrun new lands, carrying with them their flocks, their arms, and those personal habits which no man can leave behind. But they have carried no constitutions, no systems of law, no circles of schools, no colleges or universities, no institutions as a moral artillery through which the zeal of the people should utter itself.

But our own people, scarcely less nomadic than the tented Arab, scarcely less impetuous than the Goth and Hun, pour abroad along the western wilderness in swarming millions, countless, with implements, with wealth of flocks and herds, and with a breadth and depth of civilization such as never emigrated before. They drive schools along with them, as shepherds drive flocks. They have herds of churches, academies, lyceums; and their religious and educational institutions go lowing along the western plains as Jacob's herds lowed along the Syrian hills.

You cannot inoculate a nation with institutions whose animating ideas are foreign. Institutions must be indigenous. They are so with us. Nothing expresses the very American spirit so much as the fourfold forms of institutions, commercial, civil, religious, and educational. The family is a natural institution and is the mother and nurse of all others.

It is this very wealth of institutions that brings from the West such an appeal for help. We have sent to the fairest fields that the sun ever lightened or showers enriched, our sons and daughters, who know nothing but to rear along the vast intervales and valleys of the West a civilization as deep, as wide, as compact of social refinement, of intellectual culture, of moral richness, as that which hovers in their memory of dear old New England. But it is not possible for youthful States to lift up society in its whole breadth and depth at one lift. The spirit of institutions quickens their hearts, but how to give them bodies is their exceeding great task. It is enough to say of their willingness that it is worthy of their parentage. To perform the duties of life it is necessary first to live. A living is the first duty and necessity of emigrants. But with the burden of all the material tasks which underlay society suddenly upon them, they are called to upheave, in gigantic proportions, the forms of higher institutions. Ships are first built and then sent on voyages. But western States are as if men were rafted to sea with materials and were obliged to build the ship under them while they sailed,— yea, and to grapple in desperate conflict with piratical errors and red rovers of ignorance while yet they are laying down the decks and setting up the rigging.

Now an appeal for help from such men is like the cry of mariners whom the ocean threatens, and storms and cruel enemies. Our colleges lie out on ocean prairies with their flags reversed — token of imminent peril. God has given into the hand of wealth the power of saving them.

1. Indeed, it is well, in our golden age, when all the influences of the world are commercial, when governments are swayed by commercial influences, when camps are ruled by the bourse, when even morals and religion are almost obliged to ask leave to be of the till and the coffer,— that we should console ourselves with the truth that money is as susceptible of moral influence as of secular. It is a power without moral character. We do not repeat the monk's exhortation and urge men to yield their money to the church, but the church ought to yield their riches to the world. Inspired with a moral purpose, money is stronger than a king's sceptre or imperial armies. It cannot control nature, nor open the eyes of the blind, nor awake the dumb to speak. Riches will not make a man eloquent that is slow of speech, nor wise if stupid, nor powerful and swift to sail along the courses of thought which set through the age in which he lives. Yet it will give him control of learning, of eloquence, of science, of moral influence. A rich man may rake open the haunts of ignorance and bring forth a thousand gifts of power and wisdom. Riches have in them no æsthetic fineness, no creative art. But the æsthetic spirit is often borne in the bosom of poverty and cannot move. It is in the power of wealth to touch that victim whom poverty, like a fabled sorcerer, has enchanted, and set it free.

Wealth cannot preach, but it can rear up a thousand fiery tongues, like golden-mouthed Chrysostom, that shall go through the standing corn of the Philistines and burn it to ashes. It can build, not alone canals, aqueducts, warehouses, ships, stores and stately mansions. It can build schoolhouses as well as churches, academies and colleges. Wealth gotten of the seas may turn again, and, standing on the shore, in a hundred voices and a hundred languages, speak to every island of the ocean.

Riches gotten of the spices of India, and precious offerings of the East, may gather up from the immortal tree of life gayer fruits, sweeter incense, more fragrant and dripping gums and spices of the gospel, and send them back in life-giving exchange. Why should money be forever stigmatized as sordid, as selfish, as groveling, and penurious? Why should it not rise up and assert its moral power and take its own appropriate honor as a supreme dispenser of benevolence?

Have you repined that your hand was not gifted with the pen of literature? Then let a hundred hands be created by your beneficence which would not have moved but for your wealth.

Have you repined that your tongue, like a dull and heavy ship, carried your thoughts with slow voyages? Then avenge yourself by chartering clipper-tongues of other men that shall go over the deep, free as the winds.

There was never an hour when it was so much given to riches to stand in the robes of universal benefaction. It is the grand propelling force. It is the creative and stimulant influence of the world, and, like the natural sun, it calls up all manner of growths, good and bad alike. It is the province of piety to exclude the weeds and poisonous fungi, and to give growth, by wealth, to the fragrant and fruit bearing.

2. But while a spirit of true benevolence cannot be channeled and confined to any single course, and should not be; while it should abound with daily generosities to meet the

ever-fresh aspects of recurring want, and to nourish the heart of the giver with the love and gratitude of the receiver, yet wealth has a right to employ itself in works which are made noble by the elements of time and endurance.

It is a poor and miserable vanity to be known only by name; to take measures for an empty immortality; for being vocalized as a name, echoing from age to age, significant of nothing; to lie in the calendar of history as the dead names of Shephuphan, and Huram, and Gedor, and Shashack, and Shimhi lie in the Hebrew chronicles, to tell us how utterly dead a man may be who has nothing to leave behind him but his name.

But there is a generous and worthy desire of posthumous power. One may well wish not to cease working at the grave's mouth. One may hope to live so as to vitalize with his spirit institutions or physical agencies, so that they shall work on in the spirit and power of Elias when the prophet is long dead.

Do you think it would have been a joy unworthy of Bunyan if he could have foreseen the errand of his immortal Pilgrim, who, having travelled to heaven himself, hath never ceased since to convoy travellers thither ? The darkness of Bedford jail would have been wonderfully irradiated, as when sunrise comes upon night, could all the joy of afterdays have flooded backward and poured in prophetic rays upon the imprisoned wretch whose immortality of earthly glory was too fine and spiritual for the gross eyes of his contemporaries.

Do you not think that a man might yearn with a heavenly ambition to catch the notes which blossomed in his soul of mighty joys, and give them form, so that they should go out of himself and enter into the world as a music, and go singing down the ages, bringing joy to those that lacked it and expressing it fitly to those whose joy lacked a tongue ?

If a man's heart, caught up into the womb of imagination, gives birth to hymns, the children of his life, the offspring of his soul, may he not compose himself with something of the temperate raptures of heaven itself when he thinks what work he shall yet do upon the earth by the ministration of his songs and hymns that will bear his life forward and with noble metempsychosis give it scope again and life beyond the touch of death,— to minister only for good until the day come when earthly hymns and praises are caught up and mingled with the eternal choir ?

The sound of coming ages should be in every man's ears ! That is a voice which will inspire us as no hoary prophet or mighty philosopher. And he who in life becomes vital with the Spirit of God and yearns with a divine longing to give himself for the life of the world shall have imparted to him something of divine immortality and be permitted to rear up and send forth airy but stately purposes to sail upon the sea of Time, unharmed by winds and unfoundered by the waves.

But who can measure the scope and breadth of that working which he shall perpetuate who trusts his spirit, not upon the bird-wing of song or in the crystal vase of a book, but who incarnates himself in an institution suited to the universal want, common to all times, and whose nature it is to be a parent power, prolific of subsidiary powers, sending forth whatever influences and agencies are required by society in all its depths ? Your hand may work yet a thousand years hence; your thoughts may beat in the veins of life in ages to come. From heaven you may look back and see your life yet on earth, and in Time, as a mirror, behold your form and spirit.

But men must rise to the pattern of the age in which they live. As yet we have had very little individual heroism. The power that is in men to work through all time, single-handed, for the world, is little felt. Men are too modest or too selfish to suspect their possible usefulness.

We are a nation whose peculiarity it is to develop the strongest state of society and the most intense individualism of the citizen. The independence, the enterprise, the universal resource, the executive power of our people is in the mouth of the world. What such men can do for industry, for commerce, for all material forms of public good, we know. But we have a right to expect from such men new ideas, new developments and new examples in Christian beneficence.

We have a right to expect that men will seek wealth with precisely the same ambitions and purposes as men seek learning, not to be absorbed in their own selfish enjoyment, but as the means of acting upon the public, and of shaping the age in which they live.

While we have not as yet tried or proved one half the power which there is in the accumulation of small sums gathered from the whole mass of the community,— single drops that accumulate and gather force and swell to rivers,— so we have as yet but faintly conceived the power of individualism in beneficence. Laboring men, commercial men, all men of mere business, have it in their power to institute great principles in such a way that their work on earth shall not end for centuries.

Professorships should be the work of single churches. Nay, they should be the work of single men. Why should not young men, who know that God has given them genius for accumulation, rise from the paltry precedents of expenditure which ostentatious vanity sets, from the miserable methods of pride, and give the world to see what glory wealth may achieve, how it may associate itself with the noblest history of one's country and become a moral power of superior influence.

And men must remember that the world is moving on no mean pattern. As God in every age is infusing himself more and more in human affairs, so events are swelling and affairs moving through larger circuits and with statelier steps. And if men mean to give moral dignity to their wealth and wing it for immortal flight, they must not take counsel of selfishness or of mammon; they must rise to a nobler conception of the power that is in them, and of the offices which God offers to their wealth.

Why should whole States be canvassed to endow single colleges? There are single churches in every city of our land who might, without the slightest inconvenience, plant once in five years, and completely endow, a seminary of learning on whose summit the sun of a thousand years should shine.

But why do I speak of churches? One Sampson was enough to take the gates and posts of Gaza and march away unhelped. And there are men among us,— many of them,— if aroused to the consciousness of the strength that is in them, who might carry away the gates and posts of the castles of ignorance — might do better — build castles of knowledge right over against them and kill darkness by thrusting it through with light.

Why should not men be found who alone should rear up their monuments before they are dead, that shall never let them die?

We do not reproach one for cutting his name upon his monument. But time and wasting soon rub out the very granite and waste the marble letters. The grave itself grows smooth, and at length all memorial perishes. Only invisible letters last. The name of Harvard is as sharp cut to-day as a hundred years ago. Two hundred years men have walked the halls of Harvard, and not one hour of that time has its founder's name been unsyllabled.

The stone that began to hold the name of Yale has long since let go and relinquished its trust. But every year his monument has grown, and the letters of his name, changed to light, cast forth a mild radiance through every State to the Pacific.

ORATION AT THE RAISING OF "THE OLD FLAG" AT FORT SUMTER

DELIVERED APRIL 14, 1865

ON this solemn and joyful day we again lift to the breeze our fathers' flag, now again the banner of the *United* States, with the fervent prayer that God would crown it with honor, protect it from treason, and send it down to our children with all the blessings of civilization, liberty, and religion. Terrible in battle, may it be beneficent in peace. Happily no bird or beast of prey has been inscribed upon it. The stars that redeem night from darkness, and the beams of red light that beautify the morning, have been united upon its folds. As long as the sun endures, or the stars, may it wave over a nation neither enslaved nor enslaving. Once, and but once, has treason dishonored it. In that insane hour, when the guiltiest and bloodiest rebellion of time hurled their fires upon this fort, you, sir [turning to

General Anderson], and a small heroic band, stood within these now crumbled walls and did gallant and just battle for the honor and defence of the nation's banner.

In that cope of fire this glorious flag still peacefully waved to the breeze above your head, unconscious of harm as the stars and skies above it. Once it was shot down. A gallant hand, in whose care this day it has been, plucked it from the ground and reared it again—" cast down, but not destroyed." After a vain resistance, with trembling hand and sad heart, you withdrew it from its height, closed its wings, and bore it far away, sternly to sleep amid the tumults of rebellion and the thunder of battle. The first act of war had begun. The long night of four years had set in. While the giddy traitors whirled in a maze of exhilaration, dim horrors were already advancing, that were ere long to fill the land with blood.

To-day you are returned again. We devoutly join with you in thanksgiving to Almighty God that he has spared your honored life and vouchsafed you the honors of this day. The heavens over you are the same; the same shores; morning comes, and evening, as they did. All else, how changed! What grim batteries crowd the burdened shores! What scenes have filled this air and disturbed these waters! These shattered heaps of shapeless stone are all that is left of Fort Sumter. Desolation broods in yonder sad city; solemn retribution hath avenged our dishonored banner! You have come back with honor who departed hence, four years ago, leaving the air sultry with fanaticism. The surging crowds that rolled up their frenzied shouts as the flag came down are dead, or scattered, or silent; and their habitations are desolate. Ruin sits in the cradle of treason. Rebellion has perished. But there flies the same flag that was insulted. With starry eyes it looks all over this bay for that banner that supplanted it, and sees it not. You that then, for the day, were humbled are here again, to triumph once and forever. In the storm of that assault this glorious ensign was often struck; but, memorable fact, not one of its stars was torn out by shot or shell. It was a prophecy.

It said: " Not one State shall be struck from this nation by treason! " The fulfilment is at hand. Lifted to the air to-day, it proclaims, after four years of war, " Not a State is blotted out! "

Hail to the flag of our fathers, and our flag! Glory to the banner that has gone through four years black with tempests of war, to pilot the nation back to peace without dismemberment! And glory be to God, who, above all hosts and banners, hath ordained victory and shall ordain peace!

Wherefore have we come hither, pilgrims from distant places? Are we come to exult that Northern hands are stronger than Southern? No, but to rejoice that the hands of those who defend a just and beneficent government are mightier than the hands that assaulted it! Do we exult over fallen cities? We exult that a nation has not fallen. We sorrow with the sorrowful. We sympathize with the desolate. We look upon this shattered fort and yonder dilapidated city with sad eyes, grieved that men should have committed such treason and glad that God hath set such a mark upon treason that all ages shall dread and abhor it.

We exult, not for a passion gratified, but for a sentiment victorious; not for temper, but for conscience; not as we devoutly believe that our will is done, but that God's will hath been done. We should be unworthy of that liberty entrusted to our care if on such a day as this we sullied our hearts by feelings of aimless vengeance; and equally unworthy if we did not devoutly thank him who hath said, " Vengeance is mine, I will repay, saith the Lord," that he hath set a mark upon arrogant Rebellion, ineffaceable while time lasts!

Since this flag went down on that dark day, who shall tell the mighty woes that have made this land a spectacle to angels and men? The soil has drunk blood and is glutted. Millions mourn for millions slain, or, envying the dead, pray for oblivion. Towns and villages have been razed. Fruitful fields have turned back to wilderness. It came to pass, as the prophet said: "The sun was turned to darkness, and the moon to blood." The course of law was ended. The sword sat chief magistrate in half the nation; industry was paralyzed; morals corrupted; the public weal invaded by rapine and anarchy; whole States ravaged by avenging armies. The world was amazed. The earth reeled. When the flag sank here, it was as if political night had come and all beasts of prey had come forth to devour.

That long night is ended! And for this returning day we have come from afar to rejoice and give thanks. No more war! No more accursed secession! No more slavery, that spawned them both!

Let no man misread the meaning of this unfolding flag! It says, "Government hath returned hitherto." It proclaims in the name of vindicated government peace and protection to loyalty; humiliation and pains to traitors. This is the flag of sovereignty. The nation, not the States, is sovereign. Restored to authority, this flag commands, not supplicates.

There may be pardon, but no concession. There may be amnesty and oblivion, but no honeyed compromises. The nation to-day has peace for the peaceful and war for the turbulent. The only condition of submission is to submit! There is the constitution, there are the laws, there is the

government.   They rise up like mountains of strength that
shall not be moved.   They are the conditions of peace.

One nation, under one government, without slavery, has
been ordained and shall stand.   There can be peace on no
other basis.   On this basis reconstruction is easy and needs
neither architect nor engineer.   Without this basis no engineer or architect shall ever reconstruct these rebellious
States.

We do not want your cities or your fields.   We do not
envy you your prolific soil or heavens full of perpetual summer.   Let agriculture revel here; let manufactures make
every stream twice musical; build fleets in every port; inspire
the arts of peace with genius second only to that of Athens;
and we shall be glad in your gladness and rich in your wealth.

All that we ask is unswerving loyalty and universal liberty.
And that, in the name of this high sovereignty of the United
States of America, we demand; and that, with the blessing of
Almighty God, we will have!

We raise our fathers' banner, that it may bring back better
blessings than those of old; that it may cast out the devil of
discord; that it may restore lawful government and a prosperity purer and more enduring than that which it protected
before; that it may win parted friends from their alienation;
that it may inspire hope and inaugurate universal liberty;
that it may say to the sword " Return to thy sheath," and to
the plow and sickle, " Go forth; " that it may heal all jealousies, unite all policies, inspire a new national life, compact
our strength, purify our principles, ennoble our national ambitions, and make this people great and strong, not for aggression and quarrelsomeness, but for the peace of the world,
giving to us the glorious prerogative of leading all nations
to juster laws, to more humane policies, to sincerer friend-

11 ship, to rational, instituted civil liberty, and to universal Christian brotherhood.

Reverently, piously, in hopeful patriotism, we spread this banner on the sky, as of old the bow was planted on the cloud, and with solemn fervor beseech God to look upon it and make it the memorial of an everlasting covenant and decree that never again on this fair land shall a deluge of blood prevail.

Why need any eye turn from this spectacle? Are there not associations which, overleaping the recent past, carry us back to times when over North and South this flag was honored alike by all? In all our colonial days we were one, in the long Revolutionary struggle, and in the scores of prosperous years succeeding. When the passage of the Stamp Act in 1765 aroused the colonies, it was Gadsden of South Carolina that cried with prescient enthusiasm: " We stand on the broad common ground of those natural rights that we all feel and know as men. There ought to be no New England man, no New Yorker, known on this continent, but all of us," said he, " Americans!" That was the voice of South Carolina. That shall be the voice of South Carolina. Faint is the echo; but it is coming. We now hear it sighing sadly through the pines; but it shall yet break upon the shore—no North, no West, no South, but one United States of America.

There is scarcely a man born in the South who has lifted his hand against this banner but had a father who would have died for it. Is memory dead? Is there no historic pride? Has a fatal fury struck blindness or hate into eyes that used to look kindly toward each other; that read the same Bible; that hung over the same historic pages of our national glory; that studied the same constitution?

Let this uplifting bring back all of the past that was good, but leave in darkness all that was bad.

It was never before so wholly unspotted; so clear of all wrong; so purely and simply the sign of justice and liberty. Did I say that we brought back the same banner that you bore away, noble and heroic sir? It is not the same. It is more and better than it was. The land is free from slavery since that banner fell.

When God would prepare Moses for emancipation he overthrew his first steps and drove him for forty years to brood in the wilderness. When our flag came down, four years it lay brooding in darkness. It cried to the Lord, " Wherefore am I deposed?" Then arose before it a vision of its sin. It had strengthened the strong and forgotten the weak. It proclaimed liberty, but trod upon slaves.

In that seclusion it dedicated itself to liberty. Behold, to-day it fulfils its vows. When it went down four million people had no flag. To-day it rises and four million people cry out, " Behold our flag!" Hark! they murmur. It is the gospel that they recite in sacred words: " It is a gospel to the poor, it heals our broken hearts, it preaches deliverance to captives, it gives sight to the blind, it sets at liberty them that are bruised." Rise up, then, glorious gospel banner and roll out these messages of God. Tell the air that not a spot now sullies thy whiteness. Thy red is not the blush of shame, but the flush of joy. Tell the dews that wash thee that thou art pure as they. Say to the night that thy stars lead toward the morning; and to the morning that a brighter day arises with healing in its wings. And then, oh! glorious flag, bid the sun pour light on all thy folds with double brightness whilst thou art bearing around and round the world the solemn joy—a race set free! a nation redeemed!

The mighty hand of government, made strong in war by the favor of the God of Battles, spreads wide to-day the banner of liberty that went down in darkness, that arose in light; and there it streams, like the sun above it, neither parcelled out nor monopolized, but flooding the air with light for all mankind. Ye scattered and broken, ye wounded and dying, bitten by the fiery serpents of oppression everywhere in all the world, look upon this sign, lifted up, and live! And ye homeless and houseless slaves, look and ye are free! At length you too have part and lot in this glorious ensign that broods with impartial love over small and great, the poor and the strong, the bond and the free.

In this solemn hour let us pray for the quick coming of reconciliation and happiness under this common flag!

But we must build again from the foundations in all these now free southern States. No cheap exhortations " to forgetfulness of the past, to restore all things as they were," will do. God does not stretch out his hand, as he has for four dreadful years, that men may easily forget the might of his terrible acts. Restore things as they were? What! the alienations and jealousies, the discords and contentions, and the causes of them? No. In that solemn sacrifice on which a nation has offered up for its sins so many precious victims, loved and lamented, let our sins and mistakes be consumed utterly and forever.

No, never again shall things be restored as before the war. It is written in God's decree, " Old things are passed away." That new earth in which dwelleth righteousness draws near.

Things as they were! Who has an omnipotent hand to restore a million dead, slain in battle, or wasted by sickness, or dying of grief, broken-hearted? Who has omniscience to search for the scattered ones? Who shall restore the lost to broken families? Who shall bring back the squandered treasure, the years of industry wasted. and convince you that four years of guilty rebellion and cruel war are no more than dirt upon the hand, which a moment's washing removes and leaves the hand clean as before? Such a war reaches down to the very vitals of society.

Emerging from such a prolonged rebellion, he is blind who tells you that the State, by a mere amnesty and benevolence of government, can be put again, by a simple decree, in its old place. It would not be honest, it would not be kind or fraternal, for me to pretend that Southern revolution against the Union has not reacted and wrought revolution in the southern States themselves, and inaugurated a new dispensation.

Society here is like a broken loom, and the piece which rebellion put in, and was weaving, has been cut and every thread broken. You must put in new warp and new woof, and weaving anew as the fabric slowly unwinds, we shall see in it no Gorgon figures, no hideous grotesques of the old barbarism, but the figures of liberty, vines, and golden grains, framing in the heads of Justice, Love, and Liberty!

The august convention of 1787 framed the constitution with this memorable preamble:

" We, the people of the United States, in order to form a more perfect Union, establish justice, ensure domestic tranquillity, provide for the common defence, promote the general welfare, and secure the blessings of liberty to ourselves and our posterity, do ordain this constitution for the United States of America."

Again, in the awful convention of war the people of the United States, for the very ends just recited, have debated, settled, and ordained certain fundamental truths which must henceforth be accepted and obeyed. Nor is any State or any individual wise who shall disregard them. They are to civil affairs what the natural laws are to health,—indispensable conditions of peace and happiness.

What are the ordinances given by the people, speaking out of fire and darkness of war, with authority inspired by that same God who gave the law from Sinai amid thunders and trumpet voices?

1. That these United States shall be one and indivisible.

2. That States have not absolute sovereignty and have no right to dismember the republic.

3. That universal liberty is indispensable to republican government, and that slavery shall be utterly and forever abolished!

Such are the results of war. These are the best fruits of the war. They are worth all they have cost. They are foundations of peace. They will secure benefits to all nations as well as to ours.

Our highest wisdom and duty is to accept the facts as the decrees of God. We are exhorted to forget all that has happened. Yes, the wrath, the conflict, the cruelty, but not those overruling decrees of God which this war has pronounced. As solemnly as on Mount Sinai, God says, "Remember! Remember! Hear it to-day." Under this sun, under that bright child of the sun, our banner, with the eyes of this nation and of the world upon us, we repeat the syllables of God's providence and recite the solemn decrees: No more disunion! No more secession! No more slavery!

Why did this civil war begin? We do not wonder that European statesmen failed to comprehend this conflict, and that foreign philanthropists were shocked at a murderous war that seemed to have had no moral origin, but, like the brutal fights of beasts of prey, to have sprung from ferocious animalism. This great nation,—filling all profitable latitudes, cradled between two oceans, with inexhaustible resources, with riches increasing in an unparalleled ratio by agriculture, by manufactures, by commerce, with schools and churches, with books and newspapers thick as leaves in our own forests, with institutions sprung from the people and peculiarly adapted to their genius; a nation not sluggish but active, used to excitement, practical in political wisdom, and accustomed to self-government, and all its vast outlying parts held together by a federal government mild in temper, gentle in administration, and beneficent in results,—seemed to have been formed for peace.

All at once, in this hemisphere of happiness and hope, there came drooping clouds with fiery bolts full of death and desolation. At a cannon-shot upon this fort, the nation, as if it had been a trained army lying on its arms awaiting a signal, rose up and began a war of defence which, for awfulness, rises into the first rank of eminence. The front of battle, going with the sun, was twelve hundred miles long; and the depth, measured along a meridian, was a thousand miles. In this vast area more than two million men, first and last, for four years, have, in skirmish, fight, and battle, met in more than a thousand conflicts; while a coast and river line not less than four thousand miles in length has swarmed with fleets freighted with artillery. The very industry of the country seemed to have been touched by some infernal wand, and, with sudden wheel, changed its front from peace to war. The anvils of the land beat like drums. As out of the ooze emerge monsters, so from our mines and foundries uprose new and strange iron-clad machines of war.

And so, in a nation of peaceful habits, without external provocation, there arose such a storm of war as blackened the whole horizon and hemisphere. What wonder that foreign observers stood amazed at this fanatical fury that seemed without divine guidance and inspired wholly with infernal frenzy?

The explosion was sudden, but the train had long been laid. We must consider the condition of Southern society if we would understand the mystery of this iniquity. Society in the South resolves itself into three divisions, more sharply distinguished than in any other part of the nation. At the base is the laboring class, made up of slaves. Next is the middle class, made up of traders, small farmers, and poor men. The lower edge of this class touches the slave and the upper edge reaches up to the third and ruling class. This class was a small minority in numbers, but in practical ability they had centred in their hands the whole government of the South and had mainly governed the country.

Upon this polished, cultured, exceedingly capable, and wholly unprincipled class rests the whole burden of this war. Forced up by the bottom-heat of slavery, the ruling class in all the disloyal States arrogated to themselves a superiority not compatible with republican equality or with just morals. They claimed a right of pre-eminence. An evil prophet arose who trained these wild and luxuriant shoots of ambition to the shapely form of a political philosophy.

By its re-agents they precipitated labor to the bottom of society and left at the top what they thought to be a clarified fluid. In their political economy labor was to be owned by capital. In their theory of government a few were to rule the many. They boldly avowed, not the fact alone that under all forms of government the few rule the many, but their right and duty to do so. Set free from the necessity of labor, they conceived a contempt for those who felt its wholesome regimen. Believing themselves foreordained to supremacy, they regarded the popular vote, when it failed to register their wishes, as an intrusion and a nuisance. They were born in a garden, and popular liberty, like freshets over-swelling their banks, covered their dainty walks and flowers with the slime and mud of democratic votes.

When with shrewd observation they saw the growth of the popular element in the northern States, they instinctively took in the inevitable events. It must be controlled or cut off from a nation governed by gentlemen! Their power to control that popular element became less every decade; and they prepared secretly and earnestly, with wide conference and mutual connivance, to separate the South from the North.

We are to distinguish between the pretended and the real causes of this war.

To inflame and unite the great middle class of the South who had no interest in separation and no business with war, they alleged grievances that never existed and employed arguments which they, better than all other men, knew to be specious and false. Slavery itself was cared for only as an instrument of power or of excitement. They had unalterably fixed their eyes upon empire, and all was good which would secure that, and bad which hindered it.

Thus the ruling class of the South,—an aristocracy as intense, proud, and inflexible as ever existed; not limited either by customs or institutions; not recognized and adjusted in the regular order of society, playing a reciprocal part in its machinery, but secret, disowning its own existence, baptized with the ostentatious name of democracy; obsequious to the people for the sake of governing them; this nameless, lurking aristocracy, that ran in the blood of society like a rash not yet come to the skin; this political tapeworm that produced nothing but lay coiled in the body, feeding on its nutriment, and holding the whole structure to be but a servant set up to nourish it,—this aristocracy of the plantation with firm and deliberate resolve brought on the war that they might cut the land in two, and clearing themselves from incorrigible free society, set up a sterner, statelier empire where slaves worked that gentlemen might live at ease. Nor can there be any doubt that though, at first, they meant to erect the form of republican government this was but a device; a step necessary to the securing of that power by which they should be able to change the whole economy of society.

That they never dreamed of such a war we may well believe. That they would have accepted it, though twice as bloody, if only thus they could rule, none can doubt that knows the temper of these worst men of modern society. But they miscalculated. They understood the people of the South; but they were totally incapable of understanding the character of the great working classes of the loyal States. That industry which is the foundation of independence, and so of equity, they stigmatized as stupid drudgery or as mean avarice. That general intelligence and independence of thought which schools for the common people and newspapers breed they reviled as the incitement of unsettled zeal running easily into fanaticism.

They more thoroughly misunderstood the profound sentiment of loyalty and the deep love of country which pervaded the common people. If those who knew them best had never suspected the depth and power of that loyalty and love which threw them into an agony of grief when the flag was here humbled, how should they conceive of it who were wholly disjoined from them in sympathy? The whole land rose up, you remember, when the flag came down, as if inspired unconsciously by the breath of the Almighty and the power of

Omnipotence. It was as when one pierces the banks of the Mississippi for a rivulet and the whole raging stream plunges through with headlong course. There they calculated and miscalculated.

And more than all, they miscalculated the bravery of men who have been trained under law; who are civilized and hate personal brawls; who are so protected by society as to have dismissed all thought of self-defence; the whole force of whose life is turned to peaceful pursuits. These arrogant conspirators against government, with Chinese vanity, believed that they could blow away the self-respecting citizens as chaff from the battle-field. Few of them are left alive to ponder their mistake.

Here, then, are the roots of this civil war. It was not a quarrel of wild beasts; it was an inflection of the strife of ages between power and right, between ambition and equity. An armed band of pestilent conspirators sought the nation's life. Her children rose up and fought at every door and room and hall to thrust out the murderers and save the house and household. It was not legitimately a war between the common people of the North and South. The war was set on by the ruling class, the aristocratic conspirators, of the South. They suborned the common people with lies, with sophistries, with cruel deceits and slanders, to fight for secret objects which they abhorred and against interests as dear to them as their own lives.

I charge the whole guilt of this war upon the ambitious, educated, plotting political leaders of the South. They have shed this ocean of blood. They have desolated the South. They have poured poverty through all her towns and cities. They have bewildered the imagination of the people with phantasms and led them to believe that they were fighting for their homes and liberty, whose homes were unthreatened and whose liberty was in no jeopardy.

These arrogant instigators of civil war have renewed the plagues of Egypt, not that the oppressed might go free but that the free might be oppressed. A day will come when God will reveal judgment and arraign at his bar these mighty miscreants; and then every orphan that their bloody game has made and every widow that sits sorrowing and every maimed and wounded sufferer and every bereaved heart in all the wide regions of this land, will rise up and come before the Lord to lay upon these chief culprits of modern history their awful witness. And from a thousand battle-fields shall rise up armies of airy witnesses, who, with the memory of their awful sufferings, shall confront these miscreants with shrieks of fierce accusation; and every pale and starved prisoner shall raise his skinny hand in judgment. Blood shall call out for vengeance and tears shall plead for justice, and grief shall silently beckon, and love, heart-smitten, shall wail for justice. Good men and angels will cry out, " How long, oh Lord, how long wilt thou not avenge ? "

And then those guiltiest and most remorseless traitors, these high and cultured men with might and wisdom used for the destruction of their country; these most detested of all criminals that have drenched a continent in needless blood and moved the foundations of their times with hideous crimes and cruelty, shall be plunged downward forever and forever in an endless retribution, while God shall say " Thus shall it be to all who betray their country;" and all in heaven and upon the earth will say " Amen!"

But for the people misled, for the multitudes drafted and driven into their civil war, let not a trace of animosity remain. The moment their willing hand drops the musket and they return to their allegiance, then stretch out your own honest right hand to greet them. Recall to them the old days of kindness. Our hearts wait for their redemption. All the resources of a renovated nation shall be applied to rebuild their prosperity and smooth down the furrows of war.

Has this long and weary period of strife been an unmingled evil? Had nothing been gained? Yes, much. This nation has attained its manhood.

Among Indian customs is one which admits young men to the rank of warriors only after severe trials of hunger, fatigue, pain, endurance. They reach their station, not through years, but ordeals. Our nation has suffered and now is strong.

The sentiment of loyalty and patriotism, next in importance to religion, has been rooted and grounded. We have something to be proud of and pride helps love. Never so much as now did we love our country.

But four such years of education in ideas, in the knowledge of political truth, in the lore of history, in the geography of our own country, almost every inch of which we have probed with the bayonet, have never passed before. There is half a hundred years' advance in four.

We believed in our institutions and principles before; but now we know their power. It is one thing to look upon artillery and be sure that it is loaded; it is another thing to prove its power in battle. We believed in the hidden power stored in our institutions; we had never before seen this nation thundering like Mount Sinai at all those that worshipped the calf at the base of the mountain.

A people educated and moral are competent to all the exigencies of national life. A vote can govern better than a crown. We have proved it. A people intelligent and religious are strong in all economic elements. They are fitted for peace and competent to war. They are not easily inflamed and when justly incensed not easily extinguished. They are patient in adversity, endure cheerfully needful burdens, tax themselves for real wants more royally than any prince would dare to tax his people. They pour forth without stint relief for the sufferings of war, and raise charity out of the realm of a dole into a munificent duty of beneficence.

The habit of industry among freemen prepares them to meet the exhaustion of war with increase of productiveness commensurate with the need that exists. Their habits of skill enable them at once to supply such armies as only freedom can muster with arms and munition such as only free industry can create. Free society is terrible in war and afterward repairs the mischief of war with celerity almost as great as that with which the ocean heals the seams gashed in it by the keels of ploughing ships.

Free society is fruitful of military genius. It comes when called; when no longer needed it falls back, as waves do to the level of the common sea, that no wave may be greater than the undivided water. With proof of strength so great, yet in its infancy, we stand up among the nations of the world, asking no privileges, asserting no rights, but quietly assuming our place, and determine to be second to none in the race of civilization and religion.

Of all nations we are the most dangerous and the least to be feared. We need not expound the perils that wait upon enemies that assault us. They are sufficiently understood. But we are not a dangerous people because we are warlike. All the arrogant attitudes of this nation, so offensive to foreign governments, were inspired by slavery under the administration of its minions. Our tastes, our habits, our interests, and our principles incline us to the arts of peace.

This nation was founded by the common people for the common people. We are seeking to embody in public economy more liberty, with higher justice and virtue, than have been organized before. By the necessity of our doctrines we are put in sympathy with the masses of men in all nations. It is not our business to subdue nations, but to augment the powers of the common people. The vulgar ambition of mere domination, as it belongs to universal human nature, may tempt us; but it is withstood by the whole force of our principles, our habits, our precedents, and our legends.

We acknowledge the obligation which our better political principles lay upon us to set an example more temperate, humane, and just than monarchical governments can. We will not suffer wrong, and still less will we inflict it upon other nations. Nor are we concerned that so many, ignorant of our conflict, for the present misconceive the reasons of our invincible military zeal. "Why contend," say they, "for a little territory that you do not need?" Because it is ours. Because it is the interest of every citizen to save it from becoming a fortress and refuge of iniquity. This nation is our house, and our fathers' house; and accursed be the man who will not defend it to the uttermost. More territory than we need? England, that is not large enough to be our pocket, may think that it is more than we need because it is more than it needs; but we are better judges of what we need than others are.

Shall a philanthropist say to a banker who defends himself against a robber, "Why do you need so much money?" But we will not reason with such questions. When any foreign nation will willingly divide its terrritory and give it cheerfully away, we will answer the question why we are fighting for territory.

At present, for I pass to the consideration of benefits that accrue to the South in distinction from the rest of the nation, the South reaps only suffering; but good seed lies buried under the furrows of war that peace will bring to harvest.

Deadly doctrines have been purged away in blood. The subtle poison of seccession was a perpetual threat of revolution. The sword has ended that danger. That which reason had affirmed as a philosophy the people have settled as a fact. Theory pronounces, "There can be no permanent government where each integral particle has liberty to fly off." Who would venture upon a voyage on a ship each plank and timber of which might withdraw at its pleasure? But the people have reasoned by the logic of the sword and of the ballot, and they have declared that States are inseparable parts of national government. They are not sovereign. State rights remain; but sovereignty is a right higher than all others; and that has been made into a common stock for the benefit of all. All further agitation is ended. This element must be cast out of political problems. Henceforth that poison will not rankle in the blood.

Another thing has been learned: the rights and duties of minorities. The people of the whole nation are of more authority than the people of any section. These United States are supreme over northern, western, and southern States. It ought not to have required the awful chastisement of this war to teach that a minority must submit the control of the nation's government to a majority. The army and navy have been good political schoolmasters. The lesson is learned. Not for many generations will it require further illustration.

No other lesson will be more fruitful of peace than the dispersion of those conceits of vanity which on either side have clouded the recognition of the manly courage of all Americans. If it be a sign of manhood to be able to fight, then Americans are men. The North, certainly, is in no doubt whatever of the soldierly qualities of Southern men. Southern soldiers have learned that all latitudes breed courage on this continent. Courage is a passport to respect. The people of all the regions of this nation are likely hereafter to cherish a generous admiration of each other's prowess. The war has bred respect, and respect will breed affection, and affection, peace and unity.

No other event of the war can fill an intelligent Southern man, of candid nature, with more surprise than the revelation of the capacity, moral and military, of the black race. It is a revelation indeed. No people were ever less understood by those most familiar with them. They were said to be lazy, lying, impudent, and cowardly wretches, driven by the whip alone to the tasks needful to their own support and the functions of civilization. They were said to be dangerous, bloodthirsty, liable to insurrection; but four years of tumultuous distress and war have rolled across the area inhabited by them, and I have yet to hear of one authentic instance of the misconduct of a colored man. They have been patient, and gentle, and docile, and full of faith, and hope, and piety; and, when summoned to freedom they have emerged with all the signs and tokens that freedom will be to them what it was to us, the swaddling-band that shall bring them to manhood. And after the government, honoring them as men, summoned them to the field, when once they were disciplined and had learned the arts of war they proved themselves to be not second to their white brethren in arms. And when the roll of men that had shed their blood is called in the other land, many and many a dusky face will rise, dark no more when the light of eternal glory shall shine upon it from the throne of God.

The industry of the southern States is regenerated and now rests upon a basis that never fails to bring prosperity. Just now industry is collapsed; but it is not dead. It sleepeth. It is vital yet. It will spring like mown grass from the roots that need but showers and heat and time to bring them forth.

Though in many districts this generation may not see the wanton wastes of self-invoked war repaired, and though many portions may lapse again to wilderness; yet in our lifetime we shall see States, as a whole, raised to a prosperity vital, wholesome, and immovable.

The destruction of class interests, working with a religion which tends toward true democracy in proportion as it is pure and free, will create a new era of prosperity for the common laboring people of the South. Upon them have come the labor, the toil, and the loss of this war. They have fought blindfolded. They have fought for a class that sought their degradation while they were made to believe that it was for their own homes and altars. Their leaders meant a supremacy which would not long have left them political liberty save in name. But their leaders are swept away. The sword has been hungry for the ruling classes. It has sought them out with remorseless zeal. New men are to rise up; new ideas are to bud and blossom; and there will be men with different ambition and altered policy.

Meanwhile the South, no longer a land of plantations but of farms; no longer filled by slaves, but by freemen, will find no hindrance to the spread of education. Schools will multiply. Books and papers will spread. Churches will bless every hamlet. There is a good day coming for the South. Through darkness and tears and blood she has sought it. It has been an unconscious *via dolorosa*. But in the end it will be worth all it has cost. Her institutions before were deadly; she nourished death in her bosom; the greater her secular prosperity the more sure was her ruin; and every year of delay but made the change more terrible. Now, by an earthquake, the evil is shaken down, and her own historians, in a better day, shall write that from the day the sword cut off the cancer she began to find her health.

What, then, shall hinder the rebuilding of this republic? The evil spirit is cast out; why should not this nation cease to wander among tombs cutting itself? Why should it not come clothed, and in its right mind, to sit at the feet of Jesus? Is it feared that the government will oppress the conquered States? What possible motive has the government to narrow the base of that pyramid on which its own permanence depends?

It is feared that the rights of the States will be withheld? The South is not more jealous of State rights than the North. State rights from the earliest colonial days have been the peculiar pride and jealousy of New England. In every stage of national formation it was peculiarly northern, and not southern, statesmen that guarded State rights as we were forming the constitution. But once united, the loyal States gave up forever that which had been delegated to the national government. And now, in the hour of victory, the loyal States do not mean to trench upon southern State rights. They will not do it or suffer it to be done. There is not to be one rule for high latitudes and another for low. We take nothing from the southern States that has not already been taken from the northern. The South shall have just those rights that every eastern, every middle, every western State has—no more or less.

We are not seeking our own aggrandizement by impoverishing the South. Its prosperity is an indispensable element of our own. We have shown by all that we have suffered in war how great is our estimate of the southern States of this Union; and we will measure that estimate now in peace by still greater exertions for their rebuilding.

Will reflecting men not perceive, then, the wisdom of accepting established facts, and, with alacrity of enterprise, begin to retrieve the past?

Slavery cannot come back. It is the interest therefore of every man to hasten its end. Do you want more war? Are you not yet weary of contest? Will you gather up the unexploded fragments of this prodigious magazine of all mischief and heap them up for continued explosions? Does not the South need peace? And since free labor is inevitable will you have it in its worst forms or its best? Shall it be ignorant, impertinent, indolent; or shall it be educated, self-respecting, moral, and self-supporting? Will you have men as drudges or will you have them as citizens? Since they have vindicated the government and cemented its foundation-stones with their blood may they not offer the tribute of their support to maintain its laws and its policy? It is better for religion; it is better for political integrity; it is better for industry; it is better for money, if you will have that ground-motive, that you should educate the black man, and by education make him a citizen. They who refuse education to the black man would turn the South into a vast poorhouse, and labor into a pendulum, incessantly vibrating between poverty and indolence.

From this pulpit of broken stone we speak forth our earnest greeting to all our land.

We offer to the President of these United States our solemn congratulations that God has sustained his life and health under the unparalleled burdens and sufferings of four bloody years and permitted him to behold this auspicious consummation of that national unity for which he has waited with so much patience and fortitude and for which he has labored with such disinterested wisdom.

To the members of the government associated with him in the administration of perilous affairs in critical times, to the senators and representatives of the United States who have eagerly fashioned the instruments by which the popular will might express and enforce itself, we tender our grateful thanks.

To the officers and men of the army and navy who have so faithfully, skilfully and gloriously upheld their country's authority by suffering, labor, and sublime courage, we offer a heart-tribute beyond the compass of words.

Upon those true and faithful citizens, men and women, who have borne up with unflinching hope in the darkest hour and covered the land with their labor of love and charity, we invoke the divinest blessing of him whom they have so truly imitated.

But chiefly to thee, God of our fathers, we render thanksgiving and praise for that wondrous providence that has brought forth from such a harvest of war the seed of so much liberty and peace.

We invoke peace upon the North. Peace be to the West. Peace be upon the South!

In the name of God we lift up our banner and dedicate it to peace, union, and liberty, now and forever more. Amen.

DOUGLAS

STEPHEN ARNOLD DOUGLAS was born at Brandon in the State of Vermont in 1813. He studied for three years at the Academy of Canandaigua, and in 1833 settled in Jacksonville, Illinois, where, for a time, he supported himself by keeping a school. Called to the bar in 1834, he quickly obtained a lucrative practice, and in the following year was chosen Attorney-General of the State. In 1835 he was elected a member of the Legislature and five years later became Secretary of State of Illinois. He was a Judge of the Supreme Court of the State from 1841 until 1843, when he resigned the office to become a Representative in the Federal Congress. In 1847 he was sent from Illinois to the United States Senate. In 1852, and again in 1856, he received strong support as a candidate for the Presidency in the Democratic National Convention. In January, 1854, he reported to the Senate what became known as the Nebraska Bill, a measure which repealed the Missouri Compromise of 1820, and declared the people of any Territory free to regulate their domestic institutions in their own way, subject only to the Constitution of the United States. In 1857 Douglas distinguished himself by his opposition to the admission of Kansas into the Union under the Lecompton Constitution, and in the following year engaged in a close and exciting contest for the United States Senatorship with Abraham Lincoln, the Republican candidate. He was successful in this struggle, but alienated most of the slaveholding States, who refused to support him for the Presidency in 1860. The Democratic National Convention, held in that year, was rent asunder, but Douglas was nominated by one of the fragments, and received a large popular vote. Upon the outbreak of the Civil War, he urged all patriotic men to sustain the Union and the Constitution. He died at Chicago on June 3, 1861, only a little more than forty-eight years old.

ON THE KANSAS-NEBRASKA BILL

UNITED STATES SENATE, MARCH 3, 1854

IT HAS been urged in debate that there is no necessity for these territorial organizations; and I have been called upon to point out any public and national considerations which require action at this time. Senators seem to forget that our immense and valuable possessions

on the Pacific are separated from the States and organized Territories on this side of the Rocky Mountains by a vast wilderness, filled by hostile savages—that nearly a hundred thousand emigrants pass through this barbarous wilderness every year, on their way to California and Oregon—that these emigrants are American citizens, our own constituents, who are entitled to the protection of law and government, and that they are left to make their way, as best they may, without the protection or aid of law or government. The United States mails for New Mexico and Utah, and official communications between this government and the authorities of those Territories, are required to be carried over these wild plains, and through the gorges of the mountains, where you have made no provisions for roads, bridges, or ferries to facilitate travel, or forts or other means of safety to protect life. As often as I have brought forward and urged the adoption of measures to remedy these evils, and afford security against the damages to which our people are constantly exposed, they have been promptly voted down as not being of sufficient importance to command the favorable consideration of Congress. Now, when I propose to organize the Territories, and allow the people to do for themselves what you have so often refused to do for them, I am told that there are not white inhabitants enough permanently settled in the country to require and sustain a government. True; there is not a very large population there, for the very reason that your Indian code and intercourse laws exclude the settlers, and forbid their remaining there to cultivate the soil. You refuse to throw the country open to settlers, and then object to the organization of the Territories, upon the ground that there is not a sufficient number of inhabitants. . . .

I will now proceed to the consideration of the great principle involved in the bill, without omitting, however, to notice some of those extraneous matters which have been brought into this discussion with the view of producing another anti-slavery agitation. We have been told by nearly every Senator who has spoken in opposition to this bill, that at the time of its introduction the people were in a state of profound quiet and repose, that the anti-slavery agitation had entirely ceased and that the whole country was acquiescing cheerfully and cordially in the compromise measures of 1850 as a final adjustment of this vexed question. Sir, it is truly refreshing to hear Senators, who contested every inch of ground in opposition to those measures, when they were under discussion, who predicted all manner of evils and calamities from their adoption, and who raised the cry of appeal, and even resistance, to their execution, after they had become the laws of the land—I say it is really refreshing to hear these same Senators now bear their united testimony to the wisdom of those measures, and to the patriotic motives which induced us to pass them in defiance of their threats and resistance, and to their beneficial effects in restoring peace, harmony, and fraternity to a distracted country. These are precious confessions from the lips of those who stand pledged never to assent to the propriety of those measures, and to make war upon them, so long as they shall remain upon the statute book. I well understand that these confessions are now made, not with the view of yielding their assent to the propriety of carrying those enactments into faithful execution, but for the purpose of having a pretext for charging upon me, as the author of this bill, the responsibility of an agitation which they are striving to produce. They say that I, and not they, have revived the agitation. What have I done to render me obnoxious to this charge? They say that I wrote and introduced this Nebraska Bill. That is true; but I was not a volunteer in the transaction. The Senate, by a unanimous vote, appointed me chairman of the Territorial Committee, and associated five intelligent and patriotic Senators with me, and thus made it our duty to take charge of all Territorial business. In like manner, and with the concurrence of these complaining Senators, the Senate referred to us a distinct proposition to organize this Nebraska Territory, and required us to report specifically upon the question. I repeat, then, we were not volunteers in this business. The duty was imposed upon us by the Senate. We were not unmindful of the delicacy and responsibility of the position. We were aware that, from 1820 to 1850, the abolition doctrine of Congressional interference with slavery in the Territories and new States had so far prevailed as to keep up an incessant slavery agitation in Congress, and throughout the country, whenever any new Territory was to be acquired or organized. We were also aware that, in 1850, the right of the people to decide this question for themselves, subject only to the Constitution, was submitted for the doctrine of Congressional intervention. This first question, therefore, which the committee were called upon to decide, and indeed the only question of any material importance in framing this bill, was this: Shall we adhere to and carry out the principle recognized by the compromise measures of 1850, or shall we go back to the old exploded doctrine of Congressional interference, as established in 1820, in a large portion of the country, and which it was the object of the Wilmot Proviso to give a universal application, not only to all the territory which we then possessed, but all which we might hereafter acquire? There are no alternatives. We were compelled to frame the bill upon the one or the other of these two principles. The doctrine of 1820 or the doctrine of 1850 must prevail. In the discharge of the duty imposed upon us by the Senate, the committee could not hesitate upon this point, whether we consulted our own individual opinions and principles, or those which were known to be entertained and boldly avowed by a large majority of the Senate. The two great political parties of the country stood solemnly pledged before the world to adhere to the compromise measures of 1850, "in principle and substance." A large majority of the Senate—indeed, every member of the body, I believe, except the two avowed Abolitionists (Mr. Chase and Mr. Sumner)—profess to belong to one or the other of these parties, and hence were supposed to be under a high moral obligation to carry out "the principle and substance" of those measures in all new Territorial organizations. The report of the committee was in accordance with this obligation. I am arraigned, therefore, for having endeavored to represent the opinions and principles of the Senate truly—for having performed my duty in conformity with parliamentary law—for having been faithful to the trust imposed in me by the Senate. Let the vote this night determine whether I have thus faithfully represented your opinions. When a majority of the Senate shall have passed the bill— when the majority of the States shall have indorsed it through their representatives upon this floor—when a majority of the South and a majority of the North shall have sanctioned it—when a majority of the Whig party and a majority of the Democratic party shall have voted for it— when each of these propositions shall be demonstrated by the vote this night on the final passage of the bill, I shall be willing to submit the question to the country, whether, as the organ of the committee, I performed my duty in the report and bill which have called down upon my head so much denunciation and abuse.

Mr. President, the opponents of this measure have had much to say about the mutations and modifications which this bill has undergone since it was first introduced by myself, and about the alleged departure of the bill, in its present form, from the principle laid down in the original report of the committee as a rule of action in all future Territorial organizations. Fortunately there is no necessity, even if your patience would tolerate such a course of argument at this late hour of the night, for me to examine these speeches in detail, and reply to each charge separately. Each speaker seems to have followed faithfully in the footsteps of his leader in the path marked out by the Abolition confederates in their manifesto, which I took occasion to expose on a former occasion. You have seen them on their winding way, meandering the narrow and crooked path in Indian file, each treading close upon the heels of the other, and neither venturing to take a step to the right or left, or to occupy one inch of ground which did not bear the footprint of the Abolition champion. To answer one, therefore, is to answer the whole. The statement to which they seem to attach the most importance, and which they have repeated oftener, perhaps, than any other, is, that, pending the compromise measures of 1850, no man in or out of Congress ever dreamed of abrogating the Missouri Compromise; that from that period down to the present session nobody supposed that its validity had been impaired, or anything done which rendered it obligatory upon us to make it inoperative hereafter; that at the time of submitting the report and bill to the Senate, on the fourth of January last, neither I nor any member of the committee ever thought of such a thing; and that we could never be brought to the point of abrogating the eighth section of the Missouri act until after the Senator from Kentucky introduced his amendment to my bill.

Mr. President, before I proceed to expose the many misrepresentations contained in this complicated charge, I must call the attention of the Senate to the false issue which these gentlemen are endeavoring to impose upon the country for the purpose of diverting public attention from the real issue contained in the bill. They wish to have the people believe that the abrogation of what they call the Missouri Compromise was the main object and aim of the bill, and that the only question involved is, whether the prohibition of slavery north of 36° 30′ shall be repealed or not? That which is a mere incident they choose to consider the principle. They make war on the means by which we propose to accomplish an object, instead of openly resisting the object itself. The principle which we propose to carry into effect by the bill is this: That Congress shall neither legislate slavery into any Territories or States, nor out of the same; but the people shall be left free to regulate their domestic concerns in their own way, subject only to the Constitution of the United States.

In order to carry this principle into practical operation, it becomes necessary to remove whatever legal obstacles might be found in the way of its free exercise. It is only for the purpose of carrying out this great fundamental principle of self-government that the bill renders the eighth section of the Missouri act inoperative and void.

Now, let me ask, will these Senators who have arraigned
me, or any one of them, have the assurance to rise in his
place and declare that this great principle was never thought
of or advocated as applicable to Territorial Bills, in 1850;
that from that session until the present, nobody ever thought
of incorporating this principle in all new Territorial organizations; that the Committee on Territories did not recom-
mend it in their report; and that it required the amendment
of the Senator from Kentucky to bring us up to that point?
Will any one of my accusers dare to make this issue, and let
it be tried by the record? I will begin with the compromises of 1850. Any Senator who will take the trouble to
examine our journals, will find that on the 25th of March
of that year I reported from the Committee on Territories
two bills including the following measures: the admission
of California, a Territorial government for New Mexico,
and the adjustment of the Texas boundary. These bills
proposed to leave the people of Utah and New Mexico
free to decide the slavery question for themselves, in the
precise language of the Nebraska Bill now under discussion. A few weeks afterward the committee of thirteen
took those two bills, and put a wafer between them, and
reported them back to the Senate as one bill, with some
slight amendments. One of these amendments was, that
the Territorial Legislatures should not legislate upon the
subject of African slavery. I objected to that provision
upon the ground that it subverted the great principle of
self-government upon which the bill had been originally
framed by the Territorial Committee. On the first trial,
the Senate refused to strike it out, but subsequently did
so, after full debate, in order to establish that principle
as the rule of action in Territorial organizations. . . .

But my accusers attempt to raise up a false issue, and thereby divert public attention from the real one, by the cry that the Missouri Compromise is to be repealed or violated by the passage of this bill. Well, if the eighth section of the Missouri act, which attempted to fix the destinies of future generations in those Territories for all time to come, in utter disregard of the rights and wishes of the people when they should be received into the Union as States, be inconsistent with the great principles of self-government and the Constitution of the United States, it ought to be abrogated. The legislation of 1850 abrogated the Missouri Compromise, so far as the country embraced within the limits of Utah and New Mexico was covered by the slavery restriction. It is true, that those acts did not in terms and by name repeal the Act of 1820, as originally adopted, or as extended by the resolutions annexing Texas in 1845, any more than the report of the Committee on Territories proposed to repeal the same acts this session. But the acts of 1850 did authorize the people of those Territories to exercise "all rightful powers of legislation consistent with the Constitution," not excepting the question of slavery; and did provide that, when those Territories should be admitted into the Union, they should be received with or without slavery as the people thereof might determine at the date of their admission. These provisions were in direct conflict with a clause in the former enactment, declaring that slavery should be forever prohibited in any portion of said Territories, and hence rendered such clause inoperative and void to the extent of such conflict. This was an inevitable consequence, resulting from the provisions in those acts, which gave the people the right to decide the slavery question for themselves, in conformity with the Constitution. It was not necessary to go further and declare that certain previous enactments, which were incompatible with the exercise of the powers conferred in the bills, are hereby repealed. The very act of granting those powers and rights has the legal effect of removing all obstructions to the exercise of them by the people, as prescribed in those Territorial bills. Following that example, the Committee on Territories did not consider it necessary to declare the eighth section of the Missouri Act repealed. We were content to organize Nebraska in the precise language of the Utah and New Mexico Bills. Our object was to leave the people entirely free to form and regulate their domestic institutions and internal concerns in their own way, under the Constitution; and we deemed it wise to accomplish that object in the exact terms in which the same thing had been done in Utah and New Mexico by the Acts of 1850. This was the principle upon which the Committee voted; and our bill was supposed, and is now believed, to have been in accordance with it. When doubts were raised whether the bill did fully carry out the principle laid down in the report, amendments were made from time to time, in order to avoid all misconstruction, and make the true intent of the act more explicit. The last of these amendments was adopted yesterday, on the motion of the distinguished Senator from North Carolina (Mr. Badger), in regard to the revival of any laws or regulations which may have existed prior to 1820. That amendment was not intended to change the legal effect of the bill. Its object was to repel the slander which had been propagated by the enemies of the measure in the North—that the Southern supporters of the bill desired to legislate slavery into these Territories. The South denies the right of Congress either to legislate slavery into any Territory or State, or out of any Territory or State. Non-intervention by Congress with slavery in the States or Territories is the doctrine of the bill, and all the amendments which have been agreed to have been made with the view of removing all doubt and cavil as to the true meaning and object of the measure. . . .

Well, sir, what is this Missouri Compromise, of which we have heard so much of late? It has been read so often that it is not necessary to occupy the time of the Senate in reading it again. It was an act of Congress, passed on the 6th of March, 1820, to authorize the people of Missouri to form a Constitution and a State government, preparatory to the admission of such State into the Union. The first section provided that Missouri should be received into the Union "on an equal footing with the original States in all respects whatsoever." The last and eighth section provided that slavery should be "forever prohibited" in all the territory which had been acquired from France north of 36° 30', and not included within the limits of the State of Missouri. There is nothing in the terms of the law that purports to be a compact, or indicates that it was anything more than an ordinary act of legislation. To prove that it was more than it purports to be on its face, gentlemen must produce other evidence, and prove that there was such an understanding as to create a moral obligation in the nature of a compact. Have they shown it?

Now, if this was a compact, let us see how it was entered into. The bill originated in the House of Representatives, and passed that body without a Southern vote in its favor. It is proper to remark, however, that it did not at that time contain the eighth section, prohibiting slavery in the Territories; but in lieu of it, contained a provision prohibiting slavery in the proposed State of Missouri. In the Senate, the clause prohibiting slavery in the State was stricken out, and the eighth section added to the end of the bill, by the terms of which slavery was to be forever prohibited in the territory not embraced in the State of Missouri north of 36° 30'. The vote on adding the section stood in the Senate, 34 in the affirmative, and 10 in the negative. Of the Northern Senators, 20 voted for it, and 2 against it. On the question of ordering the bill to a third reading as amended, which was the test vote on its passage, the vote stood 24 yeas and 20 nays. Of the Northern Senators, 4 only voted in the affirmative, and 18 in the negative. Thus it will be seen that if it was intended to be a compact, the North never agreed to it. The Northern Senators voted to insert the prohibition of slavery in the Territories; and then, in the proportion of more than four to one, voted against the passage of the bill. The North, therefore, never signed the compact, never consented to it, never agreed to be bound by it. This fact becomes very important in vindicating the character of the North for repudiating this alleged compromise a few months afterward. The act was approved and became a law on the 6th of March, 1820. In the summer of that year, the people of Missouri formed a Constitution and State government preparatory to admission into the Union in conformity with the act. At the next session of Congress the Senate passed a joint resolution declaring Missouri to be one of the States of the Union, on an equal footing with the original States. This resolution was sent to the House of Representatives, where it was rejected by Northern votes, and thus Missouri was voted out of the Union, instead of being received into the Union under the Act of the 6th of March, 1820, now known as the Missouri Com

12   promise. Now, sir, what becomes of our plighted faith, if the Act of the 6th of March, 1820, was a solemn compact, as we are now told? They have all rung the changes upon it, that it was a sacred and irrevocable compact, binding in honor, in conscience, and morals, which could not be violated or repudiated without perfidy and dishonor! . . . Sir, if this was a compact, what must be thought of those who violated it almost immediately after it was formed? I say it is a calumny upon the North to say that it was a compact. I should feel a flush of shame upon my cheek, as a Northern man, if I were to say that it was a compact, and that the section of the country to which I belong received the consideration, and then repudiated the obligation in eleven months after it was entered into. I deny that it was a compact, in any sense of the term. But if it was, the record proves that faith was not observed—that the contract was never carried into effect—that after the North had procured the passage of the act prohibiting slavery in the Territories, with a majority in the House large enough to prevent its repeal, Missouri was refused admission into the Union as a slaveholding State, in conformity with the Act of March 6, 1820. If the proposition be correct, as contended for by the opponents of this bill—that there was a solemn compact between the North and the South that, in consideration of the prohibition of slavery in the Territories, Missouri was to be admitted into the Union, in conformity with the Act of 1820—that compact was repudiated by the North, and rescinded by the joint action of the two parties within twelve months from its date. Missouri was never admitted under the act of the 6th of March, 1820. She was refused admission under that act. She was voted out of the Union by Northern votes, notwithstanding the

stipulation that she should be received; and, in consequence of these facts, a new compromise was rendered necessary, by the terms of which Missouri was to be admitted into the Union conditionally—admitted on a condition not embraced in the Act of 1820, and, in addition, to a full compliance with all the provisions of said act. If, then, the Act of 1820, by the eighth section of which slavery was prohibited in Missouri, was a compact, it is clear to the comprehension of every fair-minded man that the refusal of the North to admit Missouri, in compliance with its stipulations, and without further conditions, imposes upon us a high, moral obligation to remove the prohibition of slavery in the Territories, since it has been shown to have been procured upon a condition never performed. . . .

Mr. President, I did not wish to refer to these things. I did not understand them fully in all their bearings at the time I made my first speech on this subject; and, so far as I was familiar with them, I made as little reference to them as was consistent with my duty; because it was a mortifying reflection to me, as a Northern man, that we had not been able, in consequence of the abolition excitement at the time, to avoid the appearance of bad faith in the observance of legislation, which has been denominated a compromise. There were a few men then, as there are now, who had the moral courage to perform their duty to the country and the Constitution, regardless of consequences personal to themselves. There were ten Northern men who dared to perform their duty by voting to admit Missouri into the Union on an equal footing with the original States, and with no other restriction than that imposed by the Constitution. I am aware that they were abused and denounced as we are now—that they were branded as dough-faces—traitors to freedom, and to the section of country whence they came. . . .

I think I have shown that if the Act of 1820, called the Missouri Compromise, was a compact, it was violated and repudiated by a solemn vote of the House of Representatives in 1821, within eleven months after it was adopted. It was repudiated by the North by a majority vote, and that repudiation was so complete and successful as to compel Missouri to make a new compromise, and she was brought into the Union under the new compromise of 1821, and not under the Act of 1820. This reminds me of another point made in nearly all the speeches against this bill, and, if I recollect right, was alluded to in the abolition manifesto; to which, I regret to say, I had occasion to refer so often. I refer to the significant hint that Mr. Clay was dead before any one dared to bring forward a proposition to undo the greatest work of his hands. The Senator from New York (Mr. Seward) has seized upon this insinuation and elaborated, perhaps, more fully than his compeers; and now the Abolition press, suddenly, and, as if by miraculous conversion, teems with eulogies upon Mr. Clay and his Missouri Compromise of 1820.

Now, Mr. President, does not each of these Senators know that Mr. Clay was not the author of the Act of 1820? Do they not know that he disclaimed it in 1850 in this body? Do they not know that the Missouri restriction did not originate in the House, of which he was a member? Do they not know that Mr. Clay never came into the Missouri controversy as a compromiser until after the compromise of 1820 was repudiated, and it became necessary to make another? I dislike to be compelled to repeat what I have conclusively proven, that the compromise

which Mr. Clay effected was the Act of 1821, under which
Missouri came into the Union, and not the Act of 1820.
Mr. Clay made that compromise after you had repudiated
the first one. How, then, dare you call upon the spirit of
that great and gallant statesman to sanction your charge
of bad faith against the South on this question? . . .

Now, Mr. President, as I have been doing justice to Mr.
Clay on this question, perhaps I may as well do justice to
another great man, who was associated with him in carrying through the great measure of 1850, which mortified the
Senator from New York so much, because they defeated his
purpose of carrying on the agitation. I allude to Mr. Webster. The authority of his great name has been quoted for
the purpose of proving that he regarded the Missouri act as
a compact, an irrepealable compact. Evidently the distinguished Senator from Massachusetts (Mr. Everett) supposed
he was doing Mr. Webster entire justice when he quoted
the passage which he read from Mr. Webster's speech of
the 7th of March, 1850, when he said that he stood upon
the position that every part of the American continent was
fixed for freedom or for slavery by irrepealable law. The
Senator says that by the expression "irrepealable law," Mr.
Webster meant to include the Compromise of 1820. Now,
I will show that that was not Mr. Webster's meaning—that
he was never guilty of the mistake of saying that the Missouri Act of 1820 was an irrepealable law. Mr. Webster
said in that speech that every foot of territory in the
United States was fixed as to its character for freedom
or slavery by an irrepealable law. He then inquired if
it was not so in regard to Texas? He went on to prove
that it was; because, he said, there was a compact in express terms between Texas and the United States. He

said the parties were capable of contracting and that there was a valuable consideration; and hence he contended that in that case there was a contract binding in honor and morals and law; and that it was irrepealable without a breach of faith.

He went on to say:

"Now, as to California and New Mexico, I hold slavery to be excluded from these Territories by a law even superior to that which admits and sanctions it in Texas—I mean the law of nature—of physical geography —the law of the formation of the earth."

That was the irrepealable law which he said prohibited slavery in the Territories of Utah and New Mexico. He went on to speak of the prohibition of slavery in Oregon, and he said it was an "entirely useless and, in that connection, senseless proviso."

He went further, and said:

"That the whole territory of the States of the United States, or in the newly acquired territory of the United States, has a fixed and settled character, now fixed and settled by law, which cannot be repealed in the case of Texas without a violation of public faith, and cannot be repealed by any human power in regard to California or New Mexico; that, *under one or other of these laws*, every foot of territory in the States or in the Territories has now received a fixed and decided character."

What irrepealable laws? "One or the other" of those which he had stated. One was the Texas compact; the other, the law of nature and physical geography; and he contended that one or the other fixed the character of the whole American continent for freedom or for slavery. He never alluded to the Missouri Compromise, unless it was by the allusion to the Wilmot Proviso in the Oregon Bill, and therein said it was a useless and, in that connection, senseless thing. Why was it a useless and senseless thing? Because it was re-enacting the law of God; because slavery had already been prohibited by physical geography. Sir, that was the meaning of Mr. Webster's speech. . . .

Mr. President, I have occupied a good deal of time in exposing the cant of these gentlemen about the sanctity of the Missouri Compromise, and the dishonor attached to the violation of plighted faith. I have exposed these matters in order to show that the object of these men is to withdraw from public attention the real principle involved in the bill. They well know that the abrogation of the Missouri Compromise is the incident and not the principle of the bill. They well understand that the report of the committee and the bill propose to establish the principle in all Territorial organizations, that the question of slavery shall be referred to the people to regulate for themselves, and that such legislation should be had as was necessary to remove all legal obstructions to the free exercise of this right by the people. The eighth section of the Missouri act standing in the way of this great principle must be rendered inoperative and void, whether expressly repealed or not, in order to give the people the power of regulating their own domestic institutions in their own way, subject only to the Constitution.

Now, sir, if these gentlemen have entire confidence in the correctness of their own position, why do they not meet the issue boldly and fairly, and controvert the soundness of this great principle of popular sovereignty in obedience to the Constitution? They know full well that this was the principle upon which the Colonies separated from the crown of Great Britain, the principle upon which the battles of the Revolution were fought, and the principle upon which our Republican system was founded. They cannot be ignorant of the fact that the Revolution grew out of the assertion of the right on the part of the imperial government to interfere with the internal affairs and domestic concerns of the Colonies. . . .

The Declaration of Independence had its origin in the violation of that great fundamental principle which secured to the Colonies the right to regulate their own domestic affairs in their own way; and the Revolution resulted in the triumph of that principle, and the recognition of the right asserted by it. Abolitionism proposes to destroy the right and extinguish the principle for which our forefathers waged a seven years' bloody war, and upon which our whole system of free government is founded. They not only deny the application of this principle to the Territories, but insist upon fastening the prohibition upon all the States to be formed out of those Territories. Therefore, the doctrine of the Abolitionists—the doctrine of the opponents of the Nebraska and Kansas Bill, and the advocates of the Missouri restriction—demands Congressional interference with slavery not only in the Territories, but in all the new States to be formed therefrom. It is the same doctrine, when applied to the Territories and the new States of this Union, which the British Government attempted to enforce by the sword upon the American Colonies. It is this fundamental principle of self-government which constitutes the distinguishing feature of the Nebraska Bill. The opponents of the principle are consistent in opposing the bill. I do not blame them for their opposition. I only ask them to meet the issue fairly and openly, by acknowledging that they are opposed to the principle which it is the object of the bill to carry into operation. It seems that there is no power on earth, no intellectual power, no mechanical power, that can bring them to a fair discussion of the true issue. If they hope to delude the people and escape detection for any considerable length of time under the catchwords "Missouri Compromise" and "faith of compacts," they will find that the people of this country have more penetration and intelligence than they have given them credit for.

Mr. President, there is an important fact connected with this slavery regulation, which should never be lost sight of. It has always arisen from one and the same cause. Whenever that cause has been removed, the agitation has ceased; and whenever the cause has been renewed, the agitation has sprung into existence. That cause is, and ever has been, the attempt on the part of Congress to interfere with the question of slavery in the Territories and new States formed therefrom. Is it not wise then to confine our action within the sphere of our legitimate duties, and leave this vexed question to take care of itself in each State and Territory, according to the wishes of the people thereof, in conformity to the forms, and in subjection to the provisions, of the Constitution?

The opponents of the bill tell us that agitation is no part of their policy; that their great desire is peace and harmony; and they complain bitterly that I should have disturbed the repose of the country by the introduction of this measure! Let me ask these professed friends of peace, and avowed enemies of agitation, how the issue could have been avoided. They tell me that I should have let the question alone; that is, that I should have left Nebraska unorganized, the people unprotected, and the Indian barrier in existence, until the swelling tide of emigration should burst through, and accomplish by violence what it is the part of wisdom and statesmanship to direct and regulate by law. How long could you have postponed action with safety? How long could you maintain that Indian barrier, and restrain the onward march of civilization, Christianity, and free government by a barbarian wall? Do you suppose that you could keep that vast country a howling wilderness in all time to come, roamed over by hostile savages, cutting off all safe communication between our Atlantic and Pacific possessions? I tell you that the time for action has come, and cannot be postponed. It is a case in which the "let alone" policy would precipitate a crisis which must inevitably result in violence, anarchy, and strife.

You cannot fix bounds to the onward march of this great and growing country. You cannot fetter the limbs of the young giant. He will burst all your chains. He will expand, and grow, and increase, and extend civilization, Christianity, and liberal principles. Then, sir, if you cannot check the growth of the country in that direction, is it not the part of wisdom to look the danger in the face, and provide for an event which you cannot avoid? I tell you, sir, you must provide for lines of continuous settlement from the Mississippi Valley to the Pacific Ocean. And in making this provision, you must decide upon what principles the Territories shall be organized; in other words, whether the people shall be allowed to regulate their domestic institutions in their own way, according to the provisions of this bill, or whether the opposite doctrine of Congressional interference is to prevail. Postpone it, if you will; but whenever you do act, this question must be met and decided.

The Missouri Compromise was interference; the Compromise of 1850 was non-interference, leaving the people to exercise their rights under the Constitution. The Committee on Territories were compelled to act on this subject. I, as their chairman, was bound to meet the question. I chose to take the responsibility regardless of consequences personal to myself. I should have done the same thing last year, if there had been time; but we know, considering the late period at which the bill then reached us from the House, that there was not sufficient time to consider the question fully, and to prepare a report upon the subject. I was therefore persuaded by my friends to allow the bill to be reported to the Senate, in order that such action might be taken as should be deemed wise and proper. The bill was never taken up for action—the last night of the session having been exhausted in debate on a motion to take up the bill. This session, the measure was introduced by my friend from Iowa (Mr. Dodge), and referred to the Territorial Committee during the first week of the session. We have abundance of time to consider the subject; it is a matter of pressing necessity, and there was no excuse for not meeting it directly and fairly. We were compelled to take our position upon the doctrine either of intervention or non-intervention. We chose the latter for two reasons: first, because we believed that the principle was right; and, second, because it was the principle adopted in 1850, to which the two great political parties of the country were solemnly pledged.

There is another reason why I desire to see this principle recognized as a rule of action in all time to come. It will have the effect to destroy all sectional parties and sectional agitations. If, in the language of the report of the committee, you withdraw the slavery question from the halls of Congress and the political arena, and commit it to the arbitrament of those who are immediately interested in and alone responsible for its consequences, there is nothing left out of which sectional parties can be organized. It never was done, and never can be done on the bank, tariff, distribution, or any party issue which has existed, or may exist, after this slavery question is withdrawn from politics. On every other political question these have always supporters and opponents in every portion of the Union—in each State, county, village, and neighborhood—residing together in harmony and good fellowship, and combating each other's opinions and correcting each other's errors in a spirit of kindness and friendship. These differences of opinion between neighbors and friends, and the discussions that grow out of them, and the sympathy which each feels with the advocates of his own opinions in every portion of this widespread Republic, add an overwhelming and irresistible moral weight to the strength of the Confederacy. Affection for the Union can never be alienated or diminished by any other party issues than those which are joined upon sectional or geographical lines. When the people of the North shall all be rallied under one banner, and the whole South marshalled under another banner, and each section excited to frenzy and madness by hostility to the institutions of the other, then the patriot may well tremble for the perpetuity of the Union. Withdraw the slavery question from the political arena, and remove it to the States and Territories, each to decide for itself, such a catastrophe can never happen. Then you will never be able to tell, by any Senator's vote for or against any measure, from what State or section of the Union he comes.

Why, then, can we not withdraw this vexed question from politics? Why can we not adopt the principle of this bill as a rule of action in all new Territorial organizations? Why can we not deprive these agitators of their vocation and render it impossible for Senators to come here upon bargains on the slavery question? I believe that the peace, the harmony, and perpetuity of the Union require us to go back to the doctrines of the Revolution, to the principles of the Constitution, to the principles of the Compromise of 1850, and leave the people, under the Constitution, to do as they may see proper in respect to their own internal affairs.

Mr. President, I have not brought this question forward as a Northern man or as a Southern man. I am unwilling to recognize such divisions and distinctions. I have brought it forward as an American Senator, representing a State which is true to this principle, and which has approved of my action in respect to the Nebraska Bill. I have brought it forward not as an act of justice to the South more than to the North. I have presented it especially as an act of justice to the people of those Territories and of the States to be formed therefrom, now and in all time to come. I have nothing to say about Northern rights or Southern rights. I know of no such divisions or distinctions under the Constitution. The bill does equal and exact justice to the whole Union, and every part of it; it violates the right of no State or Territory; but places each on a perfect equality, and leaves the people thereof to the free enjoyment of all their rights under the Constitution.

Now, sir, I wish to say to our Southern friends that if

most conclusive authority in the books before me. I regret that I did not conclude to participate in the discussion at a period sufficiently early to have enabled me to make the requisite preparation. If I had done so, I should have been able to compress what I have to say within a much smaller compass, and to have said it in a manner more satisfactory to myself and more intelligible to the Senate. I had supposed that the only question presented by the bill was, to determine whether the additional force provided for was necessary for the prosecution of the existing war to a speedy and honorable termination. The war has been in progress nearly two years. Its legal existence was recognized on the 13th of May, 1846, and it existed, in fact, prior to that time, as the official reports of the battles of Palo Alto and Resaca will show. The campaign of 1846 resulted in a series of the most brilliant victories that ever adorned the arms of any nation. States and territories were overrun and subjected, equal in extent to one half of the Mexican Confederacy, California, New Mexico, Chihuahua, Coahuila, New Leon, and Tamaulipas, besides many important towns and cities in other states, were reduced to our possession. The official reports of these conquests are to be found in the published documents of last session. The President of the United States, in his message at the beginning of that session, gave us a succinct history of the progress of our arms in these several Mexican provinces, and suggested the propriety of " providing for the security of these important conquests, by making an adequate appropriation for the purpose of erecting fortifications, and defraying the expenses necessarily incident to the maintenance of our possession and authority over them." In the same message he referred to the three-million appropriation which he had asked for at the previous

session, and renewed the recommendation. He referred to
the appropriations which were made in anticipation of the
Louisiana and Florida treaties as precedents in this case,
and adds, that " it was in contemplation, at the time those
appropriations were made, to acquire Louisiana from
France, and to purchase the Floridas from Spain, and that
they were intended to be applied as a part of the consideration which might be paid for those territories." Upon this
exposition of the progress of the war, and of the policy of the
government in reference to it, the President asked for more
men and money, for the purpose of conducting a campaign
into the very heart of Mexico — of reducing her capital, and
of holding possession of the whole country, until she should
accede to such terms of boundary and indemnity as we should
deem just and honorable. The men and money were freely
voted, including the three-million appropriation, which was
intended to be applied in part payment — the first instal-
ment, for instance — for such territory as we might acquire
from Mexico in a treaty of peace, in addition to what should
be deemed adequate remuneration for the expenses of the
war, and indemnity to our citizens. I shall excite no surprise, therefore, when I say that I was not prepared to hear
this unqualified denunciation of the war and of the recommendations of the President for its vigorous prosecution —
especially from those senators who voted for all the war
measures of last session and the preceding one. I was not
prepared to hear them denounce the war as unjust, unnecessary, and unconstitutional — much less as a war of conquest,
of rapine, and robbery. We have heard these denunciations,
within the last few days, poured forth from the lips of senators with a solemnity that would seem to carry conviction, at
least to the minds of those who made them, that they were

STEPHEN A. DOUGLAS

Orations—Volume seventeen

well merited; and, what is more astonishing, we have heard them from senators who, by their votes, if not their speeches, have sustained every war measure which has passed since hostilities first commenced by the act of Mexico. They now contend, not only that the war was unnecessary and unconstitutional, but that the President of the United States is the sole author of the inquity. Do gentlemen suppose that they can throw the responsibility of their own acts upon the President of the United States? Do they imagine that they can make the people believe that the executive is alone responsible for all the consequences that may flow from the faithful execution of the laws which they enact, and, under the constitution, compel him to execute? If it be a war of iniquity and injustice, you are the transgressors! If it be a war of robbery, you are the robbers! If it be a war against and in violation of the constitution, yours is the treason! You voted for it, under the solemnity of your oaths. You voted the men and the money. You voted to recognize the legal and constitutional existence of the war. You helped to pass the law, and made it the sworn duty of the President to see it faithfully executed It is your war, as much as his and ours; and you will not be permitted to escape your share of its responsibility, while you participate in the credit which you claim from having given it your support. I do not intend to cast any unkind reflections upon any senator, but I do think that I am fully justified by the record in the observations which I have just made. It would seem that a great discovery has recently been made — that the Congress of the United States has been acting under an entire misapprehension in regard to the nature and character of this war. We are now told that the President has changed his ground, and now assigns causes and reasons totally different promptly responded to, her fleet would immediately sail from the Jamaica station. The money was paid, because the demand was made in a tone that Mexico could understand. America spoke, as one sister would speak to another, in a voice of kindness and sisterly affection, but it fell upon Mexican ears as an unknown tongue. Mexico, mistaking our magnanimity for pusillanimity, treated our complaints with contempt, and our remonstrances with defiance.

The President of the United States, in the message to which I have referred, spoke of these things as just ground of complaint and indemnity, but not as the causes of the existing war. For he informed us that the war existed by the act of Mexico — that the Mexican army had " invaded our territory, and shed American blood upon American soil." The precise spot is not stated, but the locality is well known to have been on the left bank of the Rio Grande, opposite, and not far from, Matamoras. Then and there the war actually commenced, the Mexican army making the attack — the commanding general having, on the morning of the same day, given notice to General Taylor that " he considered hostilities commenced, and should prosecute them." This was on the 24th of April, 1846. The battle of Palo Alto was fought on the 8th, and Resaca de la Palma on the 9th, of May. Congress recognized the existence of the war, and placed at the disposal of the President ten millions of money and fifty thousand volunteers, besides the army, the navy, and the militia of the United States, for its vigorous prosecution. The law passed almost unanimously, there being only fourteen dissenting voices in the House, and two in the Senate. If the war is unconstitutional now, I suppose it was equally so then; and if it was unconstitutional then, it must necessarily be so now, unless that law legalized it, or (if I may be allowed to invent a more impressive term) constitutionalized it. In either event, Congress sanctioned it by a vote almost unanimous, irrespective of party distinctions; and confirmed it by furnishing men and means to an almost unlimited extent. I now submit it to the consciences, as well as the patriotism, of senators who voted for that law, if they are not estopped from saying that the war is either unjust, unnecessry or unconstitutional? But I will return to the recently made discovery, that the President has changed his grounds in regard to the causes of the war, and the objects for prosecuting it. I have shown that the causes which produced it remain unchanged, and that the President set forth the insults to our flag, and the injuries to our commerce and citizens, as grievances to be redressed, in the message to which the act of the 13th of May, 1846, was a patriotic response. I now wish to invite the attention of the Senate — especially those senators who have hitherto supported the war, and now oppose it upon the ground that the President has recently shifted positions by setting up a claim for indemnity — to the following extracts from a document which was sent to General Taylor, from the War Department, on the 4th of June, 1846, and by him promulgated to the Mexican people:

" A PROCLAMATION BY THE GENERAL COMMANDING THE ARMY OF THE UNITED STATES OF AMERICA, TO THE PEOPLE OF MEXICO:

" After many years of patient endurance, the United States are at length constrained to acknowledge that a war now exists between our government and the government of Mexico. For many years our citizens have been subjected to repeated insults and injuries, our vessels and cargoes have been seized and confiscated, our merchants have been plundered, maimed, imprisoned without cause and without reparation. At length ing what we had conquered, but for making new conquests in the very heart of Mexico. These bills received the cordial and powerful support of senators, who now tell us that we ought to withhold all further supplies, because the President has changed his whole policy, and converted it into a war of conquest.

Sir, I do not understand that it is, or at any time has been, a war of conquest, in the proper sense of that term, much less a war of robbery. It is a war of self-defence, forced upon us by our enemy, and prosecuted on our part in vindication of our honor, and the integrity of our territory. The enemy invaded our territory, and we repelled the invasion, and demanded satisfaction for all our grievances. In order to compel Mexico to do us justice, it was necessary to follow her retreating armies into her territory, to take possession of State after State, and hold them until she would yield to our reasonable demands; and inasmuch as it was certain that she was unable to make indemnity in money, we must necessarily take it in land. Conquest was not the motive for the prosecution of the war; satisfaction, indemnity, security, was the motive — conquest and territory the means.

Mr. President, I cannot dwell longer on the inconsistencies in which gentlemen on the opposite side involve themselves. I have already dwelt too long on these preliminary questions. I must proceed at once to the main point of my argument. I propose to examine the question, whether, on the 24th of May, 1846, American blood was shed on American soil by the Mexican army. That the Mexican forces crossed the Rio Grande on that day — attacked and killed American soldiers stationed on the left bank, is conceded. But it is denied that the left bank of that river was American soil; or, in other words, that the Rio Grande was the boundary line between

Mexico and the United States, after the admission of Texas into the Union. It is my present purpose to establish the affirmative of this proposition.

I will premise that, in my judgment, a radical error has generally obtained in regard to the character of the revolution which resulted in the establishment of the Republic of Texas. It seems to have been generally supposed that Texas rebelled against the constitutional authorities of Mexico, and, by means of a successful revolution, established her independence. No such thing. Texas never rebelled — never revolted. Precisely the reverse was the fact. A few military leaders, with Santa Anna at their head, conspired and rebelled against the Republic of Mexico — seized the reins of government — abolished the federal constitution and the State governments — and established a military despotism in their stead. That rebellion, which commenced in the city of Mexico, assumed the dignity of a successful revolution, and by the aid of the army extended its power from State to State, until it had reduced to subjection all that portion of the Republic of Mexico which lies to the south and west of the Rio Grande. The people on this side of the Rio Grande took up arms in defence of the constitutional government of the Republic of Mexico — state and federal — maintained their authority, and limited and confined the power of the revolutionary government to the right bank of that river. To show that I am clearly right in this position, it will be necessary for me to refer somewhat in detail to the most prominent facts connected with the history of Texas, as well as the revolution which led to the establishment of that Republic. From the date of the Louisiana treaty in 1803 to that of the Florida treaty in 1819, this government uniformly claimed the Rio Grande as the western boundary of the United States. In of Coahuila and Texas was adopted. It had been formed in conformity with the federal constitution, and in pursuance of an act of the federal Congress. This State constitution, and the constitution of the Republic, may be considered as the articles of compact — the bond of union — between the State and the confederation. They contain the terms and the conditions upon which the State of Coahuila and Texas constituted a member of the confederacy. I have these two instruments before me, and will invite the attention of the Senate to the first five articles of the constitution of the State of Coahuila and Texas.

"Article 1. The State of Coahuila and Texas is the union of all the Coahuiltexanos.

"Article 2. It is free and independent of the other Mexican States, and of every other power and dominion whatsoever.

"Article 3. The sovereignty of the State resides originally and essentially in the general mass of the individuals who compose it; but they shall not, of themselves, exercise any other acts of sovereignty than those pointed out in this constitution and in the form which it provides.

"Article 4. In all subjects relating to the Mexican Confederacy the State delegates its powers and rights to the general Congress of the same; but in all that belongs to the internal government and administration of said State it retains its liberty, independence, and sovereignty.

"Article 5. Wherefore, the right of establishing its fundamental laws through the medium of its representatives, in conformity to the basis established in the constitutive act and general constitution, belongs exclusively to the said State."

These were the conditions upon which the Texans became citizens of the Mexican confederacy, and were the terms alone upon which they could be required or expected to continue such. They had been invited and called there, through the colonization laws, with the guarantee that they should be protected in the enjoyment of all their rights as citizens, agreeably to the forms of the constitution. They were "free and independent of the other Mexican United States, and of every other power and dominion whatsoever." They continued true and law-abiding citizens, faithful to the constitution of the State and the confederation until their seat of government was invaded about the 1st of June, 1835, by a revolutionary army from the City of Mexico, a portion of the members of the legislature, which was then in session, captured and imprisoned, and the rest compelled to save their lives by flight, and seek a place of refuge on this side of the Rio Grande. The inhabitants between that river and the Sabine instantly took up arms in defence of their liberties and republican institutions, and for the purpose of checking the progress of the invading revolutionary army. For the purpose of concentrating their forces, and giving energy and a proper direction to their patriotic efforts, they assembled in convention on the 3d of November, 1835, and, after making a "solemn declaration" of the causes which had compelled them to take up arms, proceeded to organize a provisional government. I will read the first and the concluding paragraphs of this declaration:

"DECLARATION OF THE PEOPLE OF TEXAS, IN GENERAL CONVENTION ASSEMBLED.

"Whereas, General Antonio Lopez de Santa Anna and other military chieftains have, by force of arms, overthrown the federal institutions of Mexico, and dissolved the social compact which existed between Texas and the other members of the Mexican Confederacy; now, the good people of Texas, availing themselves of their natural rights, solemnly declare:

"1st. That they have taken up arms in defence of their rights and liberties, which are threatened by the encroach-

I will read another paragraph, to show the precautions which were taken by the usurpers to coerce the acquiescence of the people in the military despotism which they were about to establish on the ruins of the republican system:

"Symptoms of opposition having been exhibited in some of the States against this act of Congress, levelling the whole structure of their State governments, and in fact annihilating the very name of State, provision was made by Congress for a large increase of the standing army, and a considerable force was ordered to be permanently quartered in each State, under the command of the new governors now to be appointed by the president."

The decree for the establishment of the new government bears date the 3d of October, 1835, and is "formed upon the plan of Toluca for a basis." I have no less than three other histories before me, in which the same transactions are recorded, and all agree on every material point. I will read from them if any senator shall desire it. The presence of the military kept the people in subjection, and the revolution was complete so far as the capital was concerned. Its power extended in every direction. State after State submitted unconditionally before the march of the revolutionary army, until it took up its position on the borders of Zacatecas. Here, for the first time, it met with formidable opposition. Alvarez, the republican governor of that State, had raised an army of five thousand men, and awaited the approach of the revolutionists, for the purpose of deciding the fate of the republic, its constitution and liberties, by the wager of battle. Santa Anna, who commanded his troops in person, knew too well the character of these stern republicans to hazard his life and fortunes upon the issue of an engagement with them. They had fought with him and under him in achieving the

13 liberties of the country — they had been his main reliance in many a hard-fought battle in resisting the encroachments of despotism — they had been instrumental in his elevation to the Presidency, under the conviction that he, who had contributed so much to achieve, would exert himself to preserve their liberties. He feared, as well he might, a trial of strength with such men in such a cause. In this emergency he resorted to his usual recourse — stratagem. Several of his most reliable officers in the revolutionary army deserted their posts, effected their escape, and joined the patriots, with the avowed purpose of fighting in defence of the constitution. They tendered their services to command the patriot army, and unfortunately the offer was accepted. They marched the Zacatecans out to meet the enemy, and placed them in a position where Santa Anna surrounded and murdered more than one half of them before the rest were aware of the treachery of their officers. The slaughter was indiscriminate, and continued for two entire days. It was not confined to those who bore arms. The streets of the city of Zacatecas were deluged in blood. The unoffending citizens shared the fate of those who had engaged in battle. Even foreigners, who had taken no part in the contest, were not permitted to escape the general massacre.

Those who survived, now submitted unconditionally to the power of the usurper, and no further resistance ensued. The revolutionary army now turned its course towards Monclova, the seat of government for the State of Coahuila and Texas, for the purpose of chastising the Coahuiltexanos for their obstinacy in adhering to the republican constitution. The legislature of that State had solemnly protested against those revolutionary movements, and announced its determination to sustain and enforce the constitution and form of government which all were sworn to support. For this offence, General Cos, the brother-in-law of Santa Anna, dispersed the legislature by military force, captured and imprisoned a portion of the members, while the others only saved themselves by fleeing across the Rio Grande. The Senate will pardon me for reading a single paragraph on this point from the report of General Austin to the Texas convention, on the 30th of November of that year:

" The constitutional authorities of the State of Coahuila and Texas solemnly protested against the change of government, for which act they were driven by military force from office and imprisoned. The people of Texas protested against it, as they had a right to do, for which they have been declared rebels by the government in Mexico."

Prior to the capture of Monclova, and in anticipation of such an event, the legislature had authorized Governor Viesca to remove the archives of State, and convene the representatives of the people at such point on this side of the Rio Grande as he should designate. General Cos pursued and captured the governor and archives, together with the gallant Colonel Milam, who afterwards fell so gloriously while storming San Antonio, and threw them into prison. At this period the actual war commenced between the republicans on this side of the Rio Grande, and the revolutionists from the other side: the former fighting in defence of their State and federal constitutions, and the latter for their total overthrow. There is no room for controversy as to the causes of that war, and the objects to be attained by the triumph of the one party or the other. It was a direct issue between constitutional republicanism and military despotism. The revolution had already been successful to the right bank of the Rio Grande, and its victorious armies were now preparing for new conquests on this side of that river. The republicans instantly seized their arms and attacked the garrisons, which the usurper had taken the precaution to station at various points, for the purpose of over-awing the people and holding them in subjection to the new government which he was about to establish. All their early efforts were crowned with success. Victory perched upon their banners at every point. Gonzales, Conception, Goliad, San Patricio, and finally San Antonio — all surrendered to the republicans before Christmas. While these important movements were being enacted in the field, the republicans had not been unmindful of the necessity of establishing a provisional government, to combine and consolidate their resources, and give force and direction to their efforts. After the capture and imprisonment of Governor Viesca, who had been authorized by the legislature to assemble the representatives of the people at such point as he should designate, they were left to select their own time and place of meeting. They did assemble at San Felipe de Austin on the 3d day of November, 1835, and put forth the "solemn declaration," to which I have already called the attention of the Senate, and proceeded to form a provisional government. In that declaration, it should be borne in mind, they state distinctly that they had taken up arms in defence of the republican principles of the constitution of 1824. The revolutionary army, under General Cos, had passed the Rio Grande and marched upon San Antonio, and a republican army was immediately organized and sent to repel the invaders. I will not weary the Senate with the details of the movements on the plains of San Antonio. The gallant conduct of the heroic Milam, in leading the storming party into the very heart of the city, and his fall, just as victory was within his grasp, have commanded the admiration and sympathy of his countrymen. The next

in command finished the work which had been so gloriously
commenced, and General Cos and his entire army became
prisoners of war to the republicans. I hold in my hand the
terms of capitulation entered into on the 11th of December,
1835, and invite the especial attention of senators to the
articles which I shall read:

" CAPITULATION ENTERED INTO BY GENERAL MARTIN PER-
  FECTO DE COS, OF THE PERMANENT TROOPS, AND GENERAL
  EDWARD BURLESON, OF THE COLONIAL TROOPS OF TEXAS.

" 1st. That General Cos and his officers retire, with their
arms and private property, into the interior of the Republic,
under the parole of honor; that they will not in any way
oppose the re-establishment of the federal constitution of
1824. . . .
" 3d. That the General take the convicts brought in by
Colonel Ugartechea beyond the Rio Grande. . . .
" 14th. General Burleson will furnish General Cos with
such provisions as can be obtained, necessary for his troops
to the Rio Grande, at the ordinary price of the country."

Such was the fate of the first revolutionary army that
invaded Texas — defeated, captured, and dependent upon
the generosity of the Texans for provisions to enable them
to return to their own country. But there are two important
points in these articles of capitulation, which we should constantly bear in mind while discussing the boundary of the
Rio Grande. The first is, that General Cos and his army
were released upon the condition " that they will not in any
way oppose the re-establishment of the federal constitution
of 1824; " and secondly, that they should retire into the
interior of the Mexican Republic, taking with them the convicts " beyond the Rio Grande," being furnished with supplies by General Burleson to that river. The preliminary
conditions were complied with on both sides, and here ended

the first Mexican campaign into Texas. There was not a Mexican garrison nor a Mexican soldier left on this side of the Rio Grande. One campaign had placed the whole country in the acknowledged and undisputed possession of the Texans. The withdrawal of the enemy's troops gave the Texans time for deliberation to devise and establish for themselves a more perfect government. On the 2d day of March, 1836, they adopted "the unanimous declaration of independence;" and on the 17th of the same month, they signed and published the constitution which I hold in my hand. It is the "Constitution of the Republic of Texas;" which, on all essential points, conforms to the principles of the Mexican constitution of 1824, and our own free institutions. By looking over the signatures to this constitution, as well as the declaration of independence which preceded it, I find an important fact, which may throw some light on the question of boundary. From the municipality or county of Bexar, I find the following names, namely: Francisco Rouis, Antonio Navarro, J. B. Bodgett. From the municipality or county of San Patricio, are the names of John Turner, B. B. Goodrich, Jesse Grimes, J. G. Swisher, G. W. Burnett. Now, sir, by reference to Mitchell's map, which I have before me, I find these municipalities or counties laid down as extending from the Nueces to the Rio Grande; and in Mrs. Holley's "Texas" I find a very interesting account of the town of San Patrick, on the west side of the Nueces, and which, I understand, was the seat of justice of the county of San Patricio, until it was removed to Corpus Christi, by the act of the 18th of January, 1845.

I will read Mrs. Holley's description of San Patrick, written in the year 1836:

"San Patrick.—This is an Irish colony, situated in Mc-Mullen's and McGloin's grant, on the right bank of the Nueces. A number of Irish families have settled here, and many others will probably find an asylum, with the certain prospect of plenty and independence. The settlement of Irish colonies in this grant is the great object of the Empresarios, who are themselves ' exiles of Erin.' The Mexican garrison at this place surrendered to the patriots on the 3d of October, 1835."

I shall have occasion, before I close my remarks, to refer to the various acts of the Texan Congress, fixing the times of holding courts in the counties of San Patricio and Bexar, and especially the act of the 24th of May, 1838, establishing the dividing line between them. I will here content myself with the remark that, by that act, the boundary was declared to be a direct line from a certain point on the Rio Frio, thirty miles above its junction with the Nueces, to the town of Laredo, on the left bank of the Rio Grande. I am not now discussing the question as to the boundaries of the department called Bexar or Texas under the Spanish government, or during the revolutionary struggle of the Mexican people for independence; much less the idle and useless question as to the imaginary boundary, during the period that Texas and Coahuila constituted one state in the Mexican confederacy. I care not whether Coahuila and Tamaulipas were supposed to have theoretical possessions on this side of the Rio Grande prior to the overthrow of the federal constitution of 1824. If they had such possessions, they lost them when they lost their State sovereignty, by acquiescing in the revolution, and submitting to the degradation of becoming a mere department in Santa Anna's military despotism, with their diminished and curtailed limits. By that act of submission they forfeited all right to require their fellow citizens on this side of the Rio Grande to become co-sufferers in their degradation. The bond of union was dissolved by their own act, and by their wrong; and the people on this side, in the counties of San Patricio and Bexar, had a right to be represented, as they were represented, in the convention which proclaimed the independence and formed the constitution of the Republic of Texas. The question now to be determined is, what were the boundaries of the Republic, not the department of Texas. I have shown that the first invading army had been captured, and sent beyond the Rio Grande, and that, on the 1st day of January, 1836, there was not a Mexican soldier on this side of that river. While the Texans were engaged in improving and remodeling their civil institutions, Santa Anna was preparing and organizing a new army of invasion. He crossed the Rio Grande, and entered the settlements of Texas with two invading columns — the one in the direction of San Antonio, and the other upon Goliad. The slaughter of Travis and his fellow patriots in the Alamo, and the murder of Fannin and his entire command at Goliad, after they had entered into a capitulation and become prisoners of war, foreshadowed the fate of all who might fall into the hands of the Dictator. The work of destruction continued, with fire and sword, until the two hostile armies met on the banks of the San Jacinto. There, on the 21st of April, 1836, the gallant little Texan army, under the command of the distinguished senator before me, literally annihilated the Mexican forces, leaving more than one-half of them dead upon the field, and capturing the rest — not allowing even one to escape to tell the tale of the terrible retribution which the God of Battles had inflicted upon them for their merciless crimes. The murderer of Fannin and his men was now a captive pleading for his life in the hands of the Texan general. The generals of the two armies, and the executives of the two nations (for such they were now acknowledged to be) immediately opened negotiations for a treaty of peace, independence, and boundaries. At length, on the 12th of May, 1836, the treaty was signed by President Burnett and his cabinet on the part of the Republic of Texas, and General Santa Anna on the part of Mexico. The caption shows who were the parties to this treaty. I will read it:

" Articles of agreement and solemn compact, made and adopted by James G. Burnet, President of the Republic of Texas, and the undersigned members of the cabinet thereof, on the one part, and Don Antonio Lopez de Santa Anna, President of the Republic of Mexico, and Don Vincente Filisola, general of division, Don José Urea, Don Joaquim Ramires y Sesma, and Don Antonio Goana, generals of brigades of the armies of Mexico."

After a preamble, the first article proceeds as follows:

" Therefore, it is agreed by the President Santa Anna, and the Generals Don Vincente Filisola, Don José Urea, Don Joaquim Ramires y Sesma, and Don Antonio Goana—
" 1st. That the armies of Mexico shall, with all practicable expedition, evacuate the territory of Texas, and retire to Monterey, beyond the Rio Grande."

The second article provides that the Mexican army " shall abstain from all pillage and devastation " on their retreat. I will invite especial attention to the third, and a part of the fourth articles, as follows:

" 3d. That the army of Texas are to march westwardly, and to occupy such posts as the commanding general may think proper, on the east side of the Rio Grande or Rio Bravo del Norte.
" 4th. That the President Santa Anna, in his official character as chief of the Mexican nation, and the Generals Don

Vincente Filisola, Don José Urea, Don Joaquim Ramires y Sesma, and Don Antonio Goana, as chiefs of armies, do solemnly acknowledge, sanction, and ratify the full, entire, and perfect independence of the Republic of Texas, with such boundaries as are hereafter set forth and agreed upon for the same."

The fifth article prescribes the boundaries of the Republic of Texas. I will read so much as relates to the southwestern boundary:

" 5th. That the following be, and the same are hereby, established and made the lines of demarcation between the two Republics of Mexico and Texas, to wit: The line shall commence at the estuary or mouth of the Rio Grande, on the western bank thereof, and shall pursue the same bank of the said river to the point where the river assumes the name of the Rio Bravo del Norte, from which point it shall proceed on the said western bank to the head waters, or source of said river, it being understood that the terms Rio Grande and Rio Bravo del Norte apply to and designate one and the same stream."

The sixth and seventh articles relate to the release of prisoners, and the restoration to Texas of all fortresses, artillery, and munitions of war within her limits.

In article eighth, Texas undertakes, in consideration of the foregoing provisions, to spare the life of Santa Anna and his officers, and to restore them to their liberty.

Article ninth is as follows:

" 9th. The release of the President Santa Anna shall be made immediately on receiving the signatures of Generals Don Vincente Filisola, Don José Urea, Don Joaquim Ramires y Sesma, and Don Antonio Goana, to this agreement, and his conveyance to Vera Cruz as soon afterward as may be convenient."

It will be borne in mind that the generals named in the

ninth article were not prisoners, and that after the capture of Santa Anna, General Filisola succeeded to his powers as commander-in-chief of the Mexican army. The remaining articles relate to the mode in which these were to be executed. General Filisola, and the other officers named in the ninth article, did subsequently sign and ratify this treaty; and, in pursuance of it, were permitted to retire, with the forces under their command, in peace and security beyond the Rio Grande. Here ends the history of the second invasion of Texas by Mexico. Like the first, it resulted in the total annihilation of the invading army — its defeat and capture. Texas was now free and independent, without a hostile foot upon her soil. There was not a Mexican soldier to be found on this side of the Rio Grande. Those who survived the battle of San Jacinto, and returned to their own country, did so by the permission of the Texan army, and under the sanctity of a treaty stipulation that the Rio Grande should forever remain the line of " demarcation between the two Republics of Mexico and Texas." It does seem to me that I might stop here with safety, and rest the question of the boundary of the Rio Grande upon the incontrovertible facts which I have brought to the notice of the Senate. But, sir, I am well aware that while no senator will controvert the truth of any one material fact which I have stated, or the fairness and impartiality with which all my facts have been presented, yet it will be said that the treaty to which I have alluded was not binding upon the Mexican nation, because Santa Anna was a prisoner of war, in captivity, at the time of its execution. I do not deem it necessary to make an argument on this point, so far as Santa Anna is himself concerned, for it can make no difference with the result. General Filisola, and the other generals who subsequently signed and ratified that treaty, in conjunction with him, were not prisoners of war — were not in duress or captivity when they executed it. They were at the head of their respective commands, in the full enjoyment of all their faculties, and the free exercise of all their rights, when they signed and ratified the instrument. They acted upon their own judgments and of their own volition, and made no pretext of duress or coercion. If, then, the captivity of Santa Anna deprived him of the faculties of volition and action, Filisola succeeded to his position of commander-in-chief of the army, and was duly invested with all the powers of which he had been deprived. But, sir, I cannot concede that the acts of Santa Anna were not binding upon himself and his government. We must bear in mind that the government of Mexico at that time was a military despotism, erected upon the ruins of the Republic, after the federal constitution had been abolished. Santa Anna was the head of that government (if, indeed, he was not the government itself) and the people were responsible for his acts, because they had submitted to his rule, and acquiesced in his authority. The government had no rightful existence, and no other authority than that which resulted from violence and power. It had extended its authority, by successful revolution, to the Rio Grande, and to that extent the people were bound by its acts. It had failed in two successive attempts to establish its power on this side of that river, and the evidence of that failure is to be found recorded in letters of blood in the treaty of San Jacinto, sealed with the impress of the government's captivity, and witnessed by the dead of more than one half of the revolutionary army.

The failure of Mexico to conquer and reduce to subjugation is conclusive evidence of the right of the inhabitants to govern themselves. This treaty is an acknowledgment of that right, and as such is good evidence of the independence and boundaries of the Republic of Texas. I do not insist that the treaty conferred any new rights upon Texas, either in respect to her independence or limits; for they existed before the treaty was signed and independent of its provisions. Her inalienable right of independence resulted from the subversion of the constitutional government of the Mexican confederacy; the fact of independence, with the boundary of the Rio Grande, was evidenced by the total annihilation of every revolutionary army which had presumed to enter her territory, and the expulsion of every hostile foot from her soil. The treaty is a valid acknowledgment of both the right and the fact. It was entered into for a consideration, which, it is reasonable to suppose, was not only desirable, but invaluable to Mexico. The life of her chief magistrate, and the safety of thousands of her soldiers and officers, depended upon it, and were secured by it. In fact, the whole conduct of the government of Mexico, from the date of that treaty through a long series of years, has clearly shown that she regarded the Rio Grande as the boundary of Texas: but claimed the right of reconquest, as she is pleased to term it, inasmuch as the treaty had not been ratified according to the forms of the constitution, which had been abolished nearly two years previous. Texas was permitted to remain in the undisturbed possession of the territory for years. Invasion and conquest were constantly threatened, but no attempt was ever made to carry the threat into execution by a regularly appointed army until the year 1842, six years after the battle and treaty of San Jacinto. In that year, General Vascus ventured to cross the Rio Grande, and, by a rapid movement, succeeded, on the 6th of March, in reaching and plundering San Antonio. The Texans instantly seized their arms, and prepared to chastise and repulse the invaders. The result is thus recorded in Green's "Mier Expedition":

"A large number had already assembled under their veteran leader, General Edward Burleson, always the first in the field and foremost in the fight. The enemy fled before them to the Rio Grande, one hundred and fifty miles distant."

This was the end of the third regular invasion of Texas by Mexico. The invading army only escaped the fate of the two preceding ones by a hasty flight before the Texans across the Rio Grande. Now for the fourth and last invasion which Mexico ever attempted, unless, indeed, the marauding party under Canales, which was promptly met and repulsed, is entitled to the dignity of that designation. About the 1st of September, 1842, General Woll crossed the Rio Grande with his army, and, by rapid marches, took possession of San Antonio on the 11th of that month. A few days afterwards he succeeded in capturing and murdering a small party of Texans in the vicinity of that place. For the result of this invasion, I will invite the attention of the Senate to the passages which I will read from the work I have just quoted:

"After the massacre of Dawson and his men, General Woll made a triumphal entry into San Antonio with his fifteen prisoners and some two hundred of his own wounded, and prepared for a hasty retreat toward the Rio Grande. This retreat was greatly hastened upon hearing that Colonels Mayfield, Moore, and McCullough, and others, were coming up with reinforcements to Caldwell. With all General Woll's hurry in his flight homeward, at the Rio Hondo he found Caldwell upon his heels. His retreat became a flight and a panic; and had the Texans charged him, as all now agree, and as all then seemed to be anxious to do, his whole force would have fallen an easy prey. Much has been said against Caldwell and others for not so doing; and the blame has been charged upon several; but the writer has not been able to satisfy his mind that any particular individual was to blame. It seems to be one of those mischances in war, more the result of accident, or the want of promptness, than the absence of bravery. It was, however, a national misfortune that he was permitted to escape to the west side of the Rio Grande, after murdering forty-one and carrying off sixty-seven of our best citizens."

Thus ended the fourth and last invasion of Texas by Mexico. If at any time marauding parties ever crossed the Rio Grande and approached the settlements, their flight, before Hays's and McCullough's rangers, was more rapid than their original march. The repulse and retreat of General Woll's army in the fall of 1842, again left Texas in the undisputed enjoyment of her whole territorial limits, as defined in the treaty of San Jacinto, and vindicated by her arms whenever invaded since the date of General Cos's capitulation in 1835. I have said that Hays and McCullough always held the marauding parties in check, and repulsed them whenever they invaded the country. On this point I will read a paragraph from the speech of Mr. Kaufman, of Texas, in the House of Representatives, on the 27th of June, 1846:

"Indeed, the Texas rangers, under the gallant Hays and McCullough, have for years held undisputed sway over that territory [the country between the Nueces and the Rio Grande], and we have had such occupation of it as the condition and wants of our population permitted and required. No Mexican forces have ever been stationed on the left [of the Rio Grande]—all their war manifestoes are dated on the right."

I am aware that I am accumulating evidence on this point beyond what ought to be required to convince the most incredulous mind. Yet I must be permitted to call the attention of the Senate to one item more: I allude to the armistice which was concluded between the governments of Mexico and Texas, on the 15th of February, 1844, and the proclamation of General Woll, announcing the reopening of hostilities from and after the 11th of June of that year. The hostilities which were reopened existed only on paper, if we except the cruel and barbarous treatment of the Texan prisoners who had been so unfortunate as to fall into the hands of the Mexicans in the previous campaigns. General Woll, acting under the express orders of the Mexican government, at Mier, June 20, 1844, issued an order or proclamation, of which the third section is as follows:

" 3. Every individual who may be found at the distance of one league from the left bank of the Rio Bravo [Rio Grande], will be regarded as a favorer and accomplice of the usurpers of that part of the national territory, and as a traitor to his country."

This order is important in two points of view: first, that while Mexico claimed the whole of Texas, as her national territory, she at that time regarded and acknowledged the Rio Bravo, or Grande, as the boundary. She had previously declared the inhabitants of Texas rebels and traitors, who were to be put to immediate death; and by this order that sentence was applied to every person, whether Mexican or Texan, who should be found at the distance of three miles from the Rio Grande, upon the ground that the fact of being there was conclusive evidence that they favored the Texan cause. A Mexican might cross the river to the left bank, and save his life by showing that he was not a Texan; but if he went one league from the Rio Grand , death was his portion, and no excuse or explanation would be received. The next point upon which this order is important is to be found in the fact of its express acknowledgment that the Texans were in possession of the country:

"Every individual who may be found at the distance of one league from the left bank of the Rio Bravo will be regarded as a favorer and accomplice of the usurpers of that part of the national territory."

It appears, then, that the Texans had usurped the territory on the left bank of the Rio Bravo, or Grande. To usurp, according to Webster, is "to seize and hold in possession by force or without right." I have already disposed of the question as to the right of Texas "to seize and hold in possession by force" the country between the Nueces and the Rio Grande; and it is sufficient for my purpose that Mexico, in 1844, acknowledged the fact that Texas had seized and did then hold it in possession by force. I have now traced, with a minuteness which I fear has been tedious, every important fact, bearing upon the question of boundary, since the subversion of the federal constitution of 1824. In the examination of this subject my mind has been powerfully impressed by the circumstance that, in every invasion which Mexico has ever made of the territory of Texas, the Rio Grande has been uniformly mentioned as the line which the army crossed, and beyond which it retreated whenever it was permitted to escape. The same may be said of the capitulations and treaties with the two captive armies. The Nueces is not even alluded to, nor can the name be found in any one of them. This circumstance is a powerful argument of itself, and is forced to make a deep impression upon the mind of every impartial man.

Having shown that Mexico has never held any portion of the country this side of the Rio Grande (of course I speak of the lower Rio Grande) since the subversion of the constitution of 1824, and that Texas has promptly repelled every invasion of her territory, I now propose to show that she has occupied and governed it by her civil institutions during that whole period. I have already shown that every Mexican garrison between the Nueces and the Rio Grande, as well as in all other portions of Texas, was reduced and captured in the fall of 1835 — that the counties of San Patricio and Bexar were represented in the convention which established the provisional government in November, 1835, and also in the convention which declared the independence, and formed the constitution of the Republic of Texas, in March, 1836 — and that by that constitution each of those counties constituted a congressional district, with the right of sending representatives and senators to the Congress of the Republic. I have referred also to the act of the Texan Congress of the 24th of May, 1838, defining with greater certainty the dividing line between those counties from the Nueces to the Rio Grande, and confirming the surveys of land which had been made by the county surveyors of both respectively. On the 19th of December, 1836, the Congress of Texas passed an act defining the boundaries of the Republic, and adopting those designated in the treaty of San Jacinto. On the 4th of February, 1842, an act was passed fixing the times of holding the higher courts in the counties of San Patricio and Bexar, and for other purposes. On the 18th of January, 1844, another act was passed regulating the times of holding courts in those counties; and on the 31st of December, 1844, an act was passed changing the times of holding courts in those counties. On the 18th of January, 1845, an act was passed removing the seat of justice of San Patricio county to Corpus Christi, and providing for the appointment of a presiding judge of the county court. On the 1st of February, 1845, an act providing for the resurvey of all the land in the counties of San Patricio and Refugio, the title of which was derived from the Mexican government or the State of Coahuila and Texas, and for returning the plats to the general land office of Texas. I have all these acts before me, but will not stop to read them, unless desired by some senator. During the whole of the period from the establishment of the Republic, these counties were represented in the Congress of Texas. They were also represented in the convention of the people of Texas, which agreed to the terms of annexation, and which formed the constitution of the State of Texas, with which she was admitted into our federal Union. I hold in my hand the present constitution of Texas — the same upon which our act of Congress was founded, admitting her into the Union as a State, upon an equal footing with the original States; and, in the thirtieth section of the third article, I find that the county of San Patricio is constituted a representative district with one representative, and the county of Bexar with two representatives; and in the thirty-second section of the same article is the following provision: " The county of Bexar, the eighteenth district, shall elect one senator. The counties of Goliad, Refugio and San Patricio, the nineteenth district, shall elect one senator."

The third section of the thirteenth article is as follows:

" Section 3d. All laws and parts of laws now in force in the Republic of Texas which are not repugnant to the constitution of the United States, the joint resolutions for annexing Texas to the United States, or to the provisions of this constitution, shall continue and remain in force as the laws of this State until they expire by their own limitation or shall be altered or repealed by the legislature thereof."

Now, sir, this provision ratifies and continues in force all the acts of the Texan Congress to which I have referred — the act declaring the Rio Grande to be the boundary of the

Republic — the act establishing the boundary lines of counties from the Nueces to the Rio Grande — the several acts providing for the surveys of lands and fixing the times of holding courts in those counties — all are confirmed by this section of the constitution. The Congress of the United States must be presumed to have been familiar with these laws and this section of the constitution, when the act was passed admitting her into the Union. This presumption is greatly strengthened by the fact that, within a few days after the admission of Texas, Congress passed an act extending our revenue laws over the territory of the State, and establishing a port of delivery, among other places, at Corpus Christi, in the county of San Patricio.

I have now concluded all I have to say on the question of boundary. Whether I have succeeded in establishing the boundary of the Rio Grande is for the Senate and the country to judge. One thing is certain: Mexico never dreamed of any other boundary than that of the Rio Grande or the Sabine. She was in possession of the country to the Rio Grande, and claimed the right to conquer to the Sabine. This was the position of Mexico towards Texas, as stated by herself, when the latter was annexed to this country and admitted into the Union.

The question now arises, who commenced the present war — the United States or Mexico? This seems to be a disputed point between the two great political parties in this country, although the governments of the two belligerent countries agree in relation to it. Our government has officially declared, in the form of a solemn law, all the departments concurring, that the war was commenced by "the act of Mexico." This is our statement of the question Now for the Mexican side of the case, as stated by her President and ministers of war and foreign affairs. I read from the President's annual message of December 8, 1846.

" The apprehensions of a contemplated Mexican invasion have been since fully justified by the event. The determination of Mexico to rush into hostilities with the United States was afterwards manifested from the whole tenor of the note of the Mexican minister of foreign affairs to our minister, bearing date on the 12th of March, 1846. Paredes had then revolutionized the government, and his minister, after referring to the resolution for the annexation of Texas, which had been adopted by our Congress in March, 1845, proceeds to declare that ' a fact such as this, or to speak with greater exactness, so notable an act of usurpation, created an imperious necessity that Mexico for her own honor should repel it with proper firmness and dignity. The supreme government had beforehand declared that it would look upon such an act as *casus belli;* and as a consequence of this declaration negotiation was by its very nature at an end and war was the only recourse of the Mexican government.'

" It appears also that on the 4th of April following, General Paredes, through his minister of war, issued orders to the Mexican general in command on the Texan frontier to ' attack ' our army ' by every means which war permits.' To this General Paredes had been pledged to the army and people of Mexico during the military revolution which had brought him into power. On the 18th of April, 1846, General Paredes addressed a letter to the commander on that frontier, in which he stated to him, 'At the present date I suppose you at the head of that valiant army, either fighting already or preparing for the operations of a campaign;' and ' supposing you already on the theatre of operations, and with all the forces assembled, it is indispensable that hostilities be commenced, yourself taking the initiative against the enemy.' "

Thus we find that the Mexican minister of foreign affairs, on the 12th of March, 1846, notified our minister that " negotiation was, by its very nature, at an end, and war was the only recourse of the Mexican government; " and that on the

18th day of April, 1846, the President of Mexico instructed the general of the Mexican army that it was "indispensable that hostilities be commenced, yourself taking the initiative against the enemy." Mexico avows the act. It is her pride and boast that she commenced the war — that she took the "initiative," and struck the first blow. She makes no complaint of General Taylor's march from Corpus Christi to the Rio Grande. She knew nothing of that movement at the time she gave orders for the commencement of hostilities. Her complaint was, that our armies were stationed on the west side of the Sabine — that we had incorporated the country between the Sabine and the Rio Grande into our Union, and deprived her of the right which she claimed of reconquest. This was her grievance; and for this grievance she boasted that she had the chivalry to make war against the United States, and take the initiative. She knew nothing of the distinctions in the strength of her title on the one side or the other of the Nueces until she found it explained in the speeches of American senators. Those speeches are the foundations of her better title to the country west than east of that river. Up to the commencement of this war, the name of the Nueces river cannot be found in any Mexican document — civil or military — addressed to this country or Texas, in which she claims a better or any other title to that river than to the Sabine. Her separate title to the Nueces is a Whig title, originating in this country, and derived from Whig newspapers and speeches, and adopted by the Mexican authorities, for the first time, in the negotiation with Mr. Trist "on the Chapultepec causeway." She now claims it, because she is told that it is hers; but she is unable to comprehend, much less explain, upon what principles her separate and better title rests. I repeat, that this line of the Nueces was manufactured in this country, for the purpose of erecting a platform from which to assail the President of the United States, and through him the Democratic party. The idea was conceived after the passage of the act of the 13th of May, 1846, recognizing "a state of war by the act of Mexico," and by gentlemen who voted for that law. Why did they not then tell us that the President had invaded the territory of Mexico in violation of the constitution of the United States, and instruct him to withdraw the army within the line of our rightful boundary, instead of furnishing ten millions of dollars and fifty thousand men to prosecute the invasion to the vitals of Mexico? I suppose the answer will be, if any answer shall be made, that they at that time were as ignorant as Mexico herself of the existence of any better title to the one side than the other of the Nueces.

But, sir, there is one point more to which I wish to address a few remarks. It is strenuously insisted, here and elsewhere, that the letter of the secretary of war, of the 13th of January, 1846, ordering General Taylor from Corpus Christi to the Rio Grande, was the real cause of the war. Some go so far as to charge the President with giving the order for the purpose of producing war; while others, who are more charitable, content themselves with saying that it was an act so imprudent and reckless, that any man in his senses ought to have known that war would have been the inevitable consequence. It often becomes necessary in military movements, on a theatre remote from the capital, to trust much to the superior local knowledge and discretion of the commanding general in respect to the proper disposition of the forces under his command. Such was the case in this instance. General Taylor was put in full possession of the views of the government, in sending him to Texas, and left to select his own position. Those views were, the defence of the western boundary of Texas from invasion, and the preservation of friendly relations with Mexico, if possible. He selected his position at Corpus Christi, and after remaining there several months, on the 4th of October, 1845, he wrote to the department as follows:

" Sir: I beg leave to suggest some considerations in relation to the present position of our force, and the dispositions which may become necessary for the more effectual prosecution of the objects for which it has been concentrated."

After a detailed exposition of the reasons for the recommendation which he was about to make, he proceeds as follows:

" For these reasons our position thus far has, I think, been the best possible; but now that the entire force will soon be concentrated, it may well be a question whether the views of government will be best carried out by our remaining at this point. It is with great deference that I make any suggestions on topics which may become matter of delicate negotiation; but if our government, in settling the question of boundary, makes the line of the Rio Grande an ultimatum, I cannot doubt that the settlement will be greatly facilitated and hastened by our taking possession at once of one or two suitable points on, or quite near, that river. Our strength and state of preparation should be displayed in a manner not to be mistaken. However salutary may be the effect produced upon the border people by our presence here, we are too far from the frontier to impress the government of Mexico with our readiness to vindicate by force of arms, if necessary, our title to the country as far as the Rio Grande. The ' army of occupation ' will in a few days be concentrated at this point, in condition for vigorous and efficient service. Mexico having as yet made no positive declaration of war, or committed any overt act of hostilities, I do not feel at liberty, under my instructions, particularly those of July 8, to make a forward movement to the Rio Grande without authority from the war department."

These are the recommendations of General Taylor: " I cannot doubt that the settlement will be greatly facilitated and hastened by our taking possession at once of one or two suitable points on, or quite near, that river," the Rio Grande. " I do not feel at liberty, under my instructions, particularly those of the 8th of July, to make a forward movement to the Rio Grande, without authority from the war department." General Taylor was the commanding general on the theatre of action. He had better opportunities of knowing the movements, intentions, and feelings of the Mexicans than any one else. He had previously, July 20, 1845, given the department this assurance: " and the department may rest assured that I will take no step to interrupt the friendly relations between the United States and Mexico." Relying upon the faith of this assurance, and upon his better means of information, the department complied with his request, and gave him the desired order " for a forward movement to the Rio Grande." General Taylor had recommended it as a peace measure, calculated to facilitate and hasten the settlement of the boundary question; and in that view, and on that recommendation, the order was given. It is clear, therefore, that General Taylor, and he alone, is responsible for that order. If it was right and wise, his is the merit; and if it was wrong, he ought — as I have no doubt he is perfectly willing — to take the responsibility. I have no doubt that the order was an act of policy and wisdom — nay, of necessity.

But, sir, who are the men that condemn this order, and for what purpose is the condemnation made at this time? They are the professed advocates of the election of General Taylor to the presidency, and the order is condemned for the purpose of making political capital for themselves and their candidate, against the Democratic party. Under the influence of the same patriotic motives, it has suddenly been discovered, by a portion of those who voted for the war, that it was unjust, unnecessary, and unconstitutional. They can see no hope of rescuing the ship of state from the hands of the wicked rulers who are directing its course, except by the elevation to the presidency of a man whose very name has been introduced to the knowledge of the civilized world only by his extraordinary success in shedding human blood in an unjust cause! By denouncing the war as a scheme of rapine and robbery, they, in effect, charge Generals Taylor and Scott, and all the officers and men under their command, with being a band of successful robbers, murderers, and pirates, whose only title to the gratitude of their countrymen is derived from a series of unparalleled triumphs in violation of the constitution of their country, over a weak and an unoffending people! Should it hereafter be to us a matter of surprise to hear all Europe, whose jealousy has been aroused by our growing greatness and importance among the nations of the world, denounce us as a nation of robbers and pirates, when they can refer to the speeches of American senators for the truth and justice of their statements? Suppose gentlemen succeed in making the world believe that the war in which we are engaged, and which has been sanctioned by the nation according to all the forms and solemnities known to the constitution, is unnecessary and unjust — a war of rapine and robbery — their only triumph of which they can boast will be, that they have rendered the name and the fame of their country infamous in the eyes of Christendom. Whose heart did not swell and pulsate with patriotic pride as he heard the shout of the glorious victories achieved by our countrymen wafted from the plains and mountains of Mexico, striking terror to the hearts of all enemies of republican institutions, and demonstrating that ours is the first military, as well as civil power, upon the globe? Sir, I shall never forget the proud and grateful emotions of my own breast, when the response was heard from all parts of the Union to the call for volunteers in the summer of 1846, showing that more than three hundred thousand had tendered their services, when only fifty thousand could be received. Was that response prompted by a love of plunder and robbery; or was it a patriotic response from the hearts of freemen, burning with a fervent desire to avenge their country's wrongs and vindicate her rights? Shall it be said that in republican America the only sentiment which can animate and arouse the whole people — which can quell partisan strife and obliterate party distinction, for a time — is an insatiable lust for rapine and robbery, upon our unoffending and unfortunate neighbors? Such must be the fruits of the victory, if gentlemen triumph in the efforts they are now making in regard to this war. All the emotions of my heart and the feelings of my nature revolt at the idea. National and State pride rebels at the thought. My own State has sent nearly seven thousand men to this war, and has offered up more lives on the field of battle, and sacrificed more by the diseases of the country, than any other State in the Union. Their patriotic deeds of noble daring have shed honor upon the State, as well as glory upon the American arms. I feel grateful to them — the living and the dead — for the services they have rendered and the renown they have won. Every other State has had its share in the glory of this war. If they have not furnished as many men, it was because the government declined to receive them. All have done their duty, and all ought to feel proud of their achievements.

IN THE FIRST LINCOLN AND DOUGLAS DEBATE

OPENING SPEECH DELIVERED AT OTTAWA, ILLINOIS, AUGUST 21, 1858

LADIES AND GENTLEMEN,— I appear before you to-day for the purpose of discussing the leading political topics which now agitate the public mind. By an arrangement between Mr. Lincoln and myself, we are present here to-day for the purpose of having a joint discussion, as the representatives of the two great political parties of the State and Union, upon the principles in issue between those parties; and this vast concourse of people shows the deep feeling which pervades the public mind in regard to the questions dividing us.

Prior to 1854 this country was divided into two great political parties, known as the Whig and Democratic parties. Both were national and patriotic, advocating principles that were universal in their application. An old-line Whig could proclaim his principles in Louisiana and Massachusetts alike. Whig principles had no boundary sectional line: they were not limited by the Ohio River, nor by the Potomac, nor by the line of the free and slave States, but applied and were proclaimed wherever the constitution ruled or the American flag waved over the American soil. So it was and so it is with the great Democratic party, which, from the days of Jefferson until this period, has proven itself to be the historic party of this nation. While the Whig and Democratic parties differed in regard to a bank, the tariff, distribution, the specie circular, and the sub-treasury, they agreed on the great slavery question which now agitates the Union. I say that the Whig party and the Democratic party agreed on the slavery question, while they differed on those matters of expediency to which I have referred. The Whig party and the Democratic party jointly adopted the compromise measures of 1850 as the basis of a proper and just solution of the slavery question in all its forms. Clay was the great leader, with Webster on his right and Cass on his left, and sustained by the patriots in the Whig and Democratic ranks who had devised and enacted the compromise measures of 1850.

In 1851 the Whig party and the Democratic party united in Illinois in adopting resolutions indorsing and approving the principles of the compromise measures of 1850 as the proper adjustment of that question. In 1852, when the Whig party assembled in convention at Baltimore for the purpose of nominating a candidate for the presidency, the first thing it did was to declare the compromise measures of 1850, in substance and in principle, a suitable adjustment of that question. [Here the speaker was interrupted by loud and long-continued applause.]

My friends, silence will be more acceptable to me in the discussion of these questions than applause. I desire to address myself to your judgment, your understanding, and your consciences, and not to your passions or your enthusiasm. When the Democratic convention assembled in Baltimore in the same year, for the purpose of nominating a Democratic candidate for the presidency, it also adopted the compromise measures of 1850 as the basis of Democratic action. Thus you see that up to 1853–54 the Whig party and the Democratic party both stood on the same platform with regard to the slavery question. That platform was the right of the people of each State and each Territory to decide their local and domestic institutions for themselves, subject only to the federal constitution.

During the session of Congress of 1853–54 I introduced into the Senate of the United States a bill to organize the Territories of Kansas and Nebraska on that principle which had been adopted in the compromise measures of 1850, approved by the Whig party and the Democratic party in Illinois in 1851, and indorsed by the Whig party and the Democratic party in national convention in 1852. In order that there might be no misunderstanding in relation to the principle involved in the Kansas and Nebraska bill, I put forth the true intent and meaning of the act in these words: "It is the true intent and meaning of this act not to legislate slavery into any State or Territory, or to exclude it therefrom, but to leave the people thereof perfectly free to form and regulate their domestic institutions in their own way, subject only to the federal constitution."

Thus you see that up to 1854, when the Kansas and Nebraska bill was brought into Congress for the purpose of carrying out the principles which both parties had up to that time indorsed and approved, there had been no division in this country in regard to that principle except the opposition of the Abolitionists. In the House of Representatives of the Illinois legislature, upon a resolution asserting that principle, every Whig and every Democrat in the House voted in the affirmative, and only four men voted against it, and those four were old-line Abolitionists.

In 1854 Mr. Abraham Lincoln and Mr. Lyman Trumbull entered into an arrangement, one with the other, and each with his respective friends, to dissolve the old Whig party on the one hand, and to dissolve the old Democratic party on the other, and to connect the members of both into an Abolition party, under the name and disguise of a Republican party. The terms of that arrangement between Lincoln and

Trumbull have been published by Lincoln's special friend, James H. Matheny, Esq.; and they were that Lincoln should have General Shields's place in the United States Senate, which was then about to become vacant, and that Trumbull should have my seat when my term expired.

Lincoln went to work to abolitionize the old Whig party all over the State, pretending that he was then as good a Whig as ever; and Trumbull went to work in his part of the State preaching abolitionism in its milder and lighter form, and trying to abolitionize the Democratic party, and bring old Democrats handcuffed and bound hand and foot into the Abolition camp. In pursuance of the arrangement the parties met at Springfield in October, 1854, and proclaimed their new platform.

Lincoln was to bring into the Abolition camp the old-line Whigs, and transfer them over to Giddings, Chase, Fred Douglass, and Parson Lovejoy, who were ready to receive them and christen them in their new faith. They laid down on that occasion a platform for their new Republican party, which was thus to be constructed. I have the resolutions of the State convention then held, which was the first mass State convention ever held in Illinois by the Black Republican party; and I now hold them in my hands and will read a part of them, and cause the others to be printed. Here are the most important and material resolutions of this Abolition platform: —

1. *Resolved,* That we believe this truth to be self-evident, that, when parties become subversive of the ends for which they are established, or incapable of restoring the government to the true principles of the constitution, it is the right and duty of the people to dissolve the political bands by which they may have been connected therewith, and to organize new parties upon such principles and with such

views as the circumstances and the exigencies of the nation may demand.

2. *Resolved,* That the times imperatively demand the reorganization of parties, and, repudiating all previous party attachments, names, and predilections, we unite ourselves together in defence of the liberty and constitution of the country, and will hereafter co-operate as the Republican party, pledged to the accomplishment of the following purposes: to bring the administration of the government back to the control of first principles; to restore Nebraska and Kansas to the position of free Territories; that, as the constitution of the United States vests in the States, and not in Congress, the power to legislate for the extradition of fugitives from labor, to repeal and entirely abrogate the Fugitive Slave Law; to restrict slavery to those States in which it exists; to prohibit the admission of any more slave States into the Union; to abolish slavery in the District of Columbia; to exclude slavery from all the Territories over which the general government has exclusive jurisdiction; and to resist the acquirement of any more Territories unless the practice of slavery therein forever shall have been prohibited.

3. *Resolved,* That in furtherance of these principles we will use such constitutional and lawful means as shall seem best adapted to their accomplishment, and that we will support no man for office, under the general or State government, who is not positively and fully committed to the support of these principles, and whose personal character and conduct is not a guarantee that he is reliable, and who shall not have abjured old party allegiance and ties.

Now, gentlemen, your Black Republicans have cheered every one of those propositions; and yet I venture to say that you cannot get Mr. Lincoln to come out and say that he is now in favor of each one of them. That these propositions, one and all, constitute the platform of the Black Republican party of this day, I have no doubt; and, when you were not aware for what purpose I was reading them, your Black Republicans cheered them as good Black Republican doctrines.

My object in reading these resolutions was to put the question to Abraham Lincoln this day, whether he now stands and will stand by each article in that creed, and carry it out. I desire to know whether Mr. Lincoln to-day stands as he did in 1854, in favor of the unconditional repeal of the Fugitive Slave Law. I desire him to answer whether he stands pledged to-day, as he did in 1854, against the admission of any more slave States into the Union, even if the people want them. I want to know whether he stands pledged against the admission of a new State into the Union with such a constitution as the people of that State may see fit to make. I want to know whether he stands to-day pledged to the abolition of slavery in the District of Columbia. I desire him to answer whether he stands pledged to the prohibition of the slave-trade between the different States. I desire to know whether he stands pledged to prohibit slavery in all the Territories of the United States, north as well as south of the Missouri Compromise line. I desire him to answer whether he is opposed to the acquisition of any more territory unless slavery is prohibited therein. I want his answer to these questions.

Your affirmative cheers in favor of this Abolition platform are not satisfactory. I ask Abraham Lincoln to answer these questions, in order that, when I trot him down to lower Egypt, I may put the same questions to him. My principles are the same everywhere. I can proclaim them alike in the North, the South, the East, and the West. My principles will apply wherever the constitution prevails and the American flag waves. I desire to know whether Mr. Lincoln's principles will bear transplanting from Ottawa to Jonesboro?

I put these questions to him to-day distinctly, and ask an

14   answer. I have a right to an answer; for I quote from the
platform of the Republican party, made by himself and
others at the time that party was formed, and the bargain
made by Lincoln to dissolve and kill the old Whig party,
and transfer its members, bound hand and foot, to the Abolition party, under the direction of Giddings and Fred
Douglass.

In the remarks I have made on this platform, and the position of Mr. Lincoln upon it, I mean nothing personally dis-
respectful or unkind to that gentleman. I have known him
for nearly twenty-five years. There were many points of
sympathy between us when we first got acquainted. We were
both comparatively boys, and both struggling with poverty
in a strange land. I was a school-teacher in the town of
Winchester, and he a flourishing grocery-keeper in the town
of Salem. He was more successful in his occupation than I
was in mine, and hence more fortunate in this world's goods.
Lincoln is one of those peculiar men who perform with
admirable skill everything which they undertake. I made
as good a school-teacher as I could, and, when a cabinet-
maker, I made a good bedstead and tables, although my old
boss said I succeeded better with bureaus and secretaries
than with anything else; but I believe that Lincoln was
always more successful in business than I, for his business
enabled him to get into the legislature. I met him there,
however, and had sympathy with him, because of the up-hill
struggle we both had in life. He was then just as good at
telling an anecdote as now. He could beat any of the boys
wrestling or running a foot-race, in pitching quoits or tossing
a copper; could ruin more liquor than all the boys of the
town together; and the dignity and impartiality with which
he presided at a horse-race or fist-fight excited the admiration

and won the praise of everybody that was present and participated. I sympathized with him because he was struggling with difficulties, and so was I.

Mr. Lincoln served with me in the legislature in 1836, when we both retired; and he subsided or became submerged, and he was lost sight of as a public man for some years. In 1846, when Wilmot introduced his celebrated proviso, and the Abolition tornado swept over the country, Lincoln again turned up as a member of Congress from the Sangamon district. I was then in the Senate of the United States, and was glad to welcome my old friend and companion. Whilst in Congress, he distinguished himself by his opposition to the Mexican war, taking the side of the common enemy against his own country; and, when he returned home, he found that the indignation of the people followed him everywhere, and he was again submerged, or obliged to retire into private life, forgotten by his former friends.

He came up again in 1854, just in time to make this Abolition or Black Republican platform, in company with Giddings, Lovejoy, Chase, and Fred Douglass, for the Republican party to stand upon. Trumbull, too, was one of our own contemporaries. He was born and raised in old Connecticut, was bred a Federalist, but, removing to Georgia, turned Nullifier when nullification was popular, and, as soon as he disposed of his clocks and wound up his business, migrated to Illinois, turned politician and lawyer here, and made his appearance in 1841 as a member of the legislature. He became noted as the author of the scheme to repudiate a large portion of the State debt of Illinois, which, if successful, would have brought infamy and disgrace upon the fair escutcheon of our glorious State. The odium attached to that measure consigned him to oblivion for a time. I helped to do it. I walked into a public meeting in the hall of the House of Representatives, and replied to his repudiating speeches, and resolutions were carried over his head denouncing repudiation, and asserting the moral and legal obligation of Illinois to pay every dollar of the debt she owed and every bond that bore her seal. Trumbull's malignity has followed me since I thus defeated his infamous scheme.

These two men, having formed this combination to abolitionize the old Whig party and the old Democratic party, and put themselves into the Senate of the United States, in pursuance of their bargain, are now carrying out that arrangement. Matheny states that Trumbull broke faith; that the bargain was that Lincoln should be the senator in Shields's place, and Trumbull was to wait for mine; and the story goes that Trumbull cheated Lincoln, having control of four or five abolitionized Democrats who were holding over in the Senate. He would not let them vote for Lincoln, which obliged the rest of the Abolitionists to support him in order to secure an Abolition senator. There are a number of authorities for the truth of this besides Matheny, and I suppose that even Mr. Lincoln will not deny it.

Mr. Lincoln demands that he shall have the place intended for Trumbull, as Trumbull cheated him and got his; and Trumbull is stumping the State, traducing me for the purpose of securing the position for Lincoln, in order to quiet him   It was in consequence of this arrangement that the Republican convention was impanelled to instruct for Lincoln and nobody else; and it was on this account that they passed resolutions that he was their first, their last, and their only choice. Archy Williams was nowhere, Browning was nobody, Wentworth was not to be considered; they had no man in the Republican party for the place except Lincoln, for the reason that he demanded that they should carry out the arrangement.

Having formed this new party for the benefit of deserters from Whiggery and deserters from Democracy, and having laid down the Abolition platform which I have read, Lincoln now takes his stand and proclaims his Abolition doctrines. Let me read a part of them. In his speech at Springfield to the convention which nominated him for the Senate he said: —

" In my opinion, it will not cease until a crisis shall have been reached and passed. 'A house divided against itself cannot stand.' I believe this government cannot endure permanently half slave and half free. I do not expect the Union to be dissolved,— I do not expect the house to fall,— but I do expect it will cease to be divided. It will become all one thing or all the other. Either the opponents of slavery will arrest the further spread of it, and place it where the public mind shall rest in the belief that it is in the course of ultimate extinction, or its advocates will push it forward till it shall become alike lawful in all the States,— old as well as new, North as well as South." [" Good," " Good," and cheers.]

I am delighted to hear you Black Republicans say, " Good." I have no doubt that doctrine expresses your sentiments; and I will prove to you now, if you will listen to me, that it is revolutionary and destructive of the existence of this government. Mr. Lincoln, in the extract from which I have read, says that this government cannot endure permanently in the same condition in which it was made by its framers — divided into free and slave States. He says that it has existed for about seventy years thus divided, and yet he tells you that it cannot endure permanently on the same principles and in the same relative condition in which our fathers made it. Why can it not exist divided into free and slave States? Washington, Jefferson, Franklin, Madison, Hamilton, Jay, and the great men of that day made this government divided into free States and slave States, and left each State perfectly free to do as it pleased on the subject of slavery. Why can it not exist on the same principles on which our fathers made it? They knew when they framed the constitution that in a country as wide and broad as this, with such a variety of climate, production, and interest, the people necessarily required different laws and institutions in different localities.

They knew that the laws and regulations which would suit the granite hills of New Hampshire would be unsuited to the rice plantations of South Carolina; and they therefore provided that each State should retain its own legislature and its own sovereignty, with the full and complete power to do as it pleased within its own limits, in all that was local and not national.

One of the reserved rights of the States was the right to regulate the relations between master and servant, on the slavery question. At the time the constitution was framed there were thirteen States in the Union, twelve of which were slaveholding States and one a free State. Suppose this doctrine of uniformity preached by Mr. Lincoln, that the States should all be free or all be slave, had prevailed; and what would have been the result? Of course, the twelve slaveholding States would have overruled the one free State; and slavery would have been fastened by a constitutional provision on every inch of the American republic, instead of being left, as our fathers wisely left it, to each State to decide for itself. Here I assert that uniformity in the local laws and institutions of the different States is neither possible nor desirable. If uniformity had been adopted when the government was established, it must inevitably have been the uniformity of slavery everywhere, or else the uniformity of negro citizenship and negro equality everywhere.

We are told by Lincoln that he is utterly opposed to the Dred Scott decision, and will not submit to it, for the reason that he says it deprives the negro of the rights and privileges of citizenship. That is the first and main reason which he assigns for his warfare on the supreme court of the United States and its decision.

I ask you, Are you in favor of conferring upon the negro the rights and privileges of citizenship? Do you desire to strike out of our State constitution that clause which keeps slaves and free negroes out of the State, and allow the free negroes to flow in, and cover your prairies with black settlements? Do you desire to turn this beautiful State into a free negro colony, in order that, when Missouri abolishes slavery, she can send one hundred thousand emancipated slaves into Illinois, to become citizens and voters, on an equality with yourselves? If you desire negro citizenship, if you desire to allow them to come into the State and settle with the white man, if you desire them to vote on an equality with yourselves, and to make them eligible to office, to serve on juries, and to adjudge your rights, then support Mr. Lincoln and the Black Republican party, who are in favor of the citizenship of the negro.

For one, I am opposed to negro citizenship in any and every form. I believe this government was made on the white basis. I believe it was made by white men, for the benefit of white men and their posterity forever; and I am in favor of confining citizenship to white men, men of European birth and descent, instead of conferring it upon negroes, Indians, and other inferior races.

Mr. Lincoln, following the example and lead of all the little Abolition orators who go around and lecture in the basements of schools and churches, reads from the Declaration of Independence that all men were created equal, and then asks how can you deprive a negro of that equality which God and the Declaration of Independence award to him? He and they maintain that negro equality is guaranteed by the laws of God, and that it is asserted in the Declaration of Independence. If they think so, of course they have a right to say so, and so vote. I do not question Mr. Lincoln's conscientious belief that the negro was made his equal, and hence is his brother; but, for my own part, I do not regard the negro as my equal and positively deny that he is my brother or any kin to me whatever.

Lincoln has evidently learned by heart Parson Lovejoy's catechism. He can repeat it as well as Farnsworth, and he is worthy of a medal from Father Giddings and Fred Douglass for his abolitionism. He holds that the negro was born his equal and yours, and that he was endowed with equality by the Almighty, and that no human law can deprive him of these rights which were guaranteed to him by the Supreme Ruler of the universe.

Now, I do not believe that the Almighty ever intended the negro to be the equal of the white man. If he did, he has been a long time demonstrating the fact. For thousands of years the negro has been a race upon the earth; and during all that time, in all latitudes and climates, wherever he has wandered or been taken, he has been inferior to the race which he has there met. He belongs to an inferior race, and must always occupy an inferior position. I do not hold that, because the negro is our inferior, therefore he ought to be a slave. By no means can such a conclusion be drawn from what I have said.

On the contrary, I hold that humanity and Christianity both require that the negro shall have and enjoy every right, every privilege, and every immunity consistent with the safety of the society in which he lives. On that point, I presume, there can be no diversity of opinion. You and I are bound to extend to our inferior and dependent beings every right, every privilege, every facility and immunity consistent with the public good.

The question then arises, What rights and privileges are consistent with the public good? This is a question which each State and each Territory must decide for itself. Illinois has decided it for herself. We have provided that the negro shall not be a slave; and we have also provided that he shall not be a citizen, but protect him in his civil rights, in his life, his person, and his property, only depriving him of all political rights whatsoever, and refusing to put him on an equality with the white man. That policy of Illinois is satisfactory to the Democratic party and to me, and, if it were to the Republicans, there would then be no question upon the subject; but the Republicans say that he ought to be made a citizen, and, when he becomes a citizen, he becomes your equal, with all your rights and privileges. They assert the Dred Scott decision to be monstrous because it denies that the negro is or can be a citizen under the constitution.

Now, I hold that Illinois had a right to abolish and prohibit slavery as she did, and I hold that Kentucky has the same right to continue and protect slavery that Illinois had to abolish it. I hold that New York had as much right to abolish slavery as Virginia has to continue it, and that each and every State of this Union is a sovereign power, with the right to do as it pleases upon this question of slavery and upon all its domestic institutions. Slavery is not the only question which comes up in this controversy. There is a far more important one to you; and that is, What shall be done with the free negro? We have settled the slavery question as far as we are concerned: we have prohibited it in Illinois forever, and, in doing so, I think we have done wisely, and there is no man in the State who would be more strenuous in his opposition to the introduction of slavery than I would; but, when we settled it for ourselves, we exhausted all our power over that subject.

We have done our whole duty, and can do no more. We must leave each and every other State to decide for itself the same question. In relation to the policy to be pursued toward the free negroes, we have said that they shall not vote; whilst Maine, on the other hand, has said that they shall vote. Maine is a sovereign State, and has the power to regulate the qualifications of voters within her limits. I would never consent to confer the right of voting and of citizenship upon a the free negro? We have settled the slavery question as far ing from me in opinion. Let Maine take care of her own negroes, and fix the qualifications of her own voters to suit herself, without interfering with Illinois; and Illinois will not interfere with Maine. So with the State of New York. She allows the negro to vote provided he owns two hundred and fifty dollars' worth of property, but not otherwise. While I would not make any distinction whatever between a negro who held property and one who did not, yet, if the sovereign State of New York chooses to make that distinction it is her business and not mine, and I will not quarrel with her for it. She can do as she pleases on this question if she minds her own business and we will do the same thing. Now, my friends, if we will only act conscientiously and rigidly upon this great principle of popular sovereignty, which guarantees to each State and Territory the right to do as it pleases on all things local and domestic, instead of Congress interfering, we will continue at peace one with another. Why should Illinois be at war with Missouri, or Kentucky with Ohio, or Virginia with New York, merely because their institutions differ? Our fathers intended that our institutions should differ. They knew that the North and the South, having different climates, productions, and interests, required different institutions. This doctrine of Mr. Lincoln, of uniformity among the institutions of the different States, is a new doctrine, never dreamed of by Washington, Madison, or the framers of this government.

Mr. Lincoln and the Republican party set themselves up as wiser than these men who made this government, which has flourished for seventy years under the principle of popular sovereignty, recognizing the right of each State to do as it pleased. Under that principle, we have grown from a nation of three or four millions to a nation of about thirty millions of people. We have crossed the Alleghany Mountains and filled up the whole northwest, turning the prairie into a garden, and building up churches and schools, thus spreading civilization and Christianity where before there was nothing but savage barbarism.

Under that principle we have become, from a feeble nation, the most powerful on the face of the earth; and, if we only adhere to that principle, we can go forward increasing in territory, in power, in strength, and in glory until the Republic of America shall be the north star that shall guide the friends of freedom throughout the civilized world.

And why can we not adhere to the great principle of self-government upon which our institutions were originally based? I believe that this new doctrine preached by Mr. Lincoln and his party will dissolve the Union if it succeeds. They are trying to array all the northern States in one body against the South, to excite a sectional war between the free States and the slave States, in order that the one or the other may be driven to the wall.

THURMAN

ALLEN GRANBERY THURMAN, an American jurist, the son of a Methodist clergyman, was born in Lynchburg, Virginia, November 13, 1813. At the age of six he removed with his parents to Chillicothe, Ohio, where he lived until 1853, after which he made his home in Columbus, Ohio. His early education was obtained at the Chillicothe Academy, and after some little experience in surveying he took up the study of the law and was admitted to the bar in 1835. His abilities soon secured him a large practice, and in 1845 he entered Congress as a Democrat and its youngest member. Declining a renomination after the expiration of his term, he continued his practice until 1851, when he was elected to the Ohio supreme bench and for the last year of his term was chief justice of the State. In 1867 he was an unsuccessful candidate for governor of Ohio, and in 1869 was elected to the United States Senate, of which he remained a member until 1881. During this period he was for a number of years chairman of the committee on the judiciary. He originated "the Thurman Act," which compelled Pacific railroad corporations to keep their obligations to the government, and endeavored to secure favorable reconstruction legislation for the States which had seceded. He was several times brought forward as a presidential candidate, and in 1888 ran for vice-president on the unsuccessful Cleveland ticket. He died at Columbus, Ohio, December 12, 1895. Thurman was a fair-minded, logical debater, who always retained the high regard of his political opponents.

ADDRESS AT THE UNIVERSITY OF VIRGINIA

DELIVERED AT CHARLOTTESVILLE, VIRGINIA, JUNE 26, 1872

THE theme upon which I propose to offer some observations to-night is the future of our country, or, rather, the dangers likely to menace the existence of the republic and the means of averting them.

In the outset I assume, what I believe to be true, that, whatever differences of opinion have existed or may yet exist as to the advantages or disadvantages of preserving the Union, every American citizen now wishes it to be preserved if at the same time liberty can be secured and the rights and interests of every section promoted.

(7418)

The proposition that freedom has no safe dwelling-place save in small communities is an old idea, and, whether true or false, I have no quarrel with him who sincerely believes it. Nay, more, were the sad alternative forced upon us to choose between a splendid despotism ruling over a vast territory and an oppressed people on the one hand, and, on the other, freedom in a small state and an humble community, no true man should hesitate to choose the latter.

For freedom is of such transcendent value that it far outweighs all the distinction, pomp, and power that the most successful despotism can ever achieve. But the experiment has to be made whether a vast republic may not co-exist with freedom and with advantage to all its parts; and every one of us, I am sure, whatever may be his forebodings, is anxious to give the experiment a fair trial.

Therefore it is that I speak upon this theme to-night. I know of none more appropriate for an address to an assemblage of American youth. The mature men of to-day will ere long be gone. Whatever, of good or of evil, government may confer or inflict, will soon cease to trouble them. Their mantles will fall upon your shoulders and the shoulders of those who, like you, are just entering upon manhood, and upon you and your fellows will rest the grave responsibility of contributing to the happiness or the misery, not of one only, but perhaps of many generations. Wisely to prepare for that responsibility is a task than which none can be nobler, none more elevating, none that better deserves to engage the understanding or warm the heart.

The first danger to the duration of the republic of which I shall speak is that likely to result from its magnitude. It is a trite observation that nations, like men, have their infancy, youth, manhood, old age, decay, and dissolution.

Whether this analogy be fanciful or not, the history of the world gives no small support to the idea that nature has set a limit to the growth and duration of empire. The fate of Babylon, Nineveh, Assyria, Media, Egypt, of the empires of Alexander, the Cæsars, Genghis, Tamerlane, the Caliphs, Charlemagne, and Charles V, cannot, while it strikes our imagination, fail to arrest our attention. We pause and ask: "Is it ever thus to be?"

But let us not be too hasty in our conclusions. True, those great monarchies have been rent into pieces; true, the seats of some of them are now given up to desolation; but it does not follow that a similar fate awaits us. They were, for the most part, the product of conquest, and over their wide domains despotism held unlimited sway. Their fate teaches how insecure is the empire whose sole foundation is violence, and how powerless is tyranny to perpetuate its rule over an unwilling people.

But it does not teach — at least it does not prove — that a homogeneous people, under free institutions, may not attain and preserve a greatness that none of those States ever knew. To our country it was reserved to make this mighty experiment, than which nothing grander has ever engaged the sympathies or the efforts of man. Let us not, with despondent souls, rashly predict its failure — but rather, with hopeful hearts and patriotic zeal, let us manfully strive for its successful accomplishment. That our republic, if it hold together, will attain an unexampled and perilous greatness is certainly true.

Only fifty years hence our population will probably exceed 160,000,000, or four times the present population of France. At the end of a century, in 1972, if it increase in the same ratio that has hitherto marked its growth, the United States will contain more than twice as many people as now inhabit the continent of Europe.

If it be inadmissible to suppose that this ratio of increase will continue, it is not irrational to affirm that within the lifetime of a child now born our population will equal that of the five great Powers of Europe combined. Such an aggregation of mankind, for the most part homogeneous, belonging to the most intellectual and energetic portion of the human race, speaking the same language, all more or less educated, occupying one of the fairest and most fruitful portions of the earth in that North Temperate Zone that seems to be the chosen habitation of civilization and progress, united under one government, and that a government of free institutions, will present a phenomenon such as never yet has been seen in the world.

History exhibits nothing like it, nothing that bears any close analogy to it. It strikes the imagination like the dawn of a millennium, and even the most sanguine and hopeful can scarcely regard it as more than a dream. But who is there wise enough to foresee that it will not be reality? Who is there bold enough to say that the Providence that creates will not preserve? Who is there authorized to condemn as blind and unreasoning optimism the hope that the experiment may be crowned with success?

It is true that a contrariety of interests is incident to so great and varied a territory. With but one interruption the republic extends from beyond the Arctic Circle in Alaska to the confines of the Torrid Zone, and from the Atlantic Ocean on the east to the Pacific on the west. In square miles its area nearly equals that of all Europe. It contains every variety of soil, from the most fertile plains to barren mountains and desert wastes. It holds in its bosom every earth and mineral useful to mankind. Its water boundary, with the indentations, exceeds 14,000 miles. It thus presents a field for every industry known to man. Agriculture, commerce, manufactures, mining,— every pursuit, in short, that serves to sustain or enrich a people,— are here seen in a state of unwonted and growing activity.

That there must be some clashing of interests between the different sections of such a country is obviously true. That each section, in maintaining the Union, must make some sacrifice of its peculiar interests, is almost as obvious. But the question to be answered is, not whether such sacrifices are made, but whether they are not compensated by the advantages resulting from the Union.

In my judgment they are far more than compensated. A particular section may be oppressed for a time by unjust laws — as some have been, and I think yet are; but in the long run justice is pretty sure to prevail. In the meantime the incalculable benefits of the Union — free trade between all its parts, unrestricted communication, highways that penetrate the most remote recesses, exemption from foreign aggression, and peace at home — amply repay all the local sacrifices that occur. It is no answer to this to say that peace has not always prevailed, that we have just emerged from the most fearful civil war the world ever saw.

True it is so, but for seventy-three years domestic peace did prevail. For seventy-three years no man lost his life in civil commotion, no man was executed for a political offence. The history of no other nation records a similar experience. Not one! No, not one! " To ensure domestic tranquillity " is declared in the preamble to the constitution to be one of the objects for which it is ordained. It did ensure it for nearly three quarters of a century, and if, at last, we fell upon evil times, the exception only illustrates the generality of the rule.

The diversity of races and languages among us is considered by some to be fraught with danger to the duration of the republic. American, Goth, Celt, Anglo-Saxon, Teuton, Latin, African, all contribute to form our population. But I apprehend that the danger supposed to arise from this diversity is greatly exaggerated. Of the 38,500,000 of our people in 1870 but 5,500,000 were foreign-born, and they were scattered throughout every State and Territory of the Union. And for the most part they are intelligent, industrious, thriving, and sincerely attached to free institutions. With the increase of population the proportion of foreign-born to native citizens will decrease each year. The various elements of white population will become more and more blended until a homogeneous whole will be the result.

The American of a century hence may differ from the American of the past or the present century, but yet, whatever his origin, he will be an American. What people are more homogeneous than the French? And yet in their veins runs the blood of Celt, Roman, Goth, Teuton, to say nothing of lesser subdivisions of the human race. What more composite in his origin than an Englishman, to whose blood the Celt, the Roman, the Dane, the Angle, the Saxon, the Norman, all contributed? Yet what unification more complete than that of the English people of to-day?

We have nothing, then, to fear, as it seems to me, from the diversity of race among our white population. They will, before many generations shall have passed away, be merged into one common type, the American of the future, with the same language, the same literature, the same sentiments, and substantially the same characteristics.

The African presents a more difficult problem. By some it is supposed that, following an instinct of his nature, the negro will eventually drift into a more congenial clime for him,— the tropics. But a century — nay, many centuries — map elapse before this will occur, should it ever occur. The climate of the southern States is not unfriendly to the African, as his rapid increase there for nearly two hundred years attests. His exodus, unless precipitated by a war of races, which humanity and the interest of both white and black forbid, must necessarily be slow. Practically, then, it may be assumed that he is to remain a citizen of the republic. And the question is: Will his continued existence among us endanger its duration? As long as he was a slave he was a bone of contention between the Abolitionist, seeking to set him free at whatever cost, and the Southerner, insisting upon the guarantees of the constitution.

Then, indeed, he did endanger the republic. But, though he is to some extent a bone of contention yet, I do not see that he is longer a source of peril. His race now constitutes less than thirteen per cent of our population. With each returning census, although the absolute number of the race may be greater, the proportion will be found to be less. Its numerical strength may increase, but its relative strength will constantly diminish. As a cause of strife among the whites, as a facile instrument in the hands of designing and unscrupulous men, the negro is certainly a disturbing element, but, great as are his evils, they are not beyond the rectifying power of time, prudence, and patience.

Another cause of anxiety is found in the proneness of mankind to war and their love of military glory. It was a celebrated English philosopher who said that war is the natural condition of the human race. It is to be hoped for the credit of the race that the saying is untrue. But we cannot shut our eyes to the fact that two or three hundred or more millions of people — the future population of the United States if they hold together — have never yet maintained perpetual peace. So inclined are men to war, so intoxicating is military glory, so great are the honors and emoluments awarded to successful chieftains, that peace, perpetual peace, over a continent, seems more like the dream of a visionary than the well-founded hope of common sense.

In the four hundred and fifty-odd years of the Roman republic the Temple of Janus was shut but once. In no year since history was written has peace prevailed over the entire globe. Even in this nineteenth century, which we are accustomed to call enlightened, there is scarcely a great Power in Europe that has for twenty consecutive years been exempt from war. In view of these facts it may well be asked where, if the republic be perpetuated, will be the outlet for the warlike spirit of as warlike a people as ever existed? Will it find occupation in war upon our neighbors? Where are the neighbors who could long resist? Will it make battle with the Powers of Asia or of Europe? The soldier would gather few laurels in a war necessarily waged upon the deep. Where, then, but in civil strife could the warlike temper be displayed and military honors be won? And could the republic long bear the strain of such strife? I can only answer that nations have survived the most dreadful and sanguinary civil wars. Not to multiply instances, witness France, Austria, England, Spain. It may be unwise to expect that we shall escape the calamities that have befallen other peoples, but it is not, I trust, unreasonable to believe, or at least to hope, that we may be able to survive them.

It is not uncommon to hear the remark that the passions

and prejudices excited by the late Civil War will long endure and cannot fail to imperil the Union. This is not the time or the place to discuss that war. Indeed many years must elapse before impartial and philosophic history will do exact justice to the actors in that mighty scene. But this much may now be safely affirmed, that if the North believed, as it did, that right was on its side in suppressing what it regarded as rebellion, the South had equal confidence in the justice of her cause. For four long and weary years, against the most fearful odds and in the midst of privation and suffering that might have appalled the stoutest heart, her people upheld that cause with a heroism and fortitude never surpassed.

To doubt their sincerity in the face of this fact is simply to shut one's eyes to the truth; to heap unmerited reproaches upon them is to disregard the plainest maxims of wisdom, charity, and justice. It is doubtless true that the great features of the struggle will never be forgotten. The influence of a contest that placed America in the front rank of the warlike nations of the earth; that developed characters whose names can never pass into oblivion; that made many a battle-field heroic ground to be reverentially trodden by the feet of pilgrims from age to age,— cannot be effaced in a day.

But, unless all history teaches a lesson that is false, the bitterness of feeling engendered by the strife will pass away and cease to shape the conduct of men. What nation has ever suffered more from civil wars than France, but what Frenchman now speaks of them save as of events of history? What Englishman inquires, unless from the instinct of a harmless curiosity, whether his neighbor's ancestors wore the red rose of Lancaster or the white rose of York, or whether at a later day they were Roundheads under Cromwell or Cavaliers under Charles? When were the passions of men ever more excited than in the civil wars of Rome, that followed the passage of the Rubicon and ended only when the victory at Actium placed the imperial diadem upon the brow of Octavius? Yet more than three centuries elapsed before the empire was divided, and it was not until nearly eleven centuries more had rolled around that Mahomet II placed the Crescent above the Cross on the dome of St. Sophia and put an end forever to the Empire of the East.

But why dwell upon particulars when every nation that exists or has ever existed presents an example of the forgiveness or forgetfulness of injuries given and received. A wise Providence has ordained that hate shall not reign " eternal in the human breast." The violent passions of our nature may dominate for a time, but the strain is too great to last, and in the end the better and gentler emotions prevail. Every revolving year, though it may not blot out the memories of the past, will soften their asperities, and the time may come, more speedily than the most sanguine now hope, when a fraternal feeling will animate the breasts of all who find shelter and protection under the ægis of the republic.

dollar of the expense incurred in putting down that rebellion. But we forgave them that debt, and to-day you are being taxed heavily to pay the interest on the debt that they ought to have paid. Such magnanimity as was exhibited by this nation to these rebels has never been witnessed on the earth since God made it, and, in my humble judgment, it will never be witnessed again.

Mistakes we undoubtedly made, errors we committed, but, in my judgment, the greatest mistake we made, and the gravest error we committed, was in not hanging enough of these rebels to make treason forever odious. To-day, in Congress, the men have changed but not the measures. Twenty years ago they said: "Do this, or fail to do that, and we will shoot your government to death." If I am to die, I would rather be shot to death with musketry than starved to death. These rebels — for they are just as rebellious now as they were twenty years ago, there is not a particle of difference — I know them better than any other living mortal man; I have summered and wintered with them; these rebels to-day have thirty-six members on the floor of the House of Representatives, without one single constituent, and in violation of law, those thirty-six members represent 4,000,000 people, lately slaves, who are as absolutely disfranchised as if they lived in another sphere, through shot-guns, and whips, and tissue-ballots, for the law expressly says that wherever a race or class is disfranchised, they shall not be represented upon the floor of the House. And these thirty-six members thus elected constitute three times the whole of their majority upon the floor.

This is not only a violation of the law, but it is an outrage upon all the loyal men of the United States. It ought not to be. It must not be. And it shall not be. Twelve members of the Senate — more than their whole majority — occupy their seats upon the floor by fraud and violence; and I am saying no more to you than I said to those rebel generals. With majorities thus obtained by fraud and violence in both houses they dared to dictate terms to the loyal men of these United States.

With majorities thus obtained they dared to arraign the loyal men of these United States, and say they want honest elections. They are mortally afraid of bayonets at the polls. We offered them a law forbidding any man to come within two miles of a polling-place with arms of any description, and they promptly voted it down, for they wanted their Ku-Klux. They were not afraid of the Ku-Klux, but of soldiers. In all the northern States there is less than one soldier to a county. There is about two thirds of a soldier to a county, and, of course, about two thirds of a musket. Wouldn't this great county of Cook tremble if it saw two thirds of a soldier with two thirds of a musket approaching.

But they (the South) are afraid of inspectors. Why? The law creating inspectors is imperative that one must be a Democrat and the other a Republican. They have no power whatever except to certify that the election is honest and fair. They are afraid of marshals at the polls. The inspectors can't arrest. The marshals, under the orders of a court, can arrest criminals; therefore, they said, "We will have no marshals." When we told them we could not have courts without marshals, they said, "We don't want marshals at all." And they don't. Marshals interfere with their "moonshiners" — the men who distill whiskey in the mountains of North and South Carolina, and Georgia; and they don't want any courts, because the courts interfere with their Ku-Klux at the polls.

after you have elected him judge he will not bring in a bill for lost time.

You are going to hold an election next Tuesday that is of importance far beyond the borders of Chicago. The eyes of the whole nation are upon you. By your verdict you are to send forth greeting to the people of the United States, saying either that you are in favor of honest men, honest money, patriotism, and a national government, or that you are in favor of soft money, repudiation, and rebel rule. I want every single man in this vast audience to consider himself a committee of one, to work from now until the close of the polls; to go to the polls early and stay late; and let every mother's son of you decide that you will take one man besides yourself to the polls, who would not otherwise go. Find a man who might stay away, and see to it that he and yourself vote the Republican ticket.

If you cannot find just such a man, try to convert some sinner from the error of his ways. You have too much at stake to risk it at this election. The times are too good. You cannot afford to turn this government over to the hands of the repudiating rebels. Shut up your stores. Shut up your manufactories. Go to work for your country and spend two days, and on the night of the election send me, Mr. Chairman, a dispatch that Chicago has gone overwhelmingly Republican.